BROADSIDES

Mordecai Richler's novels include *St Urbain's Horseman*, shortlisted for the Booker Prize, *The Apprenticeship of Duddy Kravitz*, *Cocksure* and *Joshua Then and Now*. He is also the author of the children's books *Jacob Two-Two Meets the Hooded Fang* and *Jacob Two-Two and the Dinosaur*, as well as two essay collections, *Hunting Tigers Under Glass* and *Home Sweet Home*. He lived in London for twenty years, where he wrote for the *New Statesman*, *Encounter*, *London Magazine* and several national newspapers. In 1972 he returned to Canada with his wife and five children, and now lives in Montreal, where he was born.

Solomon Gursky Was Here, his most recent novel, was shortlisted for the Booker Prize in 1990 and won the Commonwealth Writers Prize 1990. It is also published in paperback by Vintage.

Mordecai Richler

BROADSIDES: REVIEWS AND OPINIONS

VINTAGE

VINTAGE
20 Vauxhall Bridge Road, London SW1V 2SA

An imprint of the Random Century Group

London Melbourne Sydney Auckland
Johannesburg and agencies throughout
the world

First published by Viking Penguin Books Canada Ltd, 1990
Vintage edition 1991

Set in 10½/12 Sabon by Input Typesetting Ltd, London

Printed and bound in Great Britain by
Cox & Wyman Ltd, Reading

ISBN 0 09 987690 6

These essays have been previously published, often in a somewhat different form, in the following: "Hemingway Set His Own Hours," *The New York Times Book Review*; "Deuteronomy," *Congregation* (edited by David Rosenberg); "From Batman, Through G. A. Henty, to *All Quiet on the Western Front*" (originally titled "1944: The Year I Learned to Love a German"), *The New York Times Book Review*; "Debrett's Illustrated Guide," *The Gazette* (Montreal); "All the Conspirators," *Playboy*; "The Road to Dyspepsia," *The New York Times Book Review*; "*Thy Neighbor's Wife*," *New York Magazine*; "Of Spiritual Guides, Witches and Wiccans" (originally titled "Witch's Brew," *Playboy*; "Mulroney," *The Gazette* (Montreal); "J. D. Salinger" from "Paid Liars," *The New York Times Book Review*; "Goldwyn" from "Hollywood" (originally titled "The Man Who Was Hollywood"), *The New York Times Book Review*; "Begelman" from "Hollywood," *New York Magazine*; "Journals," *Antaeus*. All other essays appeared in *Gentlemen's Quarterly* in one form or another.

M.R.

FOR BERNARD AND SYLVIA OSTRY

CONTENTS

HEMINGWAY
SET HIS
OWN HOURS

UNANSWERABLE QUESTIONS STILL surface at parties.
'What kind of novels do you write?'
Legendary. Seminal. Filthy.
'Should I know your name?'
To which I usually reply, eyes modestly lowered, 'Not
necessarily,' but, riding sufficient scotch, I become equally
capable of a bellicose 'Yes, if you're literate,' after which my
wife usually points out it is time to go home.

Strangers who accept without question a man who has put
together a life dealing in pork-belly futures or manufacturing
zippers demand to know *why you did it*. Such a weighty
query begs for an appropriately pretentious answer. Something about artistic compulsions. Muses. Inspiration. But the
truth is, everybody I knew in high school who wasn't going
to be another Hank Greenberg or Barney Ross or Maurice
'The Rocket' Richard was willing to settle for being a writer.
As far as we could make out, Hemingway set his own hours.
He seemed to go fishing whenever he felt like it. He was on
first name terms with Ingrid Bergman and Marlene Dietrich.
It had to be a good life.

What I find more intriguing than why anybody became a
writer is how some of the boys at school grew up to be
caterers, or frozen-chicken-breast packagers, or distributors
of plate glass windows. When we were sitting on the stoop
together and I was dreaming of diving out of my hotel
window to swim across the Grand Canal like Byron, or
drinking too much in Hollywood like Scott Fitzgerald, were
they secretly pledged to catering the Great American Bar

Mitzvah? Or freezing the most tasteless chicken breast? Or installing the ultimate plate glass window? The boy who grew up to be the plate glass window distributor, incidentally, is worth further mention. When a sufficient number of orders were not forthcoming, he took to creating instant demand, speeding around Montreal in the early morning hours and heaving bricks through his latest installations. Alas, his initiative earned him three years in the slammer.

The boys I grew up with are not taken in by my published novels.

'I remember you at school.'

'You were short for your age.'

'I had better looking girls.'

'You were nothing.'

'I can't understand why anybody would pay any attention to you now.'

The first writers I warmed to were George Alfred Henty, H. G. Wells, O. Henry and, for the hot stuff, Tiffany Thayer. I was only fourteen when I acquired a pipe and a lined notebook and began to write short stories that unfailingly began in a British club as Sir Bertram Digby-Howard reminisced with a chum.

'I say, Sir Archibald, do you believe in ghosts?'

'By Jove, no, old boy.'

'Then let me acquaint you with what happened to me one night at Raffles Hotel. The clock had just struck twelve when . . . '

In another story, I tried my first experiment with irony. An anti-Semitic bully is saved from drowning by a total stranger.

'I owe you my life,' the bully says, 'but I don't even know your name.'

'My name,' the stranger reveals in the last sentence of the story, 'is Isadore Lipschitz. But you can call me Izzy.'

Looking back, I fear that to begin with I did not so much want to write as to be a writer, on first name terms, if not with Ingrid Bergman, then at least with Ruth Roman. When

2

I drifted into the Algonquin Hotel, out-of-towners would gawk, nudging each other. 'Look, it's him!'

Nowadays, when I read reviews of my work, I secretly believe the worst, but at the time it never occurred to me that I might fail. Fortunately, every neophyte writer is armoured with arrogance. So, however, is many an overlooked middle-aged writer.

We have read a good deal in literary journals about the unjustly neglected novelist, but seldom a word about the many who are justly neglected, the scratch players, brandishing their little distinctions (a translation into Icelandic, a rave review in the University of British Columbia Alumni News), so I would like to say something about Harry. Harry and I were in Paris together in the early fifties, two happy scribblers, equally awash in rejection slips, yet both confident that everything was possible. Over the years, however, I won a certain recognition. He didn't. Mind you, his novels are still published, if only in Canada, where he sells maybe 1,500 copies and in one interview after another explains, 'Nothing would make me set my novels in Chicago or New York in order to pursue whorish best-sellerdom. I'm proud to be a Canadian.'

As impoverished in his fifties as we once were in Paris, he subsists on literary scraps: a Canada Council reading tour in the Northwest Territories, a term as literary resource person at an obscure Nova Scotia college, putting together an anthology of Canadian writing for Radio Finland. He is also a constant rebuke to me.

'Do you think Kafka or Martin Buber would have published in *Playboy*?'

'Certainly not.'

'Then how come I saw your name in the June issue right under the cover girl's left nipple?'

Or after the publication of *Joshua Then and Now*: 'You, you still call yourself an artist, and you let *People* take your picture.'

To which I could at least counter, 'Don't tell me you read *People* now?'

'Kitsch enriches my work.'

I am always careful to take Harry to a second-rate restaurant so as not to flaunt my bourgeois affluence. I drink beer. I don't order cognac or pay with my credit card. I feed him all the bad things that have happened to me recently. But in the end he nabs me.

'There is a magazine in Bulgaria doing a special Canadian issue. The editor is a great admirer of mine. If you let me have a story, I'll send it to him. But they only pay $1.75 a page, so you probably aren't interested.'

'Of course I'm interested. I'll send you something as soon as I get home.'

'*You own it!*'

'What?'

'The mansion in Westmount.'

'It's not a mansion, and there's a hell of a big mortgage on it.'

In the end, he will leave me a copy of his latest novel, with xeroxed endorsements by various professors.

'With your connections, maybe you can place it for me in New York. I haven't got your knack for marketing myself.'

In 1951, at the age of nineteen, I dropped out of college and sailed for England on the *Franconia*. After two weeks in London, I moved on to Paris. Devoured Malraux, Hemingway, Céline, Sartre, Camus. Determined to be a real literary man, I was scornful of my own natural material, St. Urbain Street, considering it far too commonplace for fiction. I mean, I *knew* people like that. I didn't want to *write* about them. I wanted to write like Malraux or Hemingway and, unfortunately, that's exactly what I tried in my first novel, *The Acrobats*, which I published three years later and have cunningly kept out of print ever since. The British publisher, André Deutsch, paid me an advance of £100 and Putnam's forked out $750 for the American rights. When I applied for a new passport, I no longer described myself as 'STUDENT,' but under 'occupation' printed 'WRITER,' though to myself I added 'of sorts.' I had to force two more novels through

4

the hothouse before I found my own voice and wrote *The Apprenticeship of Duddy Kravitz*, for which the pillars of Montreal's Jewish community have never forgiven me.

'Why,' I was once asked, 'couldn't you have given the boy an Italian name?'

'Why,' I was asked after I had lectured at a suburban synagogue, 'does everybody adore Sholem Aleichem, but hate your guts?'

For all that, the novel was hardly noticed when it appeared. It sold fewer than 1,000 copies in Canada, maybe 1,200 in the United States and something like 3,000 in England. But twenty-one years later, after I published *Joshua Then and Now*, the critic who blasted it in the *New York Review of Books* redeemed himself to me by observing in passing that *Duddy Kravitz* was a comic classic.

Graham Greene once said that, so far as critics were concerned, you were a young writer until you were forty and thereafter a writer who had never fulfilled his early promise. But in this game, he might have added, there is also nothing like patience.

I'm fifty-nine years old now. Only yesterday, it seems, my tonsils were plucked out on a dining-room table, but now the trendy operation for my age group is open-heart surgery. The triple bypass. An ordeal, I suspect, that is not followed by mounds of ice cream consumed on the doctor's orders. The sports and film stars of my adolescence, once indestructible, are now either gone (Peter Reiser, Rita Hayworth) or are wheeled out for television commercials promoting Preparation H, Grecian Formula or Polident. If you're an actor or an athlete, given the right agent, even the body's betrayals can be turned to a profit. The residual's residuals.

I belong to a generation that sprang to adolescence during World War II. Too young to fight, we were forever shaped by the war all the same. The headlines. The battles. The casualties. We could never wear the flag as underwear or respect those who did. Or, come to think of it, be surprised that many who did are today's stockbrokers and supply-side economists. I can remember, and bore your children and mine, with tales of the good old days, when chicken tasted of something more than sawdust, actors didn't run for high office, hockey was a winter sport, nobody had ever heard of acid rain, doctors made house calls, mail was delivered, department stores would accept cash.

We were, and remain by today's standards, a rather inhibited bunch. A friend of mine, far too proper to walk into a porn movie house to watch *Deep Throat* or *Swedish Fly Girls*, told me that he had recently stayed at a hotel in Toronto that offered on Channel C a decidedly saucy film beginning at 11 p.m. But to have it appear on his television set, he had to dial a number and provide his name and room number. 'I picked up the phone. I was about to do it. Then I hung up. I was sure if I requested the film, it would be my mother on the other end of the line. "*Bobby, whatever are you up to?*" '

After all these years, writing has become a habit. I no longer question why I do it any more than a welder wonders why he turns up at the shop every morning. Which is to say, of course we all endure our bad days, but we do get on with it. I wouldn't know what to do with myself until 4 p.m., my usual quitting time, if I couldn't sit down at my portable typewriter. Even so, I'm stuck with my original notion, which is to be an honest witness to my time, my place, and to write at least one novel that will last, that will make me remembered after death. So I'm compelled to keep trying.

Meanwhile, there are satisfactions. Fame, for instance. One year I had a letter from a university all the way out in Australia, inviting me to be writer-in-residence. But there was a problem. The invitation was addressed to Ms. Mordecai Richler. I wrote back saying I'd love to come but I just wouldn't know what to wear.

Another time, pulling into a Montreal parking lot, the car jockey began to wave me off, indicating the 'FULL' sign, but then he looked at me more closely and smiled.

'Hey, I know you. I love your books.'

Recognition at last.

'You're Farley Mowat, aren't you?'

'Damn right.'
'Let me park your car for you, sir.'

On my way back to Canada from Paris in 1953, I stopped off in London and left the manuscript of my first novel with an agent whose name had been passed to me by a poker playing crony. After a couple of rejections, she placed it, and ever since, unpublished or disappointed writers have accused me of luxuriating in connections, an ever broadening cabal made up of the right literary people. Their point is well taken. I have been to dinner with more than one influential critic. The trouble is, the critics I know, far from boosting a dinner companion, will bend over backward to prove their purity in print. Critics should be read but not seen.

Envy is not unknown among writers; there are jealousies, there are resentments. And I'm not immune. This year, I wouldn't lose any sleep if John Updike didn't win anything. I don't want to read any more about Norman Mailer's $4 million contract. But, on balance, I think writers are a much maligned group. I have never been to a dentist who did not fiercely denounce the last man to slip a filling into your mouth, but from my earliest days, I have benefited from the generosity of other writers. Beyond the cocktail party sniping, there is a commitment to the craft, a tendency to help, in Norman Mailer's phrase, anybody who is trying to add an inch to the house.

All the same, I could do with less self-pity, less dollar-a-word complaining about the lonely craft and how hell is a blank sheet of paper. We weren't drafted, we volunteered. And even as I suspected in high school, you can set your own hours. You can go fishing when you feel like it. My father, a failed scrap dealer, worked a lot harder than I do without anything like the satisfactions. On bad days, it's good to remember that.

DEUTERONOMY

TORAH WAS LITERALLY banged into me and seven other recalcitrant boys in a musty back room of the Young Israel Synagogue, our *cheder*, by a teacher I'll call Mr. Feinberg. If I got anything wrong, or if I was caught with an Ellery Queen paperback or, say, a copy of the Montreal *Herald* on my lap open at the sports pages, Mr. Feinberg would rap my knuckles with the sharp end of his ruler or twist my ear. However, what all of us feared even more than his blows was his bad breath. Grudgingly, we attended Mr. Feinberg's classes after regular school was out – while other boys, who weren't lucky enough to come from such good homes, were playing street hockey or snooker or just hanging out, smoking Turret cigarettes, five cents for a pack of five.

Our parents skimped and saved to send us to *cheder* so that we could benefit from 'a good Jewish education.' We were to learn the rules and abide by them and grow up to be a real catch for a girl from an equally respectable but preferably more prosperous home. Had our parents suspected that we were being force-fed poetry and drama in that musty back room, maybe even acquiring a taste for it, they would not have been so pleased.

Years later, when my cousin Fishl registered for a course on comparative religion at McGill, his mother wasn't thrilled. 'With you,' she said, 'the grass is always greener.'

Once I came home and told my father that Sean O'Brien's uncle, a teacher, had told me that the Flood was not only a Jewish tale; it was a myth shared by many peoples. What did he mean, *tale*? *myth*? We had studied it in the *Chummish*.

My father had a short answer for it. 'I don't want you to play with Sean O'Brien any more,' he said.

Mr. Feinberg told us again and again what an honour it would be, once we had been Bar Mitzvahed, to be called upon during the Sabbath service to bless a sentence from the Pentateuch, but I wasn't impressed. I had already heard the inside story. Members of the Young Israel congregation bid for the honour of an *aliyah*, starting with the most affluent of their number, notary and city councillor 'Uncle' Moish Takifman, a.k.a. Twelve-fifty Takifman, who unfailingly opened loud for a big twenty-five dollars, my father squeezing in late with a two-dollar bid. However, my father had revealed that regular members of the congregation were acting as shills, trying to embarrass non-members, prodding them into paying heavily for a piece of the Torah action. Bona fide members, in on the secret, were obliged to pay only half of their declared bid for an *aliyah*.

Yawning, stretching, kicking one another under the long table, we counted the minutes until *cheder* was out. Poor Mr. Feinberg, determined to knock some learning into us, tried to gain our attention with Hasidic tales. Enchanting tales of the Baal Shem Tov, Menahem Mendel of Vitebsk, Dov Baer of Mezritch. Once he told us of a legendary Lubavitcher rebbe, a prodigy, who could recite the entire Torah from memory. If a pin were put through a page, Mr. Feinberg told us, any page, protruding forty-eight pages later, or sixty-seven pages later, the rebbe, swaying in thought, could tell you exactly what word the pin had pricked. Imagine that.

Alas, a callow bunch, we were more amazed by the feats of Maurice 'The Rocket' Richard or Johnny Greco, a local welterweight who was fighting in main bouts at Madison Square Garden at the time. All the same, we certainly preferred Mr. Feinberg's Hasidic lore to the logical platitudes of Young Israel's new 'modern' rabbi, who was such a big hit with the ladies'' auxiliary, if not with the men. On Sundays, the men were now expected to attend father-and-son breakfasts featuring reviews of books by Sholem Asch or Budd Schulberg, who wrote filth about our people. The twinkly

Rabbi Bloom, a Brooklyn Dodger fan who didn't even wear a beard, made a pitch for what he called 'the kids.' Instead of a Sadie Hawkins Day Dance, like *they* were having, how about a Queen Esther Ball with a beauty contest this Purim? He also attempted to appeal to our reason. Pork, he said, was forbidden because it would have spoiled in the heat of Canaan, the children of Israel were enjoined to wear hats to protect them against sunstroke, etc. Suddenly all the magic was gone. All at once there was little to choose between the Commandments of the terrifying Jehovah, vengeful unto the tenth generation, and the Junior Red Cross's Ten Rules of Hygiene. So we argued back, equally tiresome. Now that we have iceboxes, why can't we eat bacon? Who fears sunstroke in this nutty climate? And, come to think of it, where did Cain find a wife?

Released from *cheder*, we collected our sleds and hurried over to Steinberg's supermarket, down the street, hoping to earn a quarter riding a lady's parcels home. While we waited outside in the snow, knocking our boots together to keep warm, we told puerile schoolboy Bible jokes.

– Why was God so angry with Moses?

– Because God asked him to come forth and he came fifth and lost the race.

Another story went that there were originally fifty commandments. God offered them to the Egyptians, the Amorites, the Canaanites and the Syrians, all of whom, sensibly enough, refused to cut a deal. Then Moses, our father, blundered along and offered to take ten, but no more, and we were stuck with them.

> For thou *art* an holy people, unto the LORD thy God: the LORD thy God hath chosen thee to be a special people unto himself, above all people are *are* upon the face of the earth.

In Deuteronomy, the fifth book of the Pentateuch, a repetition with comments on the Decalogue, the children of Israel – the progeny of an evil generation – are discovered this side of Jordan in the land of Moab. After forty years of wandering in the wilderness, they are at last preparing to enter the promised land of milk and honey. Moses, determined that they be bold, reminds them of what they had done unto Si-hon, king of Hesha-bon, and Og, king of Bashan, utterly destroying the men, the women and the children of every city. Or, put in today's sanitized military idiom, he recalled how they had once pacified the countryside.

Before going over Jordan, the Israelites must endure a reiteration of the Mosaic law. They are instructed once more that they are obliged to stone all false prophets, dreamers of dreams, to death. Clearly a case of the poets who wrote the Pentateuch, the most sublime poets we have ever known, advocating that short work be made of anticipated rivals. Or, looked at another way, even the greatest authors are insecure, bad-mouthing the others.

But the same harsh punishment is also due rebellious sons and adulterers and brides whose tokens of virginity fail to pass muster.

> Then they shall bring out the damsel to the door of her father's house, and the men of her city shall stone her with stones that she die: because she hath wrought folly in Israel, to play the whore in her father's house: so shalt thou put evil away from among you.

Furthermore, as we have been told by fundamentalists as disparate as Jerry Falwell, the Ayatollah Khomeini, and the Lubavitcher rebbe of 770 Eastern Parkway, gay pride was out.

> The woman shall not wear that which pertaineth unto a man, neither shall a man put on a woman's garment: for all that do so *are* abomination unto the LORD thy God.

If I may digress briefly, Christopher Sykes, in his biography of Evelyn Waugh, writes that during World War II Waugh and Randolph Churchill were parachuted into Yugoslavia as part of the British mission to aid Marshal Tito. Randolph talked incessantly, irritating Waugh no end. Then Waugh discovered that Randolph had never read the Old Testament.

Hoping to shut him up, if only for a while, Waugh offered Randolph a fiver if he would read it right through. Randolph only made it halfway before he slammed his Bible shut and exclaimed, 'I never realized that God was such a shit!'

I have repeated this anecdote often, though never in an airplane, because, such was my upbringing, the truth is it still scares me to tell it at thirty-five thousand feet. It scares me even as my first furtive taste of bacon frightened me more than my initial puff of pot, which – incidentally – is not forbidden in Deuteronomy, unlike the flesh of the eagle, the osprey, the owl, the night hawk, the swan and the pelican.

My children are not troubled by such superstitions. They had a different upbringing. Foolishly, we spared them *cheder*, short-changing them with a liberal education. I'm okay, you're okay; no hangups, but no magic, either; too bad. But now, when they sit down with my wife and me to the Passover table, there are many things they want to know. They ask more than four questions. After all these years, I have become their Mr. Feinberg.

But to return to Randolph: his point about Jehovah, albeit blasphemous and more than somewhat smart-ass, is well taken. To be fair, however, the God of Deuteronomy could also be as saucy as Dr. Ruth – an understanding God, not totally terrible.

> When a man hath taken a new wife, he shall not go out to war, neither shall he be charged with any business: *but* he shall be free at home one year, and shall cheer up his wife which he hath taken.

Obviously, Biblical draft-dodgers did not light out for Stockholm or Toronto, but instead hastily took a wife, possibly not being too fussy about her tokens of virginity. Mind you, Jehovah, a considerable strategist, did not want conscientious objectors or the chicken-hearted in the battlefield.

> And the officers shall speak further unto the people, and they shall say, What man *is there that is* fearful and fainthearted? let him go and return unto his house, lest his brethren's heart faint as well as his heart.

More than to any other book ever written, a reader brings his own baggage to the Pentateuch. What you find there depends on your sensibility. There is myth, there is drama, there is poetry. But if what you need is proof of Jewish obloquy, it is also to be found there, in lines precious to anti-Semites everywhere.

> Unto a stranger thou mayest lend upon usury; but unto thy brother thou shalt not lend upon usury.

The poetry in Deuteronomy can be vitiated by a nagging reiteration of rules, rules and more rules, tempered by threats from a God who clearly expects the worst of the people He has chosen to be special unto Himself. In fact, even as they are about to enter the promised land, God seems to be suffering from last-minute second thoughts. Possibly, the children of Israel don't deserve the freehold after all. Maybe, all things considered, He fingered the wrong bunch.

Again and again, Moses reminds the people of all God has done for them, how He delivered them out of Egypt with a mighty hand and an outstretched arm. Their most heinous crimes are recalled. They are assured that the land they are entering will be blessed in

> the fruit of thy body, and the fruit of thy ground, and the fruit of thy cattle, the increase of thy kine, and the flocks of thy sheep.

Then Moses, in a rage, lashes out against the undeserving congregation of Israel.

> For I know that after my death ye will utterly corrupt *yourselves*, and turn aside from the way which I have commanded you; and evil will befall you in the latter days; because ye will do evil in the sight of the LORD, to provoke him to anger through the work of your hands.

Late one afternoon, released from Mr. Feinberg's *cheder*, I crossed Park Avenue and slipped into Kresge's. I was caught shoplifting. The manager of the store, a Scots Presbyterian, had me into his office. He was not angry, but ashamed for my sake. 'I never would have expected such behaviour from a Jewish lad,' he said. 'You come from such a hard-working and law-abiding people. A people I greatly admire because you have always put education, sobriety and family above all.'

Yes, yes, but how did we acquire such a reputation, such habits?

Certainly our forefathers, gathered in Moab, this side of Jordan, were a loutish lot, a bunch of good ol'' boys, much given to carousing, wenching, pilfering, fighting and sacking cities. Who knew them better than Moses? Moses, his time short, who warns his flock that they will be cursed if they lead blind men astray, remove their neighbour's landmark, take advantage of widows and orphans, accept pay to murder an innocent person, or lie with their father's wife, or sisters, or beasts.

Moses, Moses.

He served a great God, yes indeed, a mighty and a terrible God, but also a God unforgiving beyond compare. Deuteronomy ends on one of the most poignant notes in the Pentateuch: the death of Moses, Moishe Rabbeinu. A hundred and twenty years old he was when he died, but his eye was not dim, nor his natural force abated.

It has been said that only five leaders of Israel lived exactly a hundred and twenty years: Moses, Hillel, Rabbi Yochanon ben Zakkai, Rabbi Yehuda HaNassi, and Rabbi Akiva. But only of Moses was it written:

> And there arose not a prophet since in Israel like unto Moses, whom the LORD knew face to face.

Moses, of the tribe of Levi, born into captivity, was set adrift by Miriam in an ark of bulrushes daubed with slime and pitch; rescued by Pharaoh's daughter, raised a prince. Moses, who turned his staff into a serpent, made the Nile run red with blood, led his people across the parting of the Red Sea, brought forth water from a rock, smashed the tablets in a rage and wandered forty years in the wilderness, was sentenced to die without entering the promised land because once or twice he had actually been given to doubts.

And the LORD said unto him, This *is* the land which I sware unto Abraham, unto Isaac, and unto Jacob, saying, I will give it unto thy seed: I have caused thee to see *it* with thine eyes, but thou shalt not go over thither.

Instead he would die on the mount, gathered unto his people, and no man would know his sepulchre unto this day. First, however, the authors of Deuteronomy would have it that the Lord appeared in the Tabernacle in a pillar of cloud and said unto Moses:

Behold, thou shalt sleep with thy fathers; and this people will rise up, and go a whoring after the gods of the strangers of the land, whither they go *to be* among them, and will forsake me, and break my covenant which I have made with them.

Then my anger shall be kindled against them in that day, and I will forsake them, and I will hide my face from them, and they shall be devoured, and many evils and troubles shall befall them.

Say what you like, He was as good as His word. Or so I said to Ornstein the last time we met and got to talking about the old days in the musty back room of the Young Israel Synagogue. Ornstein used to torment Mr. Feinberg. 'If,' he once said, 'as it is written, the LORD your God *is* God of gods, and Lord of lords, then surely this is an acknowledgement that there are other gods. Zeus, maybe. What do you think?'

Ornstein, who broke with the Communist Party long ago, is still opposed to all kinds of religious mumbo-jumbo, any sort of tribalism. A scientist of some renown, he always seems to be heading for or just coming back from an important international conference in Tokyo, London or Milan. Last year he was in Jerusalem for the first time, and he went to see the Wailing Wall. 'And you know what?' he said. 'I burst into tears. I wept and I wept.'

FROM BATMAN,
THROUGH G. A. HENTY,
TO *ALL QUIET ON THE*
WESTERN FRONT

READING WAS NOT one of my boyhood passions. Girls,
or rather the absence of girls, drove me to it. When I was
thirteen years old, short for my age, more than somewhat
pimply, I was terrified of girls. As far as I could make out,
they were only attracted to boys who were tall or played for
the school basketball team or at least shaved. Unable to
qualify on all three counts, I resorted to subterfuge. I set out
to call attention to myself by becoming a character. I acquired
a pipe, which I chewed on ostentatiously, and made it my
business to be seen everywhere, even at school basketball
games, pretending to be absorbed by books of daunting significance: say, H.G. Wells's *Outline of History*, or Paul de
Kruif's *Microbe Hunters*, or John Gunther inside one continent or another. I rented these thought-provoking books for
three cents a day from a neighbourhood lending library that
was across the street from a bowling alley where I used to
spot pins four nights a week.

O my God, I would not be thirteen again for anything.
The sweetly scented girls of my dreams, wearing lipstick
and tight sweaters and nylon stockings, would sail into the
bowling alley holding hands with the boys from the basketball team. 'Hi,' they would call out, giggly, nudging each
other, even as I bent over the pins, 'How goes the reading?'

The two ladies who ran the lending library, possibly
amused by my pretensions, tried to interest me in fiction.

'I want fact. I can't be bothered with *stories*,' I protested,
waving my pipe at them, affronted.

16

I knew what novels were, of course. I had read *Scaramouche*, by Rafael Sabatini, at school, as well as *Treasure Island* and some Ellery Queen and a couple of thumpers by G.A. Henty. Before that there had been *Action Comics, Captain Marvel, Batman* and – for educational reasons – either *Bible Comics* or *Classic Comics*. All these treasures I bought under the counter, as it were. They were passed hand to hand on dark street corners. Contraband. Our *samizdat*. The reason for this being that in 1943 the dolts who prevailed in Ottawa had adjudged American comic books unessential to the war effort, a drain on the Canadian dollar. So on the home front we were expected to make do with feeble black-and-white indigenous comic books for the duration, a blow to my crowd's morale.

Novels, I knew, were mere romantic make-believe, not as bad as poetry, to be fair, but bad enough. Our high school class master, a dedicated Scot, had been foolish enough to try to interest us in poetry. A veteran of World War I, he told us that during the nightly bombardments on the Somme he had fixed a candle to his steel helmet so that he could read poetry in the trenches. A scruffy lot, we were not moved. Instead, we exchanged knowing winks behind that admirable man's back. Small wonder, we agreed, that he drove an ancient Austin and had ended up no better than a high school teacher.

My aunts consumed historical novels like pastries. My father read *Black Mask* and *True Detective*. My mother would read anything on a Jewish subject, preferably by I. J. Singer or Sholem Asch, though she would never forgive Asch for having written *The Nazarene*, never mind *Mary* and *The Apostle*. My older brother kept a novel, *Topper Takes a Trip*, secure under his mattress in the bedroom we shared, assuring me that it was placed at just such an angle on the springs that if it were moved so much as a millimetre in his absence he would know and bloody well make me pay for it.

I fell ill with a childhood disease, I no longer remember which, but one obviously meant as a rebuke for those girls in tight sweaters who continued to ignore me. Never mind, they would mourn at my funeral, burying me with my pipe. Too late they would say, 'Boy, was he ever an intellectual!'

Aunts, who still took me for a child, brought me really dumb books *in which animals talked*. I was appalled. But the ladies from the lending library also dropped off books for me at our house. The real stuff. Fact-filled. Providing me with the inside dope on Theodore Hertzl's childhood and *Brazil Yesterday, Today, and Tomorrow*. One day they brought me a novel: *All Quiet on the Western Front*, by Erich Maria Remarque. The painting on the jacket that was taped to the book showed a soldier wearing what was unmistakably a German army helmet. What was this, I wondered, some sort of bad joke?

Nineteen forty-four that was, and I devoutly wished every German on the face of the earth an excruciating death. The invasion of France had not yet begun, but I cheered every Russian counter-attack, each German city bombed and, with the help of a map tacked to my bedroom wall, followed the progress of the Canadian troops fighting their way up the Italian boot. Boys from our street were already among the fallen. Izzy Draper's uncle. Harvey Kugelmass's older brother. The boy who was supposed to marry Gita Holtzman.

All Quiet on the Western Front lay unopened on my bed for two days. A time bomb ticking away, though I hardly suspected it. Rather than read a novel, a novel written by a German, I tuned in to radio soap operas in the afternoons: 'Ma Perkins,' 'Pepper Young's Family.' I organized a new baseball league for short players who didn't shave yet, appointing myself commissioner, the first Canadian to be so honoured. Sifting through a stack of my father's back issues of *Popular Mechanics*, I was sufficiently inspired to invent a spaceship and fly to Mars, where I was adored by everybody, especially the girls. Finally I was driven to picking up *All Quiet on the Western Front* out of boredom. I never expected that a mere novel, a stranger's tale, could actually be dangerous, creating such turbulence in my life, obliging me to question so many received ideas. About Germans. About my own monumental ignorance of the world. About what novels were.

At the age of thirteen in 1944, happily as yet untainted by English 101, I couldn't tell you whether Remarque's novel was (a) a slice of life, (b) symbolic, (c) psychological or (d) seminal. I couldn't even say if it was well or badly written. In fact, as I recall, it didn't seem to be 'written' at all. It just flowed. Now, of course, I understand that writing which doesn't advertise itself is often art of a very high order. It doesn't come easily. But at the time I wasn't capable of making such distinctions.

I also had no notion of how *All Quiet on the Western Front* rated critically as a war novel. I hadn't read Stendhal or Tolstoy or Crane or Hemingway. I hadn't even heard of them. But what I did know was that, hating Germans with a passion, I had read only twenty, maybe thirty pages before the author had seduced me into identifying with my enemy, nineteen-year-old Paul Bäumer, thrust into the bloody trenches of World War I with his schoolmates: Müller, Kemmerich and the reluctant Joseph Behm, one of the first to fall. As if that weren't sufficiently unsettling, the author, having won my love for Paul, my enormous concern for his survival, betrayed me in the last dreadful paragraphs of his book:

> He fell in October 1918, on a day that was so quiet and still on the whole front, that the army report confined itself to a single sentence: All quiet on the Western Front.
> He had fallen forward and lay on the earth as though sleeping. Turning him over one saw that he could not have suffered long; his face had an expression of calm, as though glad the end had come.

The movies, I knew from experience, never risked letting you down like that. No matter how bloody the battle, how long the odds, Errol Flynn, Robert Taylor, even Humphrey Bogart could be counted on to survive and come home to Ann Sheridan, Lana Turner, or – if they were a sensitive type –

Loretta Young. Only character actors, usually Brooklyn Dodger fans, say George Tobias or William Bendix or Dane Clark, were expendable.

Having waded into the pool of serious fiction by accident, as it were, I was not sure I liked or trusted the water. It was too deep. Anything could happen.

There was something else, a minor incident in *All Quiet on the Western Front* that would not have troubled an adult reader, but, I'm embarrassed to say, distressed that thirteen-year-old boy colliding with his first serious novel.

Sent out to guard a village that had been abandoned because it was being shelled too heavily, Katczinsky, the incomparable scrounger, surfaces with suckling pigs and potatoes and carrots for his comrades, a group of eight altogether.

> The suckling pigs were slaughtered, Kat sees to them. We want to make potato-cakes to go with the roast. But we cannot find a grater for the potatoes. However, the difficulty is soon got over. With a nail we punch a lot of holes in a pot lid and there we have a grater. Three fellows put on thick gloves to protect their fingers against the grater, two others peel the potatoes, and the business gets going.

The business, I realized, alarmed – no, *affronted* – was the making of potato *latkes*, a favorite of mine as well as of Paul Bäumer's, a dish I had always taken to be Jewish, certainly not a German concoction. What did I know? Nothing. Or, looked at another way, my real education, my lifelong addiction to fiction, began with the trifling discovery that the potato *latke* was not of Jewish origin, but something borrowed from the Germans and now a taste that Jew and German share in spite of everything.

I felt easier about my affection for the German soldier Paul Bäumer once I had been told by the ladies from the lending library that when Hitler came to power in 1932 he had burned all of Erich Maria Remarque's books, and in 1938 took away his German citizenship. Obviously Hitler grasped that novels could be dangerous, something I had learned when I was only thirteen years old. He burned them; I began to devour them. I started to read at the breakfast table and on streetcars, often missing my stop, and in bed with the benefit of a flashlight. It got me into trouble. I understood, for the first time, that I didn't live in the centre of the world but had been born into a working-class family in an unimportant country far from the cities of light: London, Paris, New York. Of course this wasn't my fault; it was my inconsiderate parents who were to blame. But there was, I now realized, a larger world out there beyond St. Urbain Street in Montreal, a world that could be available to me, even though – to my mother's despair – I had been born left-handed, ate with my elbows on the table and had failed once more to come rank one in school.

Preparing myself for the *rive gauche*, I bought a blue beret, which I didn't dare wear even in the house if anybody else was home. I looked at but lacked the courage to buy a cigarette holder. But the next time I took Goldie Zimmerman to a downtown movie and then out to Dinty Moore's for toasted tomato sandwiches, I suggested that, instead of milkshakes, we each order a glass of *vin ordinaire*. 'Are you crazy?' she asked.

As my parents bickered at the supper table, trapped in concerns far too mundane for the likes of me – what to do if Dworkin raised the rent again, how to manage my brother's college fees – I sat with, but actually apart from them in the kitchen, enthralled, reading for the first time, 'All happy families are alike but an unhappy family is unhappy after its own fashion.'

Erich Maria Remarque, his family of French descent, was born in Westphalia in 1897. He went off to war, directly from school, at the age of eighteen. He was wounded five times. He lost all his friends. After the war he worked briefly as a schoolteacher, a stone cutter, a test driver for a tire company and an editor of *Sportbild*. His first novel, *Im Westen Nicht Neues*, was turned down by several publishers before it was brought out by the Ullstein Press in Berlin in

1928. It sold 1.2 million copies in Germany and was translated into twenty-nine languages, selling 4 million copies throughout the world. A reviewer for the *Manchester Guardian* called it the greatest of all war books, and the critic for the London *Times* wrote, 'It has certain of the marks of genius which transcend nationality.' The novel has been filmed three times – the first time, memorably, by Lewis Milestone in 1930. The Milestone version, with Lew Ayres playing Paul Bäumer, won Academy Awards for Best Picture and Best Direction.

Erich Maria Remarque, who lived in the United States for the duration of World War II and then moved on to Switzerland, wrote nine other novels before he died in 1970, but none had the impact of *All Quiet on the Western Front*, a novel that endures as a testimony to a wasted generation.

Because *All Quiet on the Western Front* once meant so much to me, I picked it up again with a certain anxiety in 1986. After all this time I find it difficult to be objective about the novel. Its pages still evoke for me a back bedroom with a cracked ceiling and a sizzling radiator on St. Urbain Street, mice scrabbling in the walls, a window looking out on sheets frozen stiff on the laundry line, and all the pain of being too young to shave, an ignorant and bewildered boy of thirteen.

Over the years the novel has lost something in shock value, even as I am now missing something in purity. Once, I would happily fork out three cents a day for the pleasures any novel might have to offer; now there are editors foolish enough to pay me to pronounce. I don't know what that hungering thirteen-year-old boy would make of this fat middle-aged writer and, what's more, I don't want to know. On the other hand, what did he know anyway? He didn't really understand *Anna Karenina* the first time he rented it, and only insisted on taking it out of the lending library because one of the ladies said, 'Don't you think you ought to wait a few more years before tackling Tolstoy?' He was scornful of his father for never missing an issue of *Black Mask*, but now these magazines are collectors'' items, the subject of endless literary essays.

The original jacket copy of the 1929 edition of *All Quiet on the Western Front* warns the reader that it is 'at times crude' and 'will shock the supersensitive by its outspokenness.' Dr. Henry Seidel Canby, in his Book-of-the-Month Club report of May 1929, cautions members that the novel includes a 'liberal share of grossness which accompanies war because it must.' Obviously we've come a long way. After *The Naked and the Dead, From Here to Eternity* and *Catch-22*, not to mention a spate of Vietnam war novels, contemporary readers – far from being shocked – will be amused by the novel's discretion, the absence of explicit sex scenes, the unbelievably polite dialogue of the men in the trenches. The horrors are still there, of course. The endless artillery bombardments. The gas attacks at dawn. The bayonet warfare:

> The bayonet frequently jams on the thrust and then a man has to kick hard on the other fellow's belly to pull it out again; and in the interval he may easily get one himself. And what's more, the blade is often broken off.

And of course the rats. The fat corpse rats.

> They have shocking, evil, naked faces, and it is nauseating to see their long, nude tails.
>
> They seem to be mighty hungry. Almost every man has had his bread gnawed. Kropp wrapped his in his waterproof sheet and put it under his head, but he cannot sleep because they run over his face to get at it. Detering meant to outwit them: he fastened a thin wire to the roof and suspended his bread from it. During the night when he switched on his pocket-torch he saw the wire swinging to and fro. On the bread was riding a fat rat.

The novel also has its poignant moments, both in the trenches and when Paul Bäumer goes home on leave, an old man of nineteen, only to find insufferably pompous schoolmasters still recruiting the young with mindless prattle about the Fatherland and the glory of battle. Strong characters are deftly sketched. Himmelstoss, the postman who becomes a crazed drillmaster. Tjaden, the peasant soldier. Kantorek, the schoolmaster. On the front line the enemy is never 'the Frogs' or 'the Limeys,' but the insanity of war itself. It is the war, in fact, and not even Paul Bäumer, that is the novel's true protagonist. In a brief introduction to the novel, Remarque wrote: 'This book is to be neither an accusation nor a confession, and least of all an adventure, for death is not an adventure to those who stand face to face with it. It will try simply to tell of a generation of men who, even though they may have escaped its shells, were destroyed by the war.'

Since World War I we have become altogether too familiar with larger horrors. The Holocaust, Hiroshima, the threat of a nuclear winter. Death by numbers, cities obliterated by decree. None of this, however, diminishes the power of *All Quiet on the Western Front*, a novel that will endure because of its humanity, its honour and its refusal to lapse into sentimentality or strike a false note. It is a work that has earned its place on that small shelf of World War I classics, alongside *Goodbye to All That*, by Robert Graves, and Ernest Hemingway's *A Farewell to Arms*.

PERCOLATION, GOAL-SETTING, AND MARKETING YOUR WORK

OVER THE YEARS I've read a number of books that were more than somewhat helpful – books that promised to teach me how to make my skin glow, earn millions in real estate, cheat on my income tax or lose twenty pounds in seven days by eating more. But I never discovered anything that would really change my life. Happily, this is no longer the case. For now that I've read Kenneth Atchity's *A Writer's Time: A Guide to the Creative Process, From Vision Through Revision*, nothing will ever be the same again.

To come clean, I approached Atchity's manual with a certain suspicion, even cynicism. After all, I've read other scribblers on the writer's craft – say, Henry James, Cyril Connolly and E.M. Forster. But, interesting as these amateurs were, they never taught me a damn thing about how to Focus Gestation, Avoid Slumps and Negative Reinforcement or Do Without Crutches. Atchity, on the other hand, is a real pro, generous with guidelines and tips for the aspiring as well as the established writer. Unlike James, Connolly or Forster before him, Atchity is actually a professor of writing. He teaches the stuff at the fabled Occidental College, out there in loopy California, where, according to the blurb writer, he has already helped thousands of writers to discover (or recover) their craft by demystifying the process of writing. His fieldwork is recommended by that legend in her time, Gayle Delaney, Ph.D., founding president of the Association for the Study of Dreams, who writes, 'Atchity has a deep understanding of the creative process.' Me, I was convinced after a cursory glance at the exciting table of contents, which promised to enlighten me on Percolation, Outline vs. Road Maps, Goal-Setting, Telephone Management, Tone of Voice and Marketing Your Work.

Atchity, bless him, has an original grasp of the writer's mind as distinct from ordinary minds – like yours, for instance. As he sees it, the writer's mind is three-dimensional, composed of floating Islands of Consciousness, a Continent of Reason and a Managing Editor, which may explain why so many of us are driven to drink.

An unyielding advocate of lucid writing, or, as he puts it, a clear expression of new vision, Atchity demystifies the literary process as follows: 'Writing is the Editor's ordering of materials from all the islands into the language and structure of the Continent, managing the analytical mind to have it organize images from the nonanalytical mind.' Atchity, I should add – unnecessarily, perhaps – is also a poet, the author of *Sleeping With an Elephant: Selected Poems*.

Streetwise as well as lyrical, Atchity is aware of those publishers who exist outside the writer's three-dimensional mind, that is to say, those idiots who pronounce in publishing houses. 'When they talk about what their audiences like or want or need,' he writes, 'they deserve the author's attention.'

Yes, indeed. But imagine if you will, the Count himself sliding into a chair in his publisher's office in Moscow.

'Well, Leo, still playing the gentleman farmer at Yasnaya Polyana, or have you finally made yourself a Daily Priority Checklist?'

'I want to assure you that I've done a lot of Percolating and Goal Setting since I last came to town. I've invested in one thousand five-by-seven-inch index cards, and I've Road-Mapped your three basic types of characters: major, minor and functional. What I'm Gestating is a novel about this groovy chick, married to a pompous government official, who takes to the sack with a handsome army officer . . . '

'Hey, I like that.'

' . . . but the affair goes badly, and in the end she throws herself under a train.'

'Leo, Leo, that's not what our audiences want or need. Forget it, baby.'

Meanwhile, in a different publisher's office in Moscow, another writer, this one obviously suffering from Negative Reinforcement as well as being overwhelmed by gambling debts, is trying to cajole his publisher into a large advance. He needs it. He's been doing badly at the tables in Baden-Baden, where bruisers with mere one-dimensional minds are holding his markers.

'What have you got for me, Freddy? Not, God help us, another downer.'

'It's a cops-and-robbers caper I worked out, taking advantage of some Time-Work Management Tips I picked up recently.'

'Hey, that would make for a nice change of pace. But I do hope this time you're going to work out the story elements in your head, clearly and dramatically, before you start scribbling. Tell me about it.'

'Okay. There's this student, brainy but destitute, who robs and kills a useless old bag lady only to find himself pursued everywhere by this Kojak type . . . '

'All I ever get from you, Freddy, is sleaze, sleaze and more sleaze. We'd like to look at anything you do, sure, but if you're here for an advance, don't think telephone numbers. Not until you have learned to keep your audience in mind, their needs and desires.'

Write from the heart, Atchity advises. Convey emotion. Obviously no admirer of Céline, Faulkner and Camus, among other well-known product makers, he insists that a writer's philosophy must be optimism, unswerving optimism. Finally, there is the acid test. A writer must be able to summarize the structure and purpose of a book in a sentence of ten words or less.

'Herm, you've got a lot going for you here, especially for fish nuts and armchair adventure freaks, but we've got to think of promos in this office. So I want you to tell me, in ten words or less, why Ahab just has to hook the big white one.'

But before a writer even sits down to compose a novel, made up of Character, Action, Setting and Tone of Voice, he must, in the nature of things, have a Habitat, Materials and Filing Techniques. 'When two writers become friends,' Atchity notes, 'they inspect each other's work space to see what improvements they can make in their own.'

Well now, I hate to quibble, but that has not been my experience. In fact, my literary pals, untypically coarse perhaps, tend to inspect my bar before anything else and have never shown the least interest in a tour of what I fondly call my Habitat. Time and again, I've said, 'Sheed, how would you like to see where I Percolate and Gestate?'

'I'll have a Teacher's and a splash instead, you little twit.'

Atchity – ever helpful, never jealous of his privacy – generously includes a floor plan of his own Habitat in his book. He must be doing well. Son of a bitch has got *three* desks in there. An *electric* pencil-sharpener. A word processor. A TV set. Desk 1, the Habitat-proud Atchity writes, is his organizing and work desk. Desk 2 is taken up with just-printed material and the compact edition of the *Unabridged Oxford English Dictionary*. Desk 3 holds less frequently used reference books but is otherwise kept free for projects that need to remain out between work sessions. He also has shelves in his office (good thinking, this), a reading lamp, a rocking chair and filing cabinets with drawers full of research and ideas. Many of those ideas, I hope, as illuminating as the ones he proffers in *A Writer's Time*.

DEBRETT'S
ILLUSTRATED GUIDE
TO THE CANADIAN ESTABLISHMENT

WHEN THE GOING was good and I was living in Westmount, once a year a local entrepreneur distributed a compendium of neighbourhood tradesmen, listing their phone numbers, addresses and services provided. Useful stuff it was, too, especially if you needed a plumber or TV repairman or a pound of Kenyan coffee beans urgently. *Debrett's Illustrated Guide to the Canadian Establishment*, though it is primarily a catalogue of people in trade, is something else again. While the more modest Westmount guide was distributed free, *Debrett's* costs forty-five dollars, for which you can still buy a decent amount of pain-killing scotch, even at today's prices.

Mind you, *Debrett's* is lavishly illustrated, national in scope, and is not meant to be a functional guide to the services proffered by tradesmen. Rather, it is a celebration of the wealth and social position they have achieved by providing us, over the years, with hardware, haberdashery, booze, hamburgers, shoes and other items even people of sensibility cannot very well do without.

Beyond tradesmen, *Debrett's* also salutes money-lenders (or bankers, as they are called, if they are Protestant), property flippers, brokers and the lawyers who muddy the Establishment's dealings by rendering them into language that is necessarily incomprehensible. '*Debrett's* Six Hundred,' their honour list of Canada's most important citizens, also includes a number of people in the arts, journalism, science and medicine.

Debrett's, as I see it, is not addressed to the general reader, but to two different audiences who share at least one characteristic – a tendency to think of books as furniture.

In the first instance, I speak of the heavy-hitters whose names or photographs adorn the guide, and who are sufficiently vulgar to want it for their coffee tables. And then, if there is a burglar in your family and you are stumped as to what to give him for Christmas, *Debrett's* is just the trick. It not only reveals exactly where the truly rich live, sometimes providing helpful photographs of their homes and toys (antique cars, vintage boats, horses), but in many cases it also tells you what they collect beyond stocks and bonds and tax shelters.

If, for instance, it is oriental ivories and woodblocks your nephew the burglar is after, a good bet would be the home of Adamson, Anthony Patrick Cawthra, O.C., B.A., LL.D., F.R.A.I.C., M.C.I.P., but if it's guns and antiques he fancies, he ought to try the home of Crump, Norris Roy, C.C., M.E., D.Eng., D.Sc., LL.D., D.C.L. If, on the other hand, he is a shoe fetishist, then the pad for him belongs to Brown, Peter MacLachlan, out there in Vancouver. Pete, who obviously walks to his office, owns seventy pairs of Gucci loafers. But on no account should your nephew the burglar break into the home of Marchment, Alan Roy, B.A., F.C.A., C.T.C.I., K.St.L. Alan practises karate in his spare time.

On the front page of the handsomely produced Canadian *Debrett's*, there is a quotation from Scott Symons, which runs: 'Every nation needs an "Establishment," an elite, of some kind – or we are stuck with eternal mediocrity as a national fate.' Two photographs are placed immediately above the quotation, obviously to set the tone, as it were. One of the photographs is of Queen Elizabeth II and Prince Philip, and the other is of former Governor General Roland Michener and his missus, the latter pair royal only for a limited run.

Peter C. Newman, our entertaining chronicler of the Canadian rich, general editor of this version of *Debrett's*, writes, 'When a nation's elite is less than three generations removed from steerage it cannot afford too many pretensions.'

Even so, here they are, our very own aristos, bless each and every one of them, radiating an understandable glee in all their affluence. The progeny of storekeepers, real estate and stock market speculators, garage chain owners, bootleggers and brewers: the Eatons, the Irvings, the Bronfmans, the Molsons. Some cornucopia. K.C. Irving's three sons are nicknamed Gassy, Oily and Greasy. Tom Bata, who claims to manufacture one out of every three pairs of shoes sold in the non-Communist world, refers to his employees as Bata-men, and uses the family name as a prefix in the names of many of his company towns, among them Batawa, Ontario.

Many of our elite belong to such clubs as the Toronto, the York, the Mount Royal, the Vancouver or the Manitoba, which clubs, until recently, did not admit Jews, but now (if only for good form's sake) do tolerate the occasional toilet-trained one here and there. Mind you, the first one to wear diamond socks to lunch or bargain over his bill is bound to be shown the door.

My problem with such dreary tradesmen's luncheonettes is not that they wouldn't have me for a member, but that it ever occurred to them that I wanted to share their company in the first place. Take the Manitoba Club, for instance, which I visited in 1983 in my role as anthropologist. There is a plastic plant on the mantelpiece, the carpeting is unbelievably garish, and I could certainly not recommend the cuisine to anybody with more than a passing interest in such matters.

Peter Newman's lengthy introduction, rich in revealing anecdotes, sometimes suffers from hyperbole. Quite correctly, he mourns the passing of Montreal – the Parti Qué-becois's tribal sacrifice – but he makes too large a case for burgeoning Toronto. It is, he writes, twice as dominant in relation to its economic hinterland as is New York. Taking such an iffy logic a step further, I'm sure an even stronger case could be made for Charlottetown in relation to the rest of P.E.I. But, for all that, Toronto remains a provincial city.

It is also a bit much to talk about the 'glory' of Winston's, or to compare it to Elaine's in New York as a place where public people go to be private in public. Winston's is a very proper little gathering place for powerful lawyers, brokers and politicians. Elaine's is a rowdy haunt of writers, actors, directors and journalists. I don't think, no matter who you are, that you could get into Winston's wearing a T-shirt and blue jeans. Conversely, just about any Winston's regular dropping into Elaine's would find himself seated at a table next to the conveniences.

Don't get me wrong. I enjoyed *Debrett's* Canadian edition. We deserve a brand name compendium certifying the Canadian Establishment. After all, what interests them most is money, which is to say, even if their natures are coarse, their ambitions are touchingly modest. Consequently, they merit a volume of advertisements for themselves.

There is also, as I mentioned earlier, a section of *Debrett's* devoted entirely to the arts and journalism. I counted some 229 cultured names. On second thought, however, maybe writers were listed only because, shorn of our pretensions, we are clearly in pulp and paper. Possibly, *Debrett's* placed more emphasis on pulp than paper. Hailey, Arthur, (who enjoys yachting in the Bahamas on his thirty-eight-foot Bertram cruiser, *Sheila II*) is included, but not landlubbers Michel Tremblay or Roch Carrier.

It is also obvious, considering the one-line entries for several important writers (say, Alice Munro) that some people of discrimination, having received the *Debrett's* questionnaire, threw it into the wastepaper basket with the rest of the junk mail. Which brings me to my confession. I did fill out a form, but in such a fashion that I assumed *Debrett's* would not include it. Alas, they did run my entry, if only in part. Or, not to brag, without me there would be only 599 Very Important People in Canada. Mindful of my responsibility to the unwashed, I now look both ways before crossing the street.

On my form, asked if I owned any vintage airplanes, cars or yachts, and if I collected anything, I responded that I was still the proud owner of an eighteen-inch balsa wood Spitfire model, circa 1942, and that my collection of early Babylonian pornography was unrivalled in the non-Communist world. I listed my clubs as the Canadian Automobile Association and The Owl's Nest Society of Mansonville, P.Q. This was transposed by a snarky *Debrett's* editor to read, 'He belongs to no club more distinguished than the Canadian Automobile Association and something called The Owl's Nest Society of Mansonville, Quebec.'

Well now, let me point out that the CAA, unlike the Mount Royal Club, will give my car a tow should I run into trouble. And *something* called The Owl's Nest Society is very distinguished indeed. Even as I write, my cherished colleagues in that pub, legendary hunters, are out in the hills of the Eastern Townships, searching for venison appropriate to our winter tables.

Finally, I would like *Debrett's* to drop my name from the magical Six Hundred. I take my stand with Groucho Marx. Any club that would have me for a member is not sufficiently exclusive for me to join.

ALL THE
CONSPIRATORS

CHARLES MANSON, OSTENSIBLY vile, was actually a victim – an unwitting agent of military intelligence, programmed to kill. On the other hand, an analysis of the Commie master music plan reveals a hitherto unknown weapon called 'menticide,' concocted by the KGB to bring about suicide of the mind, rendering a generation of American youth bananas. Hence, the Rolling Stones. Lee Harvey Oswald didn't own a rifle, couldn't shoot worth a damn and was a naval intelligence officer. Like Dick Nixon. The Cult of the All-Seeing Eye, seeking to obliterate the Christian Ideal in America, counts among its covert backers the past presidents of India *and* Paramount Pictures, as well as Robert McNamara. The reason the so-called leaders of the world's nation-states can happily indulge in tranquillizers, alcohol and sodomy is that they are merely puppet-prostitutes controlled by the globe's true rulers, 'the Jewish syphilis minority.'

Hold it.

Your enemy may have another name. The Rockefeller family. No longer led by Nelson, it still deliberately manipulates the world of finance, spreading international chaos and confusion and discrediting democratic governments, as witness the 'Impeach Nixon' and Watergate frauds. The SLA, the black liberation armies and even the IRA are all CIA fronts. The air crash near Chicago's Midway Airport on December 8, 1972, which killed forty-five people – among them Mrs. Dorothy Hunt, carrying $10,000 cash and a purported $2,000,000 in American Express traveller's cheques –

was an act of sabotage. Robert Kennedy was not murdered by Sirhan Sirhan but was taken out by a second hit man, still at large. There has never been a more colossal and successful deception – nor one that has been so enormously profitable to its perpetrators – than the myth that Hitler killed six million Jews. The truth about Chappaquiddick has been suppressed by some powerful organized force of universal scope and character. The same folks, incidentally, transformed non-violent Martin Luther King, Jr., into a 'communistoid' agent. Or, conversely, America is run by an invisible government, comprised of Big Business, military intelligence and the Mafia, working together. Or maybe – just possibly – though none dare call it conspiracy, what we innocently label Communism is not managed in Moscow or Peking but is the long arm of a bigger plot controlled in London, Paris and New York by cynical men who use PID (Povery, Ignorance and Disease) as a weapon to build a prison for us all.

Spin your conspiracy wheel, pick your plot and pay your dues.

Dick Gregory, for one, is a heavy plot subscriber and proselytizer, often on tour. Pronouncing at Concordia University, Montreal, in the autumn of 1974, he ventured that the kidnapping of Patricia Hearst was a set-up job by the CIA, the motive being to foment terror, thereby giving security agents more heft, an excuse to expand on their hateful activities. 'Remember,' said Gregory, 'the whole thing happened in the doorway of her apartment. She was wearing only her negligee. When her first tape came in, we knew it was she because it came with her father's credit card. Her driver's license came with later tapes. Now, I don't sleep with many rich chicks, but I wonder whether they go to bed with their driver's license and credit cards . . . '

Gregory assured the Montreal students that Rockefeller would kill then President Ford if he got in his way. Later, in Beverly Hills, I surfaced with something more: an affable scriptwriter who actually knew who had been behind the plot to kill John Kennedy. It was H. L. Hunt's boy, Lamar. 'He brags about it openly,' said the scriptwriter.

'*He does?*'

'Yeah.'

'What does he say?'

'He says, quote, I am the most powerful man in America.'

'So?'

'Prick. Only the most powerful man in America could have killed John Kennedy.'

America, America, is crawling with conspiracy freaks, impassioned researchers, ranging from outside right to farthest left, and if the theories they clobber you with are more than somewhat contradictory, they do have one blessing in common: certitude. And none is more fiercely convinced of the absolute justice of her cause than Mrs. Mae Brussell, sole begetter of the *Conspiracy Newsletter*, a feature that in 1974 had all but gobbled whole the once bracingly sceptical *The Realist*.

Mrs. Brussell, understandably suspicious of visits from strangers, had to be approached obliquely, in my case through the distinct pleasures of a Chinese lunch in San Francisco with her editor, Paul Krassner, of *The Realist*. Krassner, unlike me, did not believe that our time was characterized by inchoate violence, chaos and mindless brutality. Instead, he espied sinister connections everywhere. G. Gordon Liddy, he pointed out, served his apprenticeship pursuing Tim Leary. 'Our country is run by an unholy trinity. Organized crime, military intelligence and corporate bureaucracy.' Maintaining a Communist threat was in their interest. 'You can't have an anti-Communist regime unless you have Communists to hold up as a spectre.'

Not altogether unreasonable, I thought, warming to Krassner, until he told me about his correspondence with Charles Manson. Though Manson's letters tended to ramble incoherently, he said that they were shot through with genius. 'Manson was let out of prison on a leash and protected, until he did what he was supposed to do, discredit the counterculture.'

After lunch, I phoned the elusive Mae Brussell in Carmel.

She still wasn't sure she would see me. Her time was valuable, she said.

'Mine, too,' I allowed.

'How do I know you're not with the FBI?'

'Aw, come on.'

'Or the CIA?'

'I'm a Canadian,' I protested, 'from Montreal.'

'*Montreal*. There's a foundation up there, Permindex, that runs an assassination school in Mexico.'

'You mean like in *The Parallax View*?'

'That film was telling you something. It was a mindblower for people new into conspiracies.'

'Do you think I'd say I was from Montreal if I had been sent out from there to, um, kill you?'

'You never know.'

Finally, grudgingly, Mrs. Brussell agreed to an interview under certain conditions. It would be taped. I would sign a prepared statement beforehand.

In the end, the interview was not taped, *at least so far as I know*, but she did present me with a statement, which I duly signed.

That I, Mordecai Richler, a White Male, Caucasian, 43 years of age, did on the 20th day of October 1974 introduce, and represent myself upon recommendation of the *Playboy* magazine to one Mae Brussell . . . for the stated purpose of writing an article for the said *Playboy* magazine having to do with current theories and research projects pertaining to Government conspiracies and assassinations;

That my reason for meeting with Mae Brussell is to put into writing, in an article, the findings of her research of the past 11 years;

That any information shared during this meeting will be credited to her name in any articles written by me, Mordecai Richler, on this subject matter;

That all findings and opinions of Mae Brussell will be described as accurately and objectively as possible, stating her findings and opinions;

That I will not follow these remarks with snide suggestions, derogatory statements or generalities and false conclusions;

That these conspiracy theories will not be intended to be accepted as having a basis in fact, inasmuch as I have spent only one or two hours interviewing the said Mae Brussell and have not done the 11 years of research on the subject matter as she has;

That all I will endeavour to do is present my viewpoint and let history decide for itself the accuracy of the conclusions reached therein;

That in the event this agreement and/or contract is broken or disrespected or dishonoured to any substantial degree, I, Mordecai Richler, agree to be sued for breach of this agreement/contract and the good faith of our visit. In addition, in the event of any adverse publicity or jeopardy accruing to the research efforts and good name of one Mae Brussell having no basis in fact, I shall agree to be sued or held liable and expect to make financial settlement with the said Mae Brussell for no less than $10,000, avoiding the necessity of legal expenses and a long delayed court procedure . . .

Before actually meeting with Mrs. Brussell, I did some homework. Cautionary homework.

Mae Brussell, the daughter of a reform rabbi, a divorced mother of four, was in her forties in 1974. She was raised in Beverly Hills and majored in philosophy at Stanford. She first became obsessed with conspiracies after reading and annotating the full twenty-six volumes of the Warren Commission Report, a study that convinced her the J.F.K. assassination was an intelligence operation and Oswald himself a government agent. Mrs. Brussell, who claimed to devour eight newspapers daily, did an hour-long weekly radio show, 'Dialogue Conspiracy,' for station KLRB-FM, Carmel, and also conducted the first accredited university course in 'Conspiracies and Assassinations,'; at Monterey Peninsula College. She had written a piece for the *Berkeley Barb*, asking, 'Is S.L.A.'s Cinqué the first black Lee Harvey Oswald?' as well as several lengthy articles for *The Realist*, all of which I read the night before I was to meet her.

Mrs. Brussell struck me as an appalling writer – her syntax unnerving, her prose muddled, lumpy and uncommonly repetitive. Put plainly, until history decided for itself, the viewpoint of this White Male Caucasian, forty-three years of age at the time, was that she wrote without wit, style or even a rudimentary grasp of language. But there was no denying that her ferocity, her flat statements, stacked one on top of another, often without connection or qualification, left me breathless.

Mrs. Brussell was convinced that a web of conspiracies threatened to strangle America. 'It is impossible,' she wrote in *The Realist* (December, 1972), 'the way the courts are constructed to force any revelations that would damage the existing power structure. If Richard Nixon moves out of office, Spiro Agnew moves in and Ronald Reagan will follow him.' In the same issue, she observed that 'J. Edgar Hoover did not have an autopsy. His body was not removed in a hearse. There was no indication of poor health. There is reason to exhume his remains; the possibility of poison in the apple pie might be discovered as his last American supper,' and she went on to promise a piece, not yet delivered so far as I know, titled 'Why was J. Edgar Hoover Murdered?' Meanwhile, she noted that Hoover, who had helped a couple of Kennedys get killed, had feared a CIA take-over and a destruction of all civil liberties.

In an earlier issue of *The Realist* (August, 1972), Mrs. Brussell stated flatly that the CIA had killed President Kennedy and that Richard Nixon was offered the money he needed for his 1968 election if he took political unknown Spiro Agnew as vice-president. Teddy Kennedy's car, she wrote, was pushed into the water at Chappaquiddick *at a time when nobody knew in what capacity Howard Hunt was serving the CIA*. Even so, she had no doubt that the entire Chappaquiddick affair 'was CIA staged for the purpose of removing Ted Kennedy as a Democratic candidate.' Furthermore, she noted that 'the widow of Drew Pearson, Jack Anderson's former boss, could have in her husband's files important information that was passed to J.F.K., on October 28, 1963, saying: "Cancel Dallas trip. Arrest Lee Harvey Oswald." ' Anderson had refused to help find this memo, passing it off as 'too far-fetched.'

Mrs. Brussell was also of the opinion that if Sirhan Sirhan and Charles Manson were free to talk, they would shake American justice to its very roots, but, in another article, she ventured that Sirhan was hypnotized and told to forget the persons who associated with him and controlled him before he became the patsy in the Robert Kennedy murder, and so one can't help wondering how much he could tell us, if he were free to speak.

In 'Why Was Patricia Hearst Kidnapped?' (*The Realist*, February, 1974), Mrs. Brussell stated in her typically unequivocal manner that the SLA was created by the CIA, their goals being no less than World War III and to plunge the Third World masses into starvation and slavery. Other motives, if needed, were to set up conditions for martial law and prevent free elections in 1976. Furthermore, she wrote that we were being brainwashed by the mass media if we believed Teddy Kennedy was actually responsible for the death of Mary Jo Kopechne.

Something else.

The CIA kidnapped Frank Sinatra, Jr., immediately after the John Kennedy assassination to divert news and attention from political events.

Illumination I: Starting out on the two-hour drive to Mae Brussell's house, tooling past the artichoke farms and seemingly endless fields of pumpkins, then turning on to the Carmel Valley Road, a sort of munchkin's suburbia, I was sorely tempted (even at the $10,000 risk of appearing irreverent) to apply philosophy major Mae Brussell's logic, her seductive mix of half-truths and unhinged speculation, to illuminate the following: The hitherto unexplained connection between the emergence of Fidel Castro, the ultimate transfer of the second Washington Senators baseball franchise to Texas, the boom in southern tobacco crops, the so-called suicide of Ernest Hemingway and the funding of Nelson Rockefeller's enormously expensive campaigns for the presidential nomination.

Look at it this way: If Fidel, reputedly a good glove man,

had not flunked in his try-out with the original Washington Senators, he would obviously not have repaired to the Sierra Maestra, wherefrom he emerged such a sorehead. Certainly, if it has not already been deep-sixed, a skilled conspiracy researcher should seek out the original scouting report on Castro. Maybe, like countrymen Tony Perez and Luis Tiant, he had the makings of a major-leaguer. Possibly, the CIA dirty (sports) tricks department, recognizing him for a grudgy type, kept him out of the original Washington Senators" undeniably porous infield because it knew he was bound to stir up the Cuban sandlots. Otherwise, how do you explain why the once threatened antitrust laws were not invoked when the Washington Senators skipped to Texas, where John Kennedy was assassinated?

By not making Fidel a bonus baby, cheap even at two hundred laundered thou, the CIA, at a stroke, accomplished the following:

1. Established a bona fide Communist menace in the hemisphere, which enabled the CIA budget to leap millions, maybe billions;

2. Which led, inevitably, to the Cuban Missile Crisis, making for higher TV Nielsen ratings, at least for slumping news shows, and, therefore, more profits for NBC, a network in which the Chase Manhattan Bank has an interest (that is to say, the ubiquitous Rockefellers, who were consequently enabled to bankroll Rocky's campaigns, not to mention his no-fault loan program to Henry Kissinger, among others).

3. In the sudden absence of Monte Cristos and other fine Havana cigars, there was a boom in inferior Southern tobacco crops. Payola for Nixon country.

4. And, most likely, murdered former Cuban resident and onetime fellow traveller Ernest Hemingway, who, if you remember, in his last days was convinced he was being pursued by IRS agents. Paranoia? Or did old Hem know too much?

*

41

Even as I ruminated over these terrifying possibilities, I found myself at Mae Brussell's door.

'May I see your driver's license?' she demanded.

'Why?'

'How do I know you are who you claim you are?'

Good thinking. Sheepishly, I turned over my tattered license. Mrs. Brussell noted the numbers on a pad and then we sat down to coffee and her delicious banana cake.

'This country,' Mrs. Brussell said, 'is run by bullets and blackmail.'

'If,' I said, quoting from one of her articles, 'J.F.K. was, indeed, the victim of a CIA plot, why didn't his brother Robert speak up?'

'The Kennedys had a proclivity for promiscuity. Robert's dalliances would have been revealed had he talked.'

'Well, maybe . . . But he would have had to have been especially vile, don't you think, to acquiesce to his brother's murder merely to conceal some commonplace adultery?'

'Why do you think they killed Marilyn Monroe?'

'I beg your pardon?'

'She was murdered. Absolutely. It was set up by military intelligence to look like suicide. In fact, it was a warning for Robert.'

'Well, O.K., then after he was killed, why didn't Teddy speak up?'

'He was warned too. Or don't you recall the private plane crash where he injured his back? Then they set up Chappaquiddick.'

'You mean . . . ?'

'His drink was drugged. They put something in it.'

Unobtrusively, I hoped, I set my unfinished slice of banana cake aside.

'Ted Kennedy,' she continued, 'still doesn't know what happened that night.'

Before I could put in a supplementary, Mrs. Brussell was into the Manson case. 'You realize that was also a military-intelligence operation. They groomed and protected him, putting him on a leash . . . '

'Why?'

'A new generation of anti-war kids had arisen, there were the communes, and if they caught on, it would have meant an end to consumer society as we know it. Manson was used to discredit the counterculture. Murray Chotiner was murdered, too; they're getting rid of the old-timers. Why, Oswald never even owned a rifle.'

'But I remember the famous photograph of him holding a rifle.'

'That's a fake. A cropped photograph. His head, another man's body. Now what's your angle? Who else are you talking to?'

'Well, I've already spoken to Nicholas Van Hoffman in Washington and – '

'He's a CIA agent.'

'Can you prove that?'

'It doesn't matter if he's actually on the payroll, his columns clearly reflect their line. There are the agents and the assholes. An asshole,' she explained, 'is anybody who spins the CIA line.'

'I see. Now, when we talked on the phone, you mentioned a foundation in Montreal, Permindex . . . ?'

'Yes. They run an assassination school in Mexico.'

'Could you give me their address, please? I'd like to look into that.'

'Remember what happened to the reporter in *The Parallax View*?'

'Ha, ha.'

Even so, she let me have the address. Later, I discovered there was no Permindex listed in the Montreal telephone directory – in fact, there was no such address. Clever bastards.

'One final question. If so many have already been murdered because they knew too much, how come you . . . ?'

'If I were reaching more people, I wouldn't be alive.'

Illumination II: *Playboy* has a circulation of 6.5 million, which means maybe 20 million readers. What if Arthur

Krechmer, *Playboy*'s editorial director, were a CIA agent, like Von Hoffman, and had cunningly brought me down from Canada only so that Mae Brussell could reach enough people to justify her being killed? That would make me an accomplice to murder. Worse. An asshole.

Los Angeles. To those of us who live smugly and bemused in North America's attic, it seems, increasingly, that America, America, is going paranoid. Certainly, my sojourn in post-Manson Beverly Hills was far from reassuring. The canyons echoed not only with affluence but also with terror. Electrified fences, Doberman pinschers, private security guards. But, above all, the fear that the coming crash, manipulated by the gnomes of Zurich, the Jewish syphilis minority, the CIA, the cynics who control PID, or whoever, might shortly render all monies, all properties, equally worthless.

Gold, that's the stuff. The overachiever's security blanket. Or was it?

The president of one of Hollywood's major studios, an astute man, told me that for months he had been professionally consulting a broker who had written a best-seller about how to make money when everyone else was losing his. They never met, but spoke on the telephone, often for an hour at a time. Again and again, the broker argued for selling absolutely everything and converting to gold. Suddenly, the dancing to bullion stopped. There was a breakthrough. 'Look here,' said the broker, 'I get the feeling, after all our talks, that you're a sophisticated man.'

'Sure.'

'Don't buy gold. It's a load of shit. It's my bag and I've got to peddle it, but the truth is there's only one thing to do. It's a four-point plan.'

'Shoot.'

'How many niggers did you see on your way to work this morning?'

'Well, I – I'm not sure.'

'*You saw lots.*'

'O.K.'

44

ALL THE CONSPIRATORS

'And where do you think they're going to be when the shit hits the fan? Out on the streets, that's where.'

'Uh-huh.'

'You've got to get yourself four guns, get it, and lots of ammo. Sink all your cash into canned and dried foods. Then you hunker down somewhere to wait it out. Me, I recommend Utah; the Mormons don't like niggers, and my guess is they can hold their territory.'

'Trouble is I'm a boat man myself.'

'Can you get to your yacht in twenty minutes?'

'Yes.'

'The only problem is you'd be inclined to sail south. Right?'

'Right.'

'No good. Those fucking Mexicans will be out there, pirating. Running amok. On the other hand, if you got yourself a couple of bazookas, that would certainly surprise them when they pulled alongside.'

Definitions.

It strikes me as neurotic, maybe, yet still reasonable, to be charged with terror on any airplane flight; but if, like me, you also tread in fear, even crossing the street, that you might be struck by an errant, possibly anti-Semitic missile, then you are more than likely paranoid.

Coming from Canada, being Jewish and a writer as well, I have impeccable paranoia credentials. Digging into my childhood, I can recall my father was utterly convinced of *the Detroit plot*, and could embellish on it lovingly at the kitchen table. Dunking his bagel into hot milk, he would assure us that *they* had long ago developed an automobile engine that required no more than a pint of gas to run a hundred miles, but the bastards were keeping it under wraps to protect the oil industry.

Many Canadian writers, most of whom tend to feel unfairly neglected, are convinced this is not due to any inadequacies of their own. They are not published abroad, they insist, because London is a closed faggots' shop and the New

York literary scene is no less than a Jewish cabal. Even more of my own countrymen, especially those inclined towards nationalism, can smell a Yankee plot beneath every bed.

Writers everywhere, myself included, are most commonly paranoid about their mail and tend to sniff conspiracy on those sour mornings that yield no offers, never mind royalty cheques, or at least letters of appreciation. A friend of mine, a well-known writer, his sanity undoubted, actually mails himself letters from time to time, if only to test the continuing integrity of the postal system.

The vast and burgeoning literature of paranoia is something else again. In our own time, it runs from just about anything by Kafka, through Evelyn Waugh's *Ordeal of Gilbert Pinfold* and Saul Bellow's *Victim*, to, most recently, Joseph Heller's *Something Happened*, wherein the protagonist tells us on the first page: 'I get the willies when I see closed doors. Even at work, where I am doing so well now, the sight of a closed door is sometimes enough to make me dread that something horrible is happening behind it, something that is going to affect me adversely . . . ' And only nine pages later he observes: 'In the office in which I work there are five people of whom I am afraid. Each of these five people is afraid of four people (excluding overlaps), for a total of twenty, and each of these twenty people is afraid of six people, making a total of a hundred and twenty people who are feared by at least one person.'

Flying over Salt Lake City, a defensible sanctuary should the niggers run amok, it occurred to me that just possibly nothing, absolutely nothing, was what it appeared to be. Looked at closely, life wasn't absurd after all. There were no accidents. The sound, the fury, *did* signify something.

Ask Skolnick.

Sherman Skolnick is a self-styled legal researcher and chairman of the Citizens'' Committee to Clean Up the Courts, whom I met in a modest, decaying duplex on the South Side of Chicago.

Skolnick, forty-four years old, a paraplegic, was attended

by a gentle aide, David Hoffman. Hoffman, thirty years old, was also crippled, his left arm severed below the elbow. Later, we were joined by the truculent Alex J. Bottos, Jr., chief staff investigator and self-proclaimed former infiltrator of a notorious airplane-robbery gang.

Skolnick, like Mrs. Brussell, was convinced that the SLA was a CIA front and that Patty Hearst was apparently brainwashed. The Hearst family was made a CIA target because, in the forties, their newspaper chain led an attack on the Rockefellers, which family was 'active in seeing to it that the atomic secrets were given to the Soviets in the early forties before the U.S. had completed its first bomb.' All the same, the ubiquitous Rockefellers were a principal force behind the creation of the CIA and took umbrage when, in 1973, the Hearst Corporation, through its Avon Books division, brought out one of the first attacks against the CIA, *The Glass House Tapes*. Hearst, fully aware of what was going on, couldn't protest because, since 1912, his publishing business had thrived on gangster lore.

I sat with the curiously touching Skolnick in his tiny kitchen, canned foods stacked everywhere, as he flicked on his tape recorder and told me, his manner self-conscious, that he didn't come from 'an elite background.' His father, a ladies'' tailor, had left him a small trust fund, inadvertently sparking Skolnick's interest in corruption and the courts. The trust, he said, was managed by a crooked broker, and Skolnick pursued him through the courts for nine years, studying law on his own. In 1963, he founded the Citizens'' Committee to Clean Up the Courts to probe cases that were in the public interest. 'We live on a shoestring,' he said.

'Ours,' said Hoffman, 'is a quasi-organization. It can't be infiltrated or taken over.'

Skolnick told me that he was working on a story for *The Realist*. 'I'm writing about the dozens and dozens of people who were murdered or died under odd circumstances in the wake of Watergate. We have contacts all over the Western world, Europe, Canada . . . '

'Who have you got in Canada?' I asked. 'Anybody I could see?'

'Well, for one thing, we don't openly discuss contacts. Some are strategically placed newsmen . . . '

Skolnick went on to say that from Dallas, through Watergate, the networks, the media, had known the facts about Oswald but didn't dare print them. I asked him, as I had asked Mae Brussell, why Robert Kennedy hadn't spoken up if there had, indeed, been a plot to assassinate John Kennedy.

'Robert Kennedy couldn't protest,' said Hoffman. 'It's like a bank robber gets caught, he has nobody to complain to.'

'Simple-minded people,' said Skolnick, 'those who are not profound researchers, like Mae, ask why the Kennedys don't speak out.'

Taking his point, I changed the subject and asked Skolnick about the crash of the United Airlines plane near Midway Airport, with Dorothy Hunt on board. 'Can you prove it was sabotage?'

'The mass media have time and again tried to protect United Airlines. They've made statements that our case is unsupported. Why? They have United Airlines as an advertiser. We have more than thirteen hundred pages of documents; they say we have no proof. Rockefeller, you know, owns all three networks, through the Chase Manhattan Bank, and the family is a major stockholder in United. So they are going to put us down, which has been our problem for two years. There are angles and angles and angles . . . '

'What evidence have you got that Mrs. Hunt was carrying two million in traveller's cheques as well as ten thousand in cash?'

'I don't know a quick answer,' said Skolnick, 'but our chief investigator can tell you a lot about that.'

Within minutes he was with us in the crowded kitchen.

'Here he is,' said Skolnick, 'Alex Bottos; one day after appearing with me in public, he was in jail on a frame-up.'

'What were you in jail for?' I asked.

Bottos, his manner icy, replied, 'Does there have to be a reason today?'

'They put him in what we call Clockwork Orange, Missouri, the behaviour modification plant. He was there for forty days.'

Immediately, Bottos presented me with a tape. An hour long, it began with spooky music, reminiscent of radio's 'Inner Sanctum.' A girl's voice announced that we would hear things new and startling from Bottos, our host. Bottos, she said, was a student of advanced experimental psychology and had personally observed brainwashing with his battalion in Korea, before being forced to submit to it himself right here in America. 'We strongly suggest,' she said, 'you don't play this tape immediately before a meal. It is brutal, shocking, at times disgusting, but also true.'

Alas, the girl's promo promised better than the tape paid. It was, for the most part, a pontifical sermon, delivered by Bottos in a slow, mournful voice. 'Words,' he began. 'How flippantly we learn to use so many of them . . . ' It was difficult to pinpoint, he said, when this country went wrong, but, clearly, we had reached a new low and were now 'the victims of mental and sexual despots.' There are many ways to assassinate a man, he continued lugubriously, but the most insidious is called zombie-ism. Total degradation. 'I have sickening news for you. As a matter of policy and law, our government is now practising zombie-ism, and doing it in your name.' Then he described the technique.

'You toss a human being, naked, into a four-by-six cell block, no sink, no toilet, nothing, and you control the lighting, sound and temperature. You keep him there for seventy-two hours to a week, creating fatigue, fear and disorientation. High temperature is induced with drugs, and if this doesn't work, you mix brutality with sexual perversions. You force the man, through beatings, to perform unnatural sexual acts and to have others perform them on him, until he is so docile he will perform the worst kind of perversion willingly.'

Bottos then went on to play an excerpt from *The Manchurian Candidate*, after which he suggested that Lee Harvey Oswald, like Laurence Harvey, may have been brainwashed. 'Lee Harvey Oswald,' he said, 'was employed at

Number Five Krashniya Street, Moscow, the Experimental Section of the Electrotechnical Institute in the Building of the Advanced Sciences. Then, at 10 a.m. on March 30, 1961, he was entered in a hospital in Minsk, Russia, for an adenoidal operation, which strangely took twelve days, for he wasn't released until April 11, when he mysteriously received a visa, enabling him to return to the United States.'

Our criminal mental health laws, modelled on Beria's, Bottos said, were introduced by the CIA and once again, the Rockefeller brothers, who wished to introduce world government, sharing control of the globe with Russia. Too bad, Bottos continued, that we didn't heed the warning of California journalist Frederick Selig, who, in June 1964, tried to tell us about the seriousness of homosexual penetration within our government. Homosexuality, Selig wrote, 'was a practising religion, worldwide, their ultimate goal to be in total control of the population and – through thought control – to condition us to believe that normal relations between men and women were a crime.'

So it goes.

Art Buchwald, whom I sought out in Washington, told me: 'The trouble with conspiracy theories is that so many of them have proved to be right. For years, I laughed at my left-wing friends when they told me their telephones were being tapped or that Nixon was a crook, and now, look, they were right all along.'

And, he might have added, though few of us would have believed it before, the truth is that idea man Liddy actually did sit in Attorney General John Mitchell's office and propose an offshore floating whorehouse wherein delegates to the Democratic Convention could be tempted and taped. There were, there's no denying, the 'plumbers' and the so-called White House horrors we all now know too much about. One of the late J. Edgar Hoover's pet projects, it has now been revealed, was Cointelpro, which meant no less than FBI infiltration of left-wing groups such as the SLA The Warren Commission Report, it must be said, leaves far too many questions unanswered. Writing in *The Washington Post* on September 27, 1974, Nicholas Von Hoffman observed: 'If it should ever be discovered that Lee Harvey Oswald was a Cuban agent, it takes no effort of the imagination to think that Fidel Castro might have dispatched the killer to Dallas to avenge the CIA's attempts on the Cuban boss's own life. When three major political figures are murdered and another is nearly so in the space of a decade, it becomes harder and harder to accept the idea they were all gunned down by lonely nuts acting out murderous and private fantasies of sickened minds.' Furthermore, from the beginning, the CIA was up to dirty tricks, some of them murderous, others ugly, more merely incredibly childish. In *The CIA and the Cult of Intelligence*, authors Victor Marchetti and John D. Marks write that for several years the agency subsidized the New York *Daily Worker*. 'In fairness to the *Worker*'s staff, it must be noted that they were unaware of the CIA's assistance, which came in the form of several thousand secretly purchased subscriptions. The CIA apparently hoped to demonstrate by this means to the American public that the threat of Communism in this country was, indeed, real.'

My problem with the conspiracy theorists is that, given a yard of provable dirty work, they want us to run another ninety-nine with them to fantasy touchdowns. Something uglier. Like Senator Joe McCarthy before them, they deal irresponsibly in rumour and innuendo. Before I saw him, poor Skolnick suspected I was an FBI informer and, afterward, he telephoned *Playboy* to say he could prove I was, in fact, a Canadian government agent. Using his and Mae Brussell's techniques, I can help by making the circumstantial case for them.

In 1958, and again in 1965, I was awarded grants by the Canada Council, ostensibly for writing. But the chairman of the council at that time was Peter Dwyer, a wartime agent with MI5. An associate of Kim Philby.

Rooted in England for eighteen years, I wrote for, among other magazines, *Encounter*, since revealed to have been secretly funded by the CIA.

After my return to Montreal in 1972, I travelled to Ottawa once a week for two years, officially a visiting professor at Carleton University, *but unofficially* . . .

A drinking companion of mine in Ottawa was Don Wall, formerly advisor on security to the cabinet.

'How do I know,' Mae Brussell asked, 'you are who you claim you are?'

The truth is I could no longer swear to it myself.

THE ROAD TO
DYSPEPSIA

ONE DAY, WHEN I was a boy, a true master of magic descended on the street corner where we used to hang out. A bona fide YO-YO champion wearing a spiffy red jacket. He shamed us, a bunch of fumble-fingers, managing every stunt conceivable with his YO-YO, ostensibly without strain. Walking the dog, racing round the moon and much more. It seemed to me that S. J. Perelman, when I first read him, could do the same with language, a tool far more daunting. Certainly the most inspired of his kamikaze flights, of which there are many, continue to yield enormous pleasure. Whatever his self-acknowledged debts to Stephen Leacock, George Ade or the still sadly underestimated Ring Lardner, he was an original, at once subversively funny, surreal and a polyglot, armed with a surprising vocabulary that sent me diving for my dictionary more than once.

Eudora Welty once observed that Perelman's prose 'is highly complex, deviously organized, the work of some master brain undoubtedly behind it – and it is more like jiu-jitsu than any prose most of us have seen.' Describing his own work in a concluding note to *Road to Miltown*, Perelman noted, 'If I were to apply for a library card in Paris, I would subscribe myself as a *feuilletoniste*, that is to say, a writer of little leaves.' But like every writer of little leaves, however perfect, he resented the overhanging trees, especially in the autumn. He objected to being described as a humorist rather than a writer.

In an affectionate but somewhat shallow letter to his daughter, Abby, written in 1954, he tries to guide her away from what I should have thought were our sturdiest oaks. He warns her against Tolstoy (who was 'writing about a historical period full of tyranny and oppression in a country full of people who take themselves very seriously") and says that he wouldn't have let her read *Crime and Punishment* if he could have prevented it. 'It's a most depressing book no matter how young or old, how high or low, one is, and that goes for all of Dostoevsky.' Instead, he recommends that Abby snack on Booth Tarkington's *Seventeen*, Mark Twain, the best of Ade and Don Marquis. 'You can be as deeply moved by laughter as you can by misery.'

Allowing that he had no purpose beyond the function to entertain, which he did so admirably, Perelman once protested that 'the humorist conjures up a picture of a man with his hat brim flopped up and a cigar in his face, popping one-liners.' Like the memorable ones he wrote for Groucho, perhaps.

By its very nature, Perelman felt, humour was an angry business, its office to deflate pretentiousness and expose man's follies. In an interview, he once said, 'Generally speaking, I don't believe in kindly humour – I don't think it exists. One of the most shameful utterances to stem from the human mouth is Will Rogers's "I never met a man I didn't like." The absolute antithesis is Oscar Wilde on the fox-hunting Englishman: "The unspeakable in full pursuit of the uneatable." Wilde's remark contains, in briefest span, the truth, whereas Rogers's is pure flatulence, crowd-pleasing and fake humility.' Bravo.

Sidney Joseph Perelman, who died in 1979 at the age of seventy-five, is enjoying something of a revival. In 1986 there was a biography, *S. J. Perelman: A Life*, by Dorothy Herrmann. A year later Penguin reissued three of his collections (*Baby, It's Cold Inside, The Rising Gorge* and *The Swiss Family Perelman*), and then along came *Don't Tread on Me: The Selected Letters of S. J. Perelman*, edited by Prudence Crowther.

Ms. Crowther became a friend of Perelman's in his last

year. It was not a vintage time for him. Laura West Perelman, his wife of forty-one years, had died of breast cancer in 1970. His sentimental attempt to resettle permanently in London had failed. Critics were beginning to complain that his work was now informed by more bile than appetite. *The New Yorker* was paying for but not publishing many of his pieces, holding them in 'inventory.' He was living alone in the Gramercy Park Hotel, only a few blocks away from the Kenmore Hall Hotel, whose assistant manager in the late twenties had been a struggling writer, Perelman's brother-in-law, Nathanael West. One night Perelman introduced West to *The Brooklyn Eagle*'s advice-to-the-lovelorn columnist, 'Susan Chester.' She showed him some of the letters she received. Four years later West published *Miss Lonelyhearts*, which sold 1,480 copies in its first edition. Then, in 1940, West and his wife Eileen were killed in a car accident. Now Perelman was being badgered by young Ph.D. candidates who had no interest in the *feuilletoniste* but wanted to know more about West.

'Those already familiar with Perelman's life,' Ms. Crowther writes in her preface, 'will note the absence of letters to some seemingly obvious correspondents. Some, of course, have chosen not to contribute.' She goes on to say that she 'made many cuts in the letters. Some were requested, most are my own doing.' This, a major irritant, is something I'd like to dispose of first.

Inadvertently, Ms. Crowther's cuts sometimes make this collection read like a Perelman parody of a dead literary man's correspondence. 'And I can't tell you how exciting is the prospect of again seeing that roll of toilet paper —— used as a face.' 'Your vignette of —— and the arty-tarty set with their "dear old sausage" talk, etc., made my blood run cold.' 'The guest of honor was ——, accompanied by that indescribable harridan, his wife.' And my favorite, 'Speaking of girls (who was speaking of girls? I'm obviously shoe-horning this into the text because it has intense meaning to me), do you know one named ——? She was married to ——, but they are now divorced.'

The publishers, sneaky smart, quote Paul Theroux's introduction to *The Last Laugh*, Perelman's posthumous collection, on the jacket flap. But I doubt that Mr. Theroux ever saw these selected letters or he couldn't have written, 'When Perelman's letters are collected, as they surely deserve to be, they will comprise the autobiography he promised and began, but never got around to finishing . . . He was always more personal and ruminative and risqué in his letters than he was in his stories.'

The letters certainly did deserve to be collected. They are interesting, charming, sometimes beautifully written, but they are also evasive, no substitute for the autobiography, and the only really risqué one in the bunch is a letter sent to Paul Theroux. Perelman was involved with many women over the years. According to his biographer, he was fond of sending them playful, decidedly erotic letters; the only one I've seen is not included in *Don't Tread on Me*, but appears in Dorothy Herrmann's book. It is an impish, spicy account of an encounter with a voluptuous, sex-crazed lady on a flight to Jakarta. It suggests that had Perelman's keepers at *The New Yorker* not been so prudish, the writer's legacy might have been enriched by some ripe sexual comedies.

Mind you, he took a dim view of John Updike's writing about sex. In a letter to Ogden Nash, reporting on a Washington reception for Presidential Scholars in 1965, he wrote, 'Also present at this was that éminence grise, J. O'Hara, and that somewhat younger eminence & literatus, J. Updike. The latter read extracts from three works of his to the assembled scholars, which I didn't personally hear as I was overtaken by the characteristic nausea that attacks me when this youth performs on the printed page. But Cheever brought me tidings that all three extracts dealt with masturbation, a favorite theme of Updike's. When I asked Cheever whether Lady Bird was present, he informed me that she was seated smack in the middle of the first row. What are we coming to?' He also seemed to disapprove of Philip Roth and Susan Sontag, among others. But he could be generous. He admired V. S. Naipaul, Kingsley Amis, Bernard Malamud and

Norman Lewis, and was largely responsible for the grant awarded Joseph Heller by the National Institute of Arts and Letters in 1963. '*Catch-22*,' he wrote, was, 'an extraordinary piece of work.'

There's a lot of juicy stuff in the letters for *New Yorker* buffs. For openers, Perelman addressed the editor who succeeded Ross not as 'Mr. Shawn,' or even 'William,' but as plain 'Bill,' which I should have thought was only God's prerogative. Followers of the recent upheaval at the *New Yorker* will be amused to discover that Mr. Shawn's promotion astonished Perelman. 'I was bowled off my pins to learn of Bill's ascension to the wheelhouse,' he wrote to the fiction editor, Gus Lobrano, in 1952. 'I suppose I had taken it for granted that if anyone were chosen for the post, it would be you, and I am still trying to puzzle it out. I of course know nothing whatever of the subterranean currents at the office, but at this distance it occurs to me there must have been an unexpected upheaval.' Only five years later he wrote, 'As for a certain 20-cent magazine called *The New Yorker*, I had another volcanic run-in with them which has effectively convinced me that by and large, that chapter of my life is closed . . . Its whole character has changed; none of the vivacity, the gaiety it used to have is apparent any more.'

In a fuller version of the same letter, published in Ms. Herrmann's *Life*, Perelman lays the blame on Katharine White. 'Following Gus Lobrano's death, [she] has consolidated her editorial power to such an extent that she sits astride the magazine and is slowly throttling the life out of it.' Then, in 1971, he wrote to the British humorist Basil Boothroyd that some of *The New Yorker*'s contributors 'tend to have a ramrod up their arse, acting as though they invented the paper. I well recall an occasion years ago when Thurber was going on ad nauseam about his influence and how he'd set the style for the whole enterprise, etc. I finally got a snootful and said mildly, "Come, come, it's just another 15-cent magazine." Though nearly blind, he leapt at me and tried to throttle me. It took two burly copy editors to drag him off me.'

The selected letters range from 1928, a year before Horace Liveright published Perelman's first collection, *Dawn Ginsberg's Revenge*, to the year of his death. Some of them, as you might expect, are very witty indeed; others sink in a sea of complaints. The correspondence reveals the breadth of Perelman's friendships. There are letters to T. S. Eliot, Groucho Marx, James Thurber, Raymond Chandler, Ogden Nash, Malcolm Cowley, E. B. White and many editors and lady friends, but, astonishingly, not one to his son Adam, who was in and out of trouble with the police.

Equally astonishing, in all the letters written between 1939 and 1945 there is hardly a reference to World War II. However, in 1947 Perelman did write a chillingly prescient letter about Indochina, as it then was, to Gus Lobrano from Bangkok. The French, he wrote, are 'in a completely untenable position in Indochina and are sure as hell going to lose it to the Vietnamese for all their 110,000 men and superior weapons. Everyone I've talked to is either overtly or secretly in sympathy with the resistance, but France is muddling ahead in a thoroughly brutal, medieval, and imperialist fashion.' Later letters establish his intense dislike of witch-hunters and 'that fearful s.o.b. Nixon.' In 1952, there is a clear-headed view of Adlai Stevenson. 'There isn't a shadow of a doubt that Stevenson is a literate, cultivated man with as sharp a sense of humor as any politician in American history has ever displayed, but he is most certainly not the Abraham Lincoln many have persuaded themselves he is.',

Several threads run through fifty-one years of correspondence – complaints about money problems, an arduous work load, hatred of Hollywood and endless bickering with editors and publishers. Through the years, Perelman protested again and again about being hard pressed for money. 'The financial picture's very murky at the moment,' he wrote, typically, in 1956, 'and there are going to be an awful lot of bailiffs nipping at my heels unless I can rustle up some of the long green.' In the early days he was obliged to write knee-slappers for Jimmy Durante, patter for a seemingly ungrateful Larry Adler, the harmonica player, and later to churn out so-so pieces for magazines he considered beneath him: 'I have about 3 weeks clear before I start my 3rd *Redbook* piece on Las Vegas.'

Perelman didn't object to being sole recipient of an Academy Award for the screenplay of the forgettable *Around The World in 80 Days*, though he was only one of the three writers entitled to credit for the script. But in later years he deeply resented being associated in the public mind with the Marx Brothers, having been one of a group of writers responsible for the incomparable *Horse Feathers* and *Monkey Business*. In 1976, when a publisher wanted to include extracts from his Marx Brothers scripts in Perelman's next book, he wrote to his British agent, Deborah Rogers, that he was 'sick and tired of my endless identification with these clowns. If it is not yet apparent after 50 years of writing for publications in the U.S., Britain, and elsewhere that my work is worth reading for its own sake; if illiterates and rock fans (synonymous) can only be led to purchase my work by dangling before them the fact that I once worked for the Marx Brothers, then let us find some other publisher.'

He could be scathing about Hollywood, whose producers 'had foreheads only by dint of electrolysis,' and where, he wrote in 1949, 'I am happy to report . . . that the cultural level hereabouts is as lofty as ever. Rouaults and Picassos are being traded like broncos.' But he deeply resented Lillian Ross's famous series in *The New Yorker* about John Huston's making of *The Red Badge of Courage*. 'There are amusing bits, conference scenes with L. B. Mayer and such, but it's a ratty job, vicious in a professional sense, and will cause a lot of totally unnecessary talk and hard feeling. I yield to nobody in my distaste for Hollywood, but I don't like the way Miss Ross presents it any more than I did Evelyn Waugh's *The Loved One*.'

There were endless quarrels with publishers, Perelman convinced that they were all inept scoundrels who admired other writers on their lists more and were out to sabotage rather than promote his books. Typical was a letter he wrote to Donald Klopfer, at Random House, in 1947. 'To the best of my information and what I myself have seen since I left New York, no advertisement for *Keep It Crisp* has appeared since early in December.' Later he would have the same complaint about a number of British publishers and about Simon & Schuster, whom he threatened to quit for Doubleday.

On the evidence of the biography and the letters collected by Prudence Crowther, the immensely talented S. J. Perelman was insufferably self-centred, a grouch, more than somewhat paranoid, a skinflint, a relentless womanizer and a remote and indifferent parent at best. Robert Gottlieb, who was his editor at Simon & Schuster for a time, told Perelman's biographer, 'He was very charming and very affable and a wonderful raconteur, a very amusing man, fun to be with, but in my view, a deeply involved, selfish and angry person, like so many great humorists . . . He ran away from trouble. He ran away from real emotional or psychic engagement. He was impeccable, but he was not generous.'

If he never risked going after the entire beast, but was content to snap at its heels, a miniaturist to the end, well then, he was superb at what he did. Time will clearly pardon S. J. Perelman, pardon him – as Auden wrote of Paul Claudel – 'for writing well.' Prudence Crowther, in her affectionate introduction to *Don't Tread on Me*, writes that Perelman once told her that someone had called out to him as he was crossing the street in the middle of the block, 'Be careful – we need you.'

Yes, indeed.

IMPOTENCE

IN THE GOOD old days of the *ancien régime* in France, when marriage was sacred, children still had respect for their parents and a *centime* would buy you a croissant and a decent cup of coffee, it was a notoriously hard time for soft men. Any fellow adjudged impotent by an ecclesiastical court was obliged to return his dowry, have his marriage annulled and suffer public ridicule. This shocking information, new to me, comes from a scholarly, occasionally hilarious book by Pierre Darmon called *Damning the Innocent: A History of the Persecution of the Impotent in Pre-Revolutionary France*.

'Without the least scruple,' Darmon writes, 'and in the most peremptory manner, the Church assumed the right to dictate the sexual behaviour of its faithful, and certain canonists set themselves up as virtuosi in what they henceforth considered to be a privileged . . . area of expertise.'

Put plainly, long before we were bombarded with sex manuals in plain brown wrappers, clerics were pronouncing on the mysteries of the orgasm. One of these *Playboy* advisors ahead of his time, Father Sanchez, asked some pertinent questions in his *De Matrimonio*:

'Is it lawful to think of another woman while in the act of fulfilling the conjugal duty?'

'Is it lawful to practice intromission elsewhere than in the appropriate orifice?'

An Italian expert in church law, Dominque de Soto, classified as impotent any husband who scattered his semen around the edges of the aforesaid a.o. (appropriate orifice). But it was left to the good surgeon Guillemeau to set the state-of-the-art standard for virility. A man must be capable of 'erecting, entering, emitting.'

This was serious stuff.

A husband accused of impotence had to provide proof of erection (or elastic tension) in court. If he failed to measure up, he was then required to ejaculate right there, never mind the absence of an a.o. And if that didn't satisfy the clerical fans, he was sentenced to pass the ultimate test – trial by congress before witnesses.

No wonder, then, that nervous young couples, determined to avoid evil spells, introduced superstitious fertility rituals into the wedding ceremony. Among these practices, condemned by the Abbé Thiers but highly recommended by freelance fertility mavens, was the following, which I dutifully pass on to you:

'Piss through the keyhole of the Church in which your marriage rites are held. Some hold that for this method to have all the success that is desired, one must piss into this hole on three or four mornings in succession.'

In the deprived seventeenth century, long before you could rent a cassette of *Night Duty Nurses* at your neighbourhood video shop, impotence cases, especially trial by congress, were understandably boffo with the Parisian public. However, I must agree with one chronicler that some complaints were brought by women of a decidedly lascivious nature. Take, for instance, the case of the shameless harpy who, having put the finger on her husband, was then charged to explain the existence of her ostensibly legitimate child. She confessed that 'she had invited a stonemason that was at work in her house to see if he could not do better than her husband . . . having lain her on a chest that was nearby, he had done in but one attempt that which her husband for all his pains had not been able to do this many a year'

Other women, even more nefarious, pretended to be virgins when this was clearly no longer the case. Happily, they could not fool the sagacious Ambroise Paré, who criticized those women who 'do insert as deep as the cervix a sponge dipped in the blood of some beast, or fill a bladder in which is contained the choleric humour of some sheep,' whereupon 'the poor ninny does believe he has had the cream when he has had only the dregs of the pot.'

The outraged Pierre Darmon suggests that behind the sang-froid with which the clergy conducted genital examinations there lurked the most impure motivations, including voyeurism. Especially, an observer complained, in the examination of women, who were often probed with a male member made of wax. Boucher d'Argis, a party pooper, recommended caution in the examination of male genitalia: 'There can be no doubt that proof of natural movement may be ordered, but experts and midwives must take great care not to exceed their mission.'

There was often learned debate in court over the quality and durability of an erection. Take, for instance, the case of the Marquis de Gesvres. Counsel for the marquis, Maître Chevalier, argued: 'He has the form, therefore he has the movement.'

Prosecution countered: 'If the Popes had reasoned thus, we would surely have no term "*De Frigidis et Maleficiatis*."'

Defence replied: 'The unfortunate marquis has been given notice to exhibit his manly vigour in the presence of four gentlemen capable of extinguishing the most ardent of fires.'

Prosecution disagreed.

'Perhaps so. But these experts possess the art of submitting their patients to all manner of prickings and spurs . . . They have secrets to excite movement, tinglings to prick sensitivity. Such excitations are by no means wrong when employed only to inform the Church.'

The marquis himself pleaded: ' . . . just looking at you makes me wilt. After all, how can you expect to see that which your very presence puts to rout? Content yourselves, therefore, with what you do see, and by that token imagine what you do not see.'

Devilishly clever, no doubt, but the marquis had to pay his wife substantial damages.

Trial by congress was defined as an occasion in which two protagonists engaged in 'virile combat,' the 'warrior' employing his 'lance' to penetrate the lair of procreation. Royal ordinances forbade duelling between noblemen, but – as one cleric put it – 'there existed no law forbidding duels and combats between those soldiers that do engage under the flag of Venus.'

A notable case involved one René de Cordouan, the Marquis de Langey. Something of a singles-bar type, the marquis looked forward to his trial with glee. Certainly the public was on his side. Crowds booed the marquis's entrance into the court, but the marquis was greeted with cheers. One cynic observed, 'Langey was proclaiming victory, you would have thought he was already *in*.'

De Langey, the author writes, had worked out in advance each stage of the ritual, down to the tiniest details. He insisted that his wife be given a hot bath to foil the effects of any astringents she might have taken. Her hair was to be left untied, to prevent her from concealing talismans that might bewitch his performance. Finally the soldiers of Venus withdrew to the field of combat – a bed – at which point the foolish marquis cried out, 'Bring me two fresh eggs, that I may get her a son at the first shot.'

A somewhat rash display of optimism, Darmon notes, because the duel was to last four hours, 'during which time,' according to the court record, 'he had not the smallest stirrings where they were needed, though he did sweat plentifully such as to change his shirt twice, the drugs he had taken having inflamed him. Next in a rage he set to praying.

' "You are not here for that," said she.'

Quite right, too.

THY NEIGHBOR'S WIFE

ERNEST HEMINGWAY, I'M told, observed that the trouble with Henry Miller was that having once been laid in the afternoon he concluded that he had invented it. On the evidence of *Thy Neighbor's Wife*, a field-study of America's changing sexual mores that was nine years in the making, the same may now be said of Gay Talese and masturbation. In 548 pages, Talese seems to describe no other sexual act quite so often or with such appetite. To be fair, this is certainly not in the service of prurience. *Thy Neighbor's Wife* is not a stroke-book, and the author attempts to justify his interest, noting that in 1968 the 'best-known character in literature was the chronic masturbator in Philip Roth's novel *Portnoy's Complaint*.' the analogy doesn't work, if only because Talese's relentless study of sexual pleasure ultimately bears the same relationship to Roth's exuberant novel as the *Reader's Digest* does to ideas.

If Talese is fascinated by what we used to call jerking-off, it is in aid of advancing a poetic *pensée*, namely, that the penis is a man's most honest organ: " . . . it has performed purposefully if not always skillfully for an eternity of centuries, endlessly searching, sensing, expanding, probing, penetrating, throbbing, wilting, and wanting more.' And not to quibble, but merely to introduce a personal note, in my case it also pisses.

The delights of masturbation are first described as early as page 8, wherein promising young Harold Rubin, who will one day run his very own massage parlour, thrusts his schoolbooks aside to fondle his whizzer as he ruminates over a nude photograph of Dianne Webber. But the lonely act does not reach its pinnacle until page 505, when we meet Betty Dodson, a painter, whom I take to be the Norma Vincent Peale of alternative life-stylists. Which is to say, this self-proclaimed Phallic Woman has overcome her Bible Belt education to such a life-enhancing degree that she can now have the other girls in to her New York apartment for what she calls 'cunt-positive' sessions. It seems that Ms. Dodson, the author of *Liberating Masturbation: a Meditation on Self-Love*, long looked to this act as her primary source of whoopee, but the poor dear feared that her habit had deformed her vaginal lips, until a knowledgeable lover disabused her of the notion. Consequently, the considerate Ms. Dodson began to conduct seminars for other worried women in her apartment, 'consciousness-raising sessions in which the participants were encouraged to scrutinize their own and each other's genitals without shame or diffidence. Using mirrors for self-examination, and then taking turns spreading their legs, the women . . . not only observed but also touched, smelled, and tasted their own genitals, and sometimes those of friends.' Well now, my immediate reaction is, *feh*! But, looked at another way, depending on where you pay your dues, it is a step forward, or two steps back, from the days when their mothers – genitally enslaved, trading fidelity for economic security – used to get together to smell and taste each other's marble cake.

Masturbation surfaces again in the concluding pages of *Thy Neighbor's Wife*, as a liberated Talese lies nude on a starched sheet on a Lexington Avenue table savouring the tender ministrations of a bare-breasted masseuse.

' "Do you want anything special?" she asked.

' "Can I have sex?" he asked. She shook her head.

' "I don't do that," she said. "I don't French either. I only give locals."

' "*Locals*?"

' "Hand jobs," she explained.

' "Okay," he said, "I'll have a local." '

*

66

In the pages between Rubin's solitary ejaculation into a Kleenex and Talese's lyrical communion (cost, $15) with another soul, we have learned a good deal about America's shifting obscenity laws, from the Comstock Act of 1873, through Justice Brennan's definition of obscenity as being 'utterly without redeeming social importance,' to the more restricting *Miller v. California* ruling with respect to community standards, endorsed by the Burger court in 1973. We have also been introduced in considerable biographical and sexual detail to the heroes and heroines of the alternative life-style, among them Dianne Webber, John Bullaro, and John and Barbara Williamson of the fabled Sandstone Retreat, about which more later. Attention is paid to Alvin Goldstein who gave us *Screw*, Dr. Alex Comfort, various bunnies, and of course Hugh Hefner. All these people are, for the most part, distressingly shallow. They are often delinquent, sometimes downright sleazy and uniformly self-regarding. Like adolescents, they believe things are happening for the first time. Ignorance is their armour, self-gratification their only concern. They are the raw material of a Terry Southern satire or, possibly, a nifty debunking job by Tom Wolfe. But Talese, who describes himself as a non-judgmental journalist, whatever that means, unfortunately accepts this vacuous lot at their own inflated value, his endless account of their couplings unredeemed by wit or humour.

Talese, who writes about himself in the third person, like General de Gaulle, is so impressed with Hugh Hefner that he describes his bed, eight-and-a-half feet in diameter, three times, and reminds us twice that the publisher of *Playboy* has been adjudged a genius. Underlying what purports to be a history of the altered sexual consciousness of middle-class America is the arrogant assumption that those of us who still put wife and family, even monogamy, over the endless searching, sensing, expanding, probing and throbbing of our most honest organ are somehow repressed, antiquated and secretly envious of Hefner and his hutch.

Hefner's notion of heavenly bliss would seem to be to lie – a Pepsi in hand, mirrors overhead – on his circular rotating bed, surrounded by half a dozen nude bunnies, each one of whom is gently massaging him with oil, while a hidden camera records the love session for future reference and his butler stands by to play and replay 'Tie a Yellow Ribbon.' But there are other men, myself included, who might honestly prefer a stationary king-size, no distracting mirrors, no leering butler, maybe a little Bach, some Remy Martin and his very own wife, and who would rather not watch a replay of last night's intimacies with his morning bagel and coffee, but instead would settle for the sports pages, horsing around with his kids before they leave for school . . . Which is to say, to each his own epiphanies.

In his exacting nine-year sexual odyssey, Talese 'lingered in the lobbies of the Holiday Inns, Ramadas, and other motels watching as the grey-suited men with attaché cases purchased at the newsstand a copy of *Playboy* or *Penthouse* before heading for their rooms,' obviously to all but tear their honest organ out by the roots. Talese's problem, possibly, was his choice of venues. There are other hotels, I can assure him, where out-of-town husbands repair to their solitary beds with paperback Dr. Johnsons or, if they have a real interest in sex, a Jane Austen novel.

Two main strands run through Talese's book: the running biography of Hugh Hefner, and the story of those people whose tangled lives led to the founding of the Sandstone Retreat, appropriately enough in California. Ah, Sandstone. Xanadu for husbands who are themselves sexual countermen, with take-out wives, available to anybody anywhere. 'Nothing in his earlier research,' Talese writes of himself in typical non-judgmental fashion, 'had quite prepared him for Sandstone – not the massage parlours, nor the swing bars, nor live shows, nor what he had read or been told by the sexual gazetteers of his acquaintance. Sandstone, during the early 1970s, was undoubtedly the most liberated fifteen acres of land in America's not-always-democratic Republic . . . '

Sandstone, in the hills of Topanga Canyon, was the inspiration of an electronics engineer named John Williamson and his wife Barbara. Williamson – who perceived organized religion as a celestial swindle and the federal government as avaricious – hoped, on this rock overlooking Malibu, to build his retreat for what he called 'change people,' those who ignored sin and guilt and celebrated pleasure. His club welcomed such paying members as Daniel Ellsberg and Anthony Russo, Betty Dodson, Max Lerner and the happily named Dr. Alex Comfort, author of *The Joy of Sex*. Upstairs, guests would shlump around starkers, shooting the breeze, having a nosh, but downstairs was the pleasure-dome – the ball room. Triads. Foursomes. Bisexuals. 'After descending the red-carpeted staircase, the visitors entered the semi-darkness of a large room where, reclining on the cushioned floor, bathed in the orange glow from the fireplace, they saw shadowed faces and interlocking limbs, rounded breasts and reaching fingers, moving buttocks, glistening backs, shoulders, nipples, navels, long blond hair spread across the pillows, thick dark arms holding soft white hips . . . Sighs of ecstasy could be heard, the slap and suction of copulating flesh . . . Or, shorn of its pretensions, what we used to call an orgy. Never mind, it was in this transcendental environment that the driven Talese at last learned to become so uninhibited as to be able to greet male friends 'with an embrace as natural as a handshake,' something some of us have been doing for years, but never thought it worth remarking on.

Thy Neighbor's Wife is not so much an immoral book as a silly one, sadly lacking in any appreciation of human dignity, of the nature of love, of the heart or the soul. It's impoverished. But it is also just possibly subversive in that it succeeds, like no other book I know of, in making of sex a mechanical bore. My, my. All that mindless sucking, licking, arching, thrusting, finally becomes oppressive. Its titillating subject aside, the book suffers because the author lacks an ear for the spoken word. Everybody I know speaks in his own voice, but in *Thy Neighbor's Wife*, all the voices seem flat and interchangeable. A good deal of information is passed on to the reader through conversation, but nowhere, in all its pages, is there an illuminating chunk of dialogue. Finally,

Thy Neighbor's Wife may also be insidious in that to dislike it, as strongly as I do, is to be open to the charge of being a prude. Don't be intimidated. It's possible to object to this book on grounds of taste alone. Indeed, if I had to describe it in a sentence, I would be bound to say it was the work of an undeniably stiff prick, but a limp mind.

BE MY FOOTSIE
WOOTSIE, YOU BUGGY
POOPOO

1

WILLIAM BETCHER, A clinical fellow in psychiatry at Harvard Medical School, has written a book called *Intimate Play: Creating Romance in Everyday Life*. It's aimed at keeping your sex life and mine creative and tender by invoking playfulness. When starting a relationship, for instance, Betcher suggests you might want to publish a 'creative' valentine to your heart's desire in the local newspaper, addressed to 'Bellybutton Blower,' "Meatball' or 'Miss Quickie,' the message running:

> Be my footsie wootsie
> Or I'll break your armsie warmsie.

I have, so help me God, not made up these endearing nicknames but plucked them from a list compiled by our fun-loving author, a list that includes Furry Bum, Hornet Toad, Pussy Lips, Applefritter, Wascally Wabbit, Cuddle Bumps and Dishdelish.

William Betcher, M.D., Ph.D., leans on case histories and anecdotes from his work as a marital therapist to illuminate his manual. Based on clinical observation, he recommends that in order to sweet-talk a shy partner into having a first go at fellatio or cunnilingus, it helps to smear the appropriate parts with food. Not bad advice, really, but I should hastily add, whatever you do, avoid horseradish.

Come to think of it, Betcher is awfully big on food as a

71

spur to healthy sex play. Take the case of Rita, whose very own Goosey Poosey once took her by surprise in the kitchen, where they shared a romantic interlude even as the onions were simmering. ' "At one point he picked up one of the carrots lying on the table and fucked me with that. Afterward, we had a good laugh about it and I told him, 'This is the first time I've ever been laid by a vegetable.' We then fantasized about other kinds of foods that would make good or bad lovers." '

Calf's liver we already know about, having read *Portnoy's Complaint*. Cucumbers – mind you, organically grown – have already figured in a fine comic passage in Lisa Alther's *Kinflicks*. But what else? Zucchini? Pickled herring? Pineapple? Rita doesn't say.

One Dr. Grunebaum, quoted on the book jacket, describes *Intimate Play* as delightful. He certainly ought to know. He's the director of the Family Psychotherapy Training Division at the Cambridge Hospital. Dr. Grunebaum writes, '[This book] should enable many couples to open up their relationships in explorative and enjoyable ways.'

You do that, according to Betcher, by indulging in free play, letting out the child in you. Betcher quotes with approval a Snookiepie who told him, ' "My happiest moments with my husband are when we can be like two kids. We might be out on a fall day raking the leaves and start playing in the piles – we like to bury each other under them or lie on our backs on a great bed of leaves and watch the cloud formations. We'll imagine things up there and describe what we see." '

Not all of Betcher's advice is asinine but harmless. Some of it is downright dangerous. He encouraged one couple, too inhibited to state clearly what they wanted in bed, to invent a numbers game in which each numeral referred to a sexual favour or specific body part. ' " . . . Carter's penis thus became '007,' after James Bond, and '7–11,' from the convenience store that stays open all night meant that I was ready to have intercourse; '8' meant I wanted to have my genitals caressed . . ." '

Calling out numbers, it seems, enabled Carter and his convenience store wife, open all night, to express their needs without suffering embarrassment. Okay, okay, but let's say Carter takes Lucy to a football game one fall afternoon, the leaves having already been raked. The first time the quarterback calls out numbers in the huddle she manages to restrain herself, but on the second play call she abandons herself to lust and leaps on to the field, shedding her clothes as she goes, shrieking, 'Yes, yes, give me an "8," you "007" devil you.'

Or Lucy's broker phones one morning to say, 'I've got sensational news for you, my little Luscious Lunchbox. The Simplex United you bought for 22 last August has just hit 69 on the ticker.'

'I'll be right over,' she replies breathlessly.

The hopelessly silly *Intimate Play* is not a publishing aberration but part of a trend, one of a subculture of books that promises to instruct us in sexual behaviour, the war between the sexes, the new man or new woman, and how to wring more joy out of sex. Usually they are written in unspeakable prose by a medical man and come festooned with praise from other doctors, all of whom have given up house calls for this far more profitable game. *Why Men Are the Way They Are*, by Warren Farrell, Ph.D., is blessed by the authors of *Open Marriage, How to Survive the Loss of Love* and *A Guide to Rational Living*. It is described as 'witty, provocative, and probing' by Carol Cassell, Ph.D., author of *Swept Away* and former president of the American Association of Sex Educators, Counselors and Therapists.

Witty, provocative, probing?

Farrell, who obviously deals out advice in a jiffy, claims to have worked with no less than 106,000 women and men 'from all walks of life' over a seventeen-year period. Say, giving him the benefit of the doubt, that he works five days a week, forty-five weeks a year. That goes to just about 6,235 sex-troubled patients a year, something like 139 a week or 28 a day. My God, now I understand why his book has also been praised by Kenneth H. Blanchard, Ph.D., co-author of *The One-Minute Manager*.

Anyway, our out-of-breath author has concluded, on the basis of a scientific study of the magazines men and women buy, that – wait for it – 'the [female] primary fantasy is glamour/beauty *and men*. Over 90 percent of the ads in women's magazines focus on glamour/beauty and men: how to get men, and what to do with them.'

Focusing his X-ray vision on men and the mags they buy, Farrell has discovered that fellas are more interested in war, sports, business and, oh, yes, women. 'If he wants part of his primary fantasy (*one* beautiful woman), he must at least be a successful performer.' His primary fantasy, by the way, is '*many* beautiful women.'

Farrell's book, a ragbag of bromides, is typically tarted up with charts and illustrations, flashy subheads on just about every page, and thoughtful hints to better behavior boxed in here and there. For example:

Guide to Listening When Someone is Upset.

The Listener during a Complaint (No One Does This Perfectly!)

Listen by using supportive eye contact and drawing out; for example, 'Tell me more . . .' 'Yes, I see . . .' 'Explain . . .'

Do not correct distortions. Instead, reach inside yourself to understand the complainer's best intent and her or his underlying hurts.

Allow time after the complainer finishes (30 seconds to one minute).

I am, in principle, against book burning, but to every rule there is an exception. Which brings me to *Men Who Hate Women and the Women Who Love Them*, by Susan Forward, Ph.D., and Joan Torres. Here, among other tales, we are told the story of Jackie, whose romance and subsequent marriage to Mark (ill-advised, you betcha) began as a blind date.

I opened the door and saw this incredibly handsome man standing there. He just smiled at me. The first words out of his mouth were, 'Can I use your phone?' I blinked and said yes, and he walked over to the phone and called the guy who had introduced us and said, 'John, you were right. She's everything you said she was.' That was only the beginning of the evening!

In fact, more than a hundred pages pass before poor, simpleminded Jackie grasps that she is stuck with something other than what good old William Betcher would affectionately dub a Buggy Poopoo.

2

Reconsidering some of the reading I have enjoyed over the years, I now understand that an alarmingly high proportion of it was based on unsubstantiated gossip about women. Mrs. Bovary. Anna Karenina. Molly Bloom. While there was a good deal of information in their stories about Money, Work and certainly Sex, it must – with hindsight – be adjudged unreliable. It was not based on either quantitative data or qualitative quotations, but, instead, on nothing more than a fallible author's instincts. Flaubert didn't send out questionnaires. Tolstoy had to wing it without benefit of computer printouts. Joyce couldn't back up Molly Bloom's zingers with convincing statistics. What I know about contemporary American couples (married, cohabiting, gay or lesbian) has largely come from other purveyors of gossip – say, John Updike, Walker Percy, Saul Bellow, and the rest. It follows, then, that my knowledge of how other couples cope with money, work and sexual problems has, until now, been shallow and unscientific.

So it was with a certain excitement that I turned to *American Couples: Money, Work, Sex*, written by two formidable sociologists, Drs. Philip Blumstein and Pepper Schwartz. To begin with, their information bank would put any mere novelist to shame. It filled 75 file drawers and more than 175,000 computer cards. With the generous support of the

National Science and Russell Sage Foundations, Blumstein and Schwartz sifted through responses to twelve thousand questionnaires and interviewed more than three hundred couples at home, sometimes more than once. They were helped by the New York *Times* wire service and that other relentless pursuer of truth, television. 'Soon after our appearance on the "Today" show,' the authors write, 'the mailroom at the University of Washington was inundated. As requests to take part in the study flowed in, we were impressed by the geographical diversity and the variety of lifestyles. There were letters from presidents of Fortune 500 companies and their wives, from ranchers, members of the clergy, and people in the military, just to name a few.'

Why, we are even told that the thirty-eight-page questionnaire from which the good doctors worked *required two years for its creation alone*, which may, in passing, tell us more than we wanted to know about the speed of foundation-supported sociologists compared with the private enterprise novelist who still functions out of a one-man shop. In any event, the questionnaire asked direct questions – thoughtful replies to be filled in on a scale of one to nine – never dreamed of by Flaubert, Tolstoy or Joyce:

> With how many people have you ever had sexual relations (including your current partner)?
> None. One. Two. 3 to 5. 6 to 10. 11 to 20. 21 to 50. 51 to 100. 101 or more.

It also asks:

> Have you had sexual relations with someone you met the same day or with a stranger?

Like you, I had to read this twice, before I concluded that Blumstein and Schwartz are not nearly so concerned with language as they are with hanky-panky. Anyway, the possible answers to this one include: Daily or almost every day. Three or four times a week. Once or twice a week. A few times. Never.

Immediately, this question posed several problems for me.

76

(a) What kind of person would answer such a questionnaire? Certainly the bunch I hang out with, though none of them are presidents of Fortune 500 companies, would consider it an insufferable intrusion and would promptly drop the questionnaire into the wastepaper basket. On the other hand, I know some of the boys I went to school with would respond that they had seduced at least 101 or more girls and that they had had sex with strangers daily or almost every day, depending on their work schedules.

(b) If a respondent claims 101 or more sexual encounters (or, like Georges Simenon, more like 10,000), is he asked to produce evidence? Testimonials? Receipts? Or has he tagged his conquests like Atlantic salmon? Otherwise couldn't he just be a braggart?

Happily, my suspicions are not supported by the many sociologists, their credentials far more impressive than mine, who have endorsed *American Couples*. The jacket blurbs from various professors claim:

'*American Couples* brings new sensitivity and understanding to age-old issues.'

'Some of the authors' findings are a surprise to both laypersons and scientists.'

'They have written the most thorough description of the new scripts in the gender drama yet to appear.'

'Blumstein's and Schwartz's revolutionary approach offers startling revelations about the universality of joys and sorrows connected with erotic love.'

Rather than sustain the suspense any longer, I will now pass on to you some of the startling revelations, surprising as they may be to both laypersons and scientists, that are at the core of this in-depth study that was so many years in the making. In true publish-and-be-damned spirit, the erudite authors introduce their section on sex with the following *pensée*: 'Having sex is an act rarely devoid of larger meaning for a couple. It always says something about the partners' feelings about each other, what kind of values they share, and the purpose of their relationship.' Other illuminations, including the following, are considered to be of such significance that they are offered in italics:

> *For employed wives, the happier they are with their job, the happier they are with their marriage. Gay men seem happier with their work if they are open about their sexual preference. The frequency of sex declines the longer couples stay together. Age can also have an impact. When the nonsexual parts of couples'' lives are going badly, their sex life suffers. In married and cohabiting couples, the more emotionally expressive a partner is, the more he or she initiates sex. When heterosexual women are attractive, they have more varied sex lives. Heterosexual men who receive oral sex are happier with their sex lives and with their relationships in general.*

The latter bombshell, like the rest, is supported by revealing interviews. As one thirty-six-year-old husband, pondering oral sex, put it, 'I enjoy the sensation so much.' Another, obviously more thoughtful husband, this one forty years old, said, 'When she gives me oral sex, I view it as an expression of her feelings for me ... She is trying to say something about our relationship ... I think she is feeling love for me.'

Women also have their say about oral sex: 'Would you call it his suggestion to me that he starts waving it toward my face?'

Another wife said: ' ... It makes him feel good, truly good. I don't find it unpleasant. I don't say I wish I could do it all the time. I don't equate it with a sale at Bloomingdale's. That I could do all the time. But it's not like going to the dentist either. It's between the two extremes. Closer to Bloomingdale's than to the dentist.'

> *Kissing occurs usually, though not always, when couples have sex. It is most consistently present among lesbians, and least present among gay men.*

As everywhere else in such a serious study, we are not trading in opinion here, or locker-room gossip, or anything so sloppy as untested insight. We are dealing in hard fact, based on a sample of twelve thousand. The statement on kissing is substantiated by a chart that reveals when heterosexuals have sex, 80 percent of them also kiss. Gay men, a rough bunch, kiss only 71 percent of the time, but loving lesbians kiss 95 percent of the time.

There is another revelation on kissing in this new script on the gender drama. As one perspicacious wife put it, 'Kissing is sensual, it's an orifice where a connection can be made.'

Remember, you read it here first.

3

The Love Test is a work that dares to ordain that you should never marry *until you find a person whose RAQ, not to mention his or her EMRF, matches your own*. This ground-breaking study, an Apple Tree Production, was written by Harold Bessell, Ph.D., an 'internationally known' authority on preventive mental health who has consulted, taught and lectured widely over the past thirty years and now works in La Jolla, California.

Bessell, a psychotherapist, is my kind of guy. He believes that at the core we are *people* people, and, damn it, he ought to know. After all, he has already racked up an impressive forty thousand counselling sessions on love. Marriage, he ventures, is a gamble. But that no longer need be the case, at least not since the good doctor developed a sentiment scale, a very personal tool: his Romantic Attraction Questionnaire (RAQ), which can be used in tandem with the Bessell Measurement of Emotional Maturity or, more properly, the Emotional Maturity Rating Form (EMRF). Though these tests boast a better than 90 percent accuracy rate for predicting future happiness, Bessell, obviously a caring *person* person, cautions readers *not to split up just because of the information you glean from his book*.

The first point Bessell makes, a veritable mindboggler, is that infatuation and true romantic attraction are not quite the same thing. In the former, his studies have proved, feelings die, while in the latter, feelings persist. There are other differences. In infatuation, strong emotion is triggered by wish-fulfilling fantasy, but in true romantic attraction, there is 'strong emotion as a normal positive biopsychological sense of excitement that is an intrinsic response not based upon a continued fantasy,' or, as we used to say, love.

Freud, in Bessell's opinion, 'missed one very big boat.' That is to say, many people do have neurotic problems, but some will live happier ever after once they have filled in their RAQ Life, however, is charged with unequal opportunities. Scientific research, and maybe a little bar-hopping, has led Bessell to conclude that *physically attractive people have more invitations to get acquainted*. Furthermore, you can also be romantically excited about a thing rather than a person. Lewis and Clark, for instance, were romantically excited about the Northwest, just as Thomas Edison was about his laboratory, and my second cousin Bernie about black silk panties with delicate lace trim.

You can save yourself a lot of trouble by carrying a copy of the love test, or RAQ, with you at parties, just in case you bump into a potential love partner. But be prepared, it asks subtle questions, psychologically loaded to rate your romantic interest on a scale of one to five. I will, in the interest of brevity, list only four of the sixty probers that make up the RAQ test.

1. I feel very lucky to know this person.
25. This person is a great companion.
41. I enjoy being with this person even when we are silent.
47. I like to touch and be touched by this person.

Bessell astutely warns that RAQ tests be filled out again and again – 'Would you please not get out of your dress just yet and lend me a pencil instead. I'm trying to concentrate' – as scores fluctuate when we are angry, sad or frightened, which in my case is most of the time.

Of course, emotionally mature people are something else again. Unfortunately, on the demanding EMRF scale, I failed to qualify. The trouble is emotionally mature chaps are not only deeply committed team players, but 'if the dishwasher is broken, they will know where to find the warranty and will make the effort to call the dealer and to be home when the repairperson [*sic*] arrives.' I even flunked out on the 'integrity' section of the EMRF, scoring embarrassingly low on the following hard-hitting criteria.

My friend shows a positive attitude about coping with unpleasantness, pain or discomfort.
My friend behaves in a neat and orderly way.
My friend willingly carries his or her share of the work load.

In order to make your love relationship work, Bessell suggests that you try your best to set aside twenty minutes a day for one-to-one time, and that if you must have a confrontation, *do it with support*. For example, you don't say, 'You're late again, you unreliable bitch,' but rather, as Bessell suggests, 'I know your tennis game was important to you. I want you to have your exercise and recreation, but it would be nice if you would show me how much you care about me by being on time.'

Bessell's language is as fresh as his ideas are original. 'Almost everything in life,' he writes, 'has its good and bad sides. For every pleasure there seems to be a price. It is said that it is an ill wind indeed that blows no good at all. We learn from the pain of our mistakes. We both love and hate to get up in the morning to go to work, to solve our daily problems.'

It comes as something of a surprise, then, to discover that Bessell is a literary man as well as a perspicacious psychotherapist. In the most challenging section of this seminal study, 'Personal Love Profile,' he offers his own analysis of famous love stories of the past, enriched by diagrams as fascinating as they are RAQ-accurate. Of Romeo and Juliet, he writes, 'Although their families were not on speaking terms, Romeo and Juliet happened to meet and fall instantly in love. It was not a case of infatuation because the relationship lasted many months, as each managed to evade disapproving families and unite. But they had two serious problems: They were young and inexperienced, and Juliet's family hired incompetent nursemaids. As a result, a relationship that might have been sweeter than a rose ended in an immature manner. With time, they probably would have become more emotionally mature and could have had a Type-One relationship. Instead, they died before their time.

'*Diagnosis*: Type-Three relationship terminated prematurely.'

Scarlett and Rhett, on the other hand, had a classic Type-Five relationship. 'Her immaturity affected every relationship she was involved in and finally drove her husband to desperate behavior. When disaster and death entered their lives, they had no way to communicate with each other. Rhett began drinking. Scarlett's immature behavior continued. Rhett knew her heart was with another man. Finally, he left her.'

Obviously, not enough one-to-one time. But in every love relationship, even the dreaded Type-Five, there is now hope if you apply Bessell's four A's to the case:

> Attention
> Acceptance
> Approval
> Affection.

OF SPIRITUAL GUIDES,
WITCHES AND
WICCANS

1

I AM GOING to come clean. Pronouncing on Shirley MacLaine's continuing spiritual journey as mapped out for discerning readers in *Dancing in the Light*, I must confess to prejudice, a certain jealousy, anger and a festering personal grievance going back to an earlier life Shirl and I shared.

My prejudice is against all autobiographies by film stars. They appal me. If, for instance, a film star had been present at the Crucifixion (a distinct possibility in the often-reincarnated MacLaine's case), she would begin by telling you what she was wearing and who had done her hair for the occasion. If she had been on the spot when Auschwitz was liberated, she would immediately have gathered survivors round her to tell them what they had missed since 1939: the films she had made, the awards she had won.

On this level, Shirley MacLaine does not disappoint. She finds every detail of her most recent life, however banal, absolutely fascinating. Were she still a tiresome adolescent, she would be asking the right questions: 'What made me the way I was? I no longer questioned whether I had lived before or whether I would live again. I was now questioning how and why?' But the fact is that at 3:57 p.m. on April 24, 1984 – as the author informs us in the very first sentence of her book – she turned fifty, an opportunity for many to pay tribute at Limelight, a New York church redone as a disco.

Following the birthday party, Simo – Miss MacLaine's housekeeper, rich in the wisdom of the mysterious East –

explained why so many people had been there. They wanted to touch Shirley to remind themselves that somebody like her was real, not an illusion, not a myth.

Shirley concurred. 'Yeah, maybe. I guess that's why celebrities are hot items. We're some kind of symbol that an thing is possible – good or bad.'

'It's everything,' said Simo. 'Your Oscar, the success of all that stuff you're talking about in *Out on a Limb* [her autobiographical tome of the previous year]. How it's so obviously working for you on the stage with this hit show. They feel you have an answer they would like to be a part of. And the people that said you didn't have all your paddles in the water a year ago are beginning to wonder what they might have missed.'

Now, after I take my morning shower (chanting my mantras, white light flowing through my bloodstream, sound waves nourishing each of my cells), I, too, would like to have my ego stroked by such a housekeeper, but my jealousy stems from stronger stuff. After *her* shower, Shirley, taking her phone messages, discovered that her publisher wanted to give her a birthday present and he hoped that afternoon would be suitable.

'I walked into the main conference room,' Shirley writes, 'where several dozen intelligent, literary-type people stood with champagne glasses in hand waiting to see what I was like.' Lou Wolfe, Bantam's president, presented her with a dozen roses and two beautifully leatherbound books, one the hardback and the other the paperback edition of *Out on a Limb*. The crowd from Bantam applauded, then asked to hear from her. Shirley obliged. She asked that conclave of 'intelligent, literary-type people' if they would please take one minute and in a collective mood, send her some positive thoughts about the book she was going to begin writing as soon as she left the building. Everybody promptly closed his or her eyes (the folks from sales possibly more tightly than the rest), and Shirley greedily sopped up the goodwill she could feel in the room.

Well, well, well. I have been published by the borzois at

Knopf for some fourteen years, allowing them to bring out five of my books, but not one of those ungrateful bastards has ever remembered my birthday. I have never seen the main conference room. Nobody closes his eyes reverently when I say I'm beginning a new novel. Instead, they say, 'I guess that will cut into your drinking time with Gordon Lish,' or 'I hope this one earns the advance.' So, of course, I'm jealous.

My anger is also rooted in my sinful life as an occasional screenwriter. Once, out there in Hollywood on a three-week rewrite, I was phoned by a gifted (that is to say, bankable) star's agent who said her client was very, very disappointed with my work. 'But the script was only delivered to her home an hour ago,' I protested. 'Surely she hasn't read it yet.'

'Well, she hasn't actually *read* it yet, but she has counted her lines twice, and there are forty-eight less in this one than in the previous draft.'

I have known actresses, overjoyed on first reading a script, to return it a week later saying their hairdresser feels it doesn't cut the mustard. Or that a script 'failed to get its shit together' for a niece who was once driven home from school by Nunnally Johnson and who has actually published poetry in the *Beverly Hills Advertiser*.

In the name of my suffering brothers who still toil on the Coast, I must protest that Shirley has taken her script consultations too far. Taking advantage of a beautiful Spiritual Guide (S.G.) of her acquaintance, a blond temporarily possessed by Ramtha (Shirl's brother in her Atlantean incarnation), she accepts *his* evaluation of a script she has been considering. My God, any fool knows they didn't even have movies in Atlantis.

Ramtha, incidentally, often works on the astral plane with another S.G., Tom McPherson, indulging in what I can only describe as otherworldly hanky-panky. Once, when Shirley felt too ill to go onstage, she pleaded with the pair to give her strength by entering her. 'Come in and help me,' she begged, failing to appreciate that this – considering her Atlantean relationship with Ramtha – would amount to no less than astral incest!!!

Shirley writes: 'Slowly, I felt my arms energize. A permeating glow ran through them. I found I could lift them. *Then I felt a current in both of my legs, a kind of mellow, activating current . . .* ' (Italics mine.)

If Ramtha didn't blink at incest, McPherson, a really naughty S.G., is a self-confessed thief. Once, Shirley entered a shop in Beverly Hills, put her purse on the floor and covered it with her jacket. 'I turned around to the rack and took down a suit jacket. I hadn't turned for longer than five seconds, *and there was no other customer there.*' But the purse was gone. 'Look,' Shirley said to the salesgirl, 'I don't care about the money or the credit cards or my passport or anything like that. I care about my spiritual tapes that were in there.'

This being Rodeo Drive and Shirley being real enough to touch (not an illusion, not a myth), the salesgirl didn't call for a padded wagon, but for the police. Nobody could find the purse. Sometime later, however, at a channelling session, McPherson came through from the astral plane, apologizing. He'd miscalculated. He hadn't meant to dematerialize the bag completely, just to move it behind the salesgirl.

Plain folks, doomed to pass through this vale of tears only once, might envy Shirley her talent, her fame, her money, but certainly not her tangled personal relationships. Ramtha advises her on the subjects of diet and exercise. Her father, back from the beyond, saw the white light when his soul briefly departed his body, and is now an enthusiastic astral hitch-hiker. As if Shirley and her parents didn't have enough problems in this life, they have been through many more together. Alan Johnson, Shirley's director-choreographer, habitually gets in touch with past-life incarnations. When Shirley falls in love with a Russian film director, whom she calls Vassily Okhlopkhov-Medvedjatnikov, they do not have just another affair, but a summit meeting. 'What fascinated each of us more than anything was the undeniable truth that our relationship was analogous to the conflicts that Russians and Americans were experiencing with each other on a global level.'

With *Out on a Limb*, Shirley started a guessing game among gossip columnists in America and England by revealng that she had had an affair with a British socialist member of Parliament – a metaphor, no doubt, for the Anglo-American alliance. In her new book she also suggests, if never quite reveals, the relationship she enjoyed with me in one of my very own earlier incarnations. The first hint comes on page 92, where Shirley, who had been born into a WASP family, writes, 'I might have had red hair and freckles and looked like the map of Ireland, but I *felt* Russian . . . When my Russian-Jewish girlfriends took me home with them after dancing class, I *knew* the food I was eating, even when it was for the first time.' Later, speaking of Russia, she tells her dad, 'Their music, their language, their food, their humor – their soul. I somehow understand it.' She suggests that her family lived there in another life. 'Look at Warren with his magnificent obsession with John Reed and the hopes for the Russian Revolution . . . I mean, wouldn't you say there might be more to this than meets the eye?'

Rest easy, *bubeleh*, there *is* more to it than meets the eye. In the fabled Galician village of Rawa-Russka in 1852, Shirley did eat her fill of *gefilte* fish, *cholent*, *kasha* knishes and *tzimmes*. In those days, in that life, she was none other than my *bubbe*, my grandmother Zippora, a rabbi's wife, otherwise notorious as 'the *rebbetsen* who danced like a shiksa.' She was trouble even then, an embarrassment to my pious grandfather. She never learned to sing Hasidic melodies properly but could belt out the Top Ten on the Moscow hit parade of the time. She couldn't cook or sew, but when the rabbi and his followers danced around the table filled with heavenly grace, my *bubbe* would burst in, kicking her legs high, anticipating Las Vegas in another life. It was a disgrace. A scandal. My grandfather was forced out of the synagogue. The entire family was obliged to hit the road, wandering from *shtetl* to *shtetl*. So in that life I grew up without benefit of a proper religious education. All because of Shirl.

There are sceptics, I know, who feel that actresses should be seen and not heard, unless they are speaking other people's lines. There are 'intelligent, literary-type people' out there who will consider *Dancing in the Light* an embarrassment. For them, I have a cautionary tale. Once, years ago, I met Lady Sheba, Queen of the Witches, and we sat down at a table to exchange ideas. 'Did I tell you,' she said, 'that I have a hand of power?'

'Not yet.'

'The great goddess — she's so beautiful, how can you describe her? — well, she took me into the astral, lifted my hand to the sky, and it lit up like neon. Look,' Lady Sheba said, showing me her palm, 'she cut a pentagram in here and the sign of the goddess right thar.'

Apologetically, I protested I couldn't make out either symbol.

'Why, of course not,' she replied, unperturbed. 'But if you had psychic vision, you could see it.'

Possibly, such a third eye, or whatever, is also essential to fully appreciate Shirley MacLaine's effusions.

2

Nineteen seventy-four it was when I had the pleasure of meeting Lady Sheba, sent out by *Playboy* to attend the Third Annual Gnostic Aquarian Festival of Astrology, Mind Power, Occult Sciences & Witchcraft in the New Age, at Hyatt Lodge, Minneapolis.

Everybody, except for the nefarious Eli, was going to be there. The astral jet-setters. Riders incomparable of the inner planes. In a word, the flower of American witchery. Philip Emmons Isaac Bonewits, a reconstructionist Druid with a B.A. in magic from the University of California, endorsed by no less than Ronnie Reagan. Bonewits, a mere twenty-two-year-old, his hair worn in a pigtail, his beard wispy, sucking on a calabash pipe and adorned in Moroccan robes, his leather belt slung low, an *athame* (a black-handled knife made or inherited by a witch) riding one hip and a hammer of Thor on the other. P.E.I. Bonewits is the sole begetter of *Real Magic*: 'Learn how to cast spells or heal a friend. Discover clairsentience (vibes), clairvoyance, telepathy, astral projection, as magic leaves the Dark Ages and enters the Age of Reason.' Gavin of Boskednan and Yvonne were also going. They are co-directors of the Church and School of Wicca (Route 2, Salem, Missouri), the craft's first mail-order college. 'Introduction: Some people would call me a wizard. They would call my mate a witch. We call ourselves flamens of the Wicca faith. Wicca is the old word meaning "wise" or "wisdom," which is now pronounced "witch." To our believers, Wicca is the oldest religion.'

Eighty-five-year-old Edmund Jones, founder of the Sabian Assembly, author of *Astrology: How & Why It Works*, had promised to appear. So had Tim Zell, of the Church of All Worlds (CAW), and his high priestess, Ms. Carolyn Clark, who was scheduled to pronounce on 'The Great Mother vs. the Great Motherfucker.' The fabled Lady Sheba, Queen of the American Witches, was going to make an appearance, and so, for that matter, was Lady Cybele, hereditary witch and professional palmist, pastor of the Church of Wicca Rede and sole proprietor of Lady Cybele's Caldron, Madison, Wisconsin. Russ Michael, who had died at the age of seventeen and returned to his physical body to finish the work he had started in two former lifetimes, would also be there, as would the inscrutable Quantz Crawford, master of the mind-blowing art of the supernatural orgasm.

There would be not only twenty-five lectures daily, with seminars and workshops, but also, every night, in the basement of the Gnostica Bookshop (a converted mortuary), a witchmeet. *For initiated witches only*. 'It will be preferred that all attending wear either street clothing or robes. For obvious reasons, no one will be sky-clad.' That is to say, starkers.

On a Wednesday, in the spring of '74, flying out to the festival, I had to confess to something like total ignorance. I went forearmed with a hastily acquired library of the occult and a certain scepticism, but only the most commonplace knowledge of the craft. There was Snow White, of blessed memory, being proffered the poisoned apple by an old crone in the traditional black pointed hat, and Judy Garland being pursued for her magical ruby slippers by another malevolent witch. But, to come clean, I had never knowingly encountered a bona fide witch until – shortly after checking into the hotel, a drummers" stopover – I was joined for drinks by Vicki Zastrow, festival director. An attractive witch, slender and blackhaired, Vicki wore a low-cut white blouse and a black pantsuit with a white trim, rather like an inverted condolence card. Vicki had also come multi-ringed, with a blue sapphire for wisdom and speed, a topaz for tact and diplomacy, and an ankh. The ankh, a T-shaped cross surmounted by a loop, was Egyptian, she explained, and symbolized life.

Vicki drove me to the Gnostica Bookshop. Philip Roth rode the same shelves as Aleister Crowley and Edgar Cayce. Another counter was choked with sabbat artifacts. Groovy Fruity Incense, magical pentagrams, brass bells and, for the deodorant-minded Wiccan, Chinese Wash. Powdered brimstone was also available, as was war water, in an economy-sized bottle.

'I would like to make it clear,' Vicki said, 'that we don't practise black magic. Our credo is, "And it hurt none, do what thou wilt shall be the whole of the law."

More Gnostic Aquarian celebrants were gathering in the lobby of the Hyatt Lodge.

'Merry witchmeet, honey.'

'Blessed be.'

Yvonne stood tippy-toe to kiss Russ on the forehead. 'I'm aiming for your third eye,' she sang out.

Me, I was aiming for the party at Carl Weschcke's twenty-four-room mansion on Summit Avenue, in adjoining St. Paul. The amiable, grey-bearded Weschcke was sponsor of the festival and president of Llewelyn Publications, a thriving occult press. Everything in his opulent living room was done up in black or gold. Even the cutlery, when it appeared, was gold-plated, the dinner plates black. The Wiccans, already gathered there, sipping wine, had come flamboyantly dressed. The wizards, many of them insurance-claim adjusters, pharmacists or government surveyors by day, favoured medieval robes or black velvet capes. Most of the witches, heavily made-up, multi-ringed, were tricked out in long skirts slit to the thigh. There was even a black cat on the prowl. But the followers of the craft, just like your friendly Lion or Rotarian, wore lapel tags for easy identification: HELLO, MY NAME IS . . . LADY CIRCE.

Gavin of Boskednan told me his Church and School of Wicca had been registered with the IRS and was now tax-deductible. The traditional church, he argued, was now a non-participating sport, like basketball. 'We participate. We do ESP, for instance.' And, yes, he was something of a psychic reader.

'Can you tell me anything about myself?' I asked hungrily.

'You're very interested in swimming and gym.'

'Sorry, no.'

'Well, you win some, you lose some.'

Yvonne, his witchmate, had enjoyed three previous incarnations. She had been a man in pre-Christian Britain and, in another life, an Arab mathematician. 'In my last reincarnation in Wales,' she said, 'I used to ride out on horseback to meet my lover. Just like in *Ryan's Daughter*. It gave the neighbours something to talk about.'

Gavin was not without a sense of responsibility about hexing people. 'But if a cabbie rooks me,' he said, 'I'm going to hex him.'

'What would you do?'

'Make him drive off the road.'

P.E.I. Bonewits confessed to even mightier powers. He could, he ventured, heal blood diseases. 'I'm also developing a nice flair for weather control.'

As we were joined by Kim Efel, the conversation turned to England, where I had been rooted for almost two decades. 'Oh,' I asked, 'have you been to England?'

Kim smiled darkly. 'Yes,' she allowed.

'When?'

'In 1248. I was also here four thousand years ago. I was a king or queen.'

'In England?'

'No. Egypt. In another life, I was buried alive.'

The editor of *Gnostica News*, twenty-seven-year-old Ron Wright, was also a traveller. He had been to Vietnam. But in this life, as it were. 'I used magic there. Creative visualization. To visualize myself out. Same as positive thinking, you know.'

Which was when I espied José Feola, parapsychologist, sinking trancelike into a chair; Yvonne, her eyes squeezed shut, was stroking his neck with her hands of power. 'He's got bad tonsils,' she explained.

Russ Michael, the warlock who had passed through death's door and back again, introduced himself. He is founder and publisher of the *Aquarian ESP Herald* and toured with the House of David basketball team for seven years. Michael has been reincarnated only twice so far. Once in India, another time in Egypt, where, as he put it, he had helped upgrade civilization. 'I was the pharaoh known as Ahmose,' he said. 'I drove the invaders out in 1600 B.C.'

Back in my hotel room, I settled into my homework. I am, I should point out, a sucker for *outré* newspapers and magazines, turning to the ads first out of habit. *Gnostica News* (paid circulation 5,000) offered witch haberdashery – robes fully lined, with pointed hoods, from $50 to $100 – and genuine rock-crystal balls, ranging from $49.95 to $6,000 (Wisconsin tax extra). There was also an ad for a 'beautiful scale replica of an authentic Spanish guillotine.' The Warlock Shop, in Brooklyn, sold hooded robes for only $15 and enjoined members of the craft to 'BOYCOTT WITCH CRAP BOOKS.' A distressed reader of *The Green Egg* was in urgent need of a female boa constrictor, eight to ten feet, at a reasonable price. *The Green Egg*, published by the Church of All Worlds, also sought help for a St. Louis man who had been possessed by a demonic being. 'We ask all of you to please get together and send him all the power you can afford so that this evil being will vanish.' The same issue also included a controversial article on 'The Craft and Homosexuality,' the authors concluding that 'the gender of the earthplane shell is not necessarily the gender of the spirit dwelling in that shell.' On balance, the authors were against homosexuals being allowed into a hetero magic circle. Makes for bad vibes. But they did feel homosexuals could form nifty covens of their own, provided polarities were balanced.

Finally, I curled up in bed with Louis T. Cullings's *Manual of Sex Magick*. The author, like many a sceptic before him, stands foursquare for 'magickal congrex,' heightened, in his case, by something he calls the Bud-Will Intelligence. As an illustration of how well it works, he tells the story of an exemplar who was driving home in California when he picked up a hitch-hiker, '100 percent woman,' who soon ended up in his cabin. 'Kiss me, Lou,' she said. 'Ever since I had titties I have dreamed about being loved by a man like you.'

The next morning, Thursday, I descended into the hotel lobby to sniff incense rising from the registration desks. Witches, witches were everywhere, collecting their festival kits and badges.

'And what's your rising house?' somebody inquired of an ebullient matron.

'I have a stationary Mercury rising in Pisces.'

'Oh-ho!' he said.

A young man, an apprentice astrologer out of Winnipeg, drove me into a corner. Standing inches from my face, he peered into my eyes. 'I'm aiming for pupil-level contact,' he explained.

Of all the simultaneous lectures being offered, I opted for P.E.I. Bonewits and his hammer of Thor, in the Regency West Room. 'During World War II,' Bonewits declared, 'occultists brought down numerous German aircraft. They also eliminated Gestapo cells. In fact, they played an unsung role in bringing down the greatest black magician of them all.'

Tim Zell was holding forth in another room. Clad in a

monk's robe, his hair worn in a pigtail, Zell explained to his audience of twenty that, as pagans, they were in the peculiar position of having a public image 'created not by ourselves but by our prosecutors. It is much as if the Nazis had succeeded in eradicating Judaism to the extent that, generations later, the common opinion of what the Jewish faith was all about was derived solely from the anti-Semitic propaganda of the Third Reich.' In Europe alone, he pointed out, nine million pagans were martyred by the Christian Church during the Inquisition and witch trials. 'Among Christians, a common accusation levelled at members of non-Jahvist religions is that they are Devil worshippers or Satanists. But Satan is a specifically Christian concept and no one outside Judeo-Christianity recognizes him at all.'

The time was ripe for a new religion, Zell felt, based on reverence for the earth and all the life that springs from it, but more than one member of his audience quarrelled with his all-embracing endorsement of paganism.

'Look here, the fertility goddess of the Aztecs was a shit-eater. I mean, literally.'

Here a thoughtful lady interjected, 'So is the earth, if you think about it.'

Zell and Carolyn Clark joined me for lunch. They were both rainmakers. 'Weather control,' Tim said, 'that's easy. Even my ten-year-old son can make blizzards in April. He has his own altar.'

Outside, it was overcast. I invited Zell and Carolyn to have a shot at rainmaking and, sportingly, they agreed, sinking to the pavement to meditate for ten minutes. On rising, Zell said, 'We'll have rain in an hour.'

Alas, the rain didn't come in one hour, or even in four, by which time I was seated in the bar with yet another witch couple, this pair out of Chicago. The male witch, a brooding young man with melancholy eyes, confided, 'It's hard to be a Jewish witch. *You'd understand.*'

'Sure.'

'If my boss knew I was Jewish, there'd be trouble. If he found out I was a witch, I'd be fired.'

His witchmate declared she was no mean rainmaker herself.

'All right, then,' I said. 'Let's go outside and make some.'

'I don't do parlour tricks,' she replied sharply.

Possibly, there was more to it than that. A sense of ecological responsibility. Lecturing to an audience of more than one hundred the same afternoon, Lady Cybele enjoined one and all not to use their power frivolously. 'I don't want any of you to raise the temperature to seventy-five degrees in St. Paul on January second, because, sure enough, if you do that, it will be thirty-five degrees and snowing on May second. Nature has its own pendulum.'

Plump, bejewelled Lady Cybele was lecturing on psychic self-defence to a rapt, largely middle-aged audience, many of whom were armed with tape recorders. When undergoing psychic attack, she advocated the construction of an instant psychic shield. Making negative static, or jamming, was also a good ploy. Vampires, she ventured, who suffer from a leaky aura, are particularly deadly. 'They latch on to your aura, make a hole and suck out energy.' Lady Cybele, a good housekeeper, suggested that self-respecting witches ought to exorcise their homes once a month, just to keep them spiritually spic-and-span. If undergoing malevolent psychic attack, she said there was nothing for it but active self-defence. 'Don't accept spells or nightmares, but send them back along the channels from whence they came. Go after your attacker with your astral sword. Rain fire and brimstone on him. Make it good.' Finally, if nothing else worked, there was always the occult cops. 'They have opted out of the reincarnation wheel,' she explained, 'but can always be summoned if you ask the Great White Brotherhood to come to your aid.'

Some fifty enthusiasts turned up in their finery for the first evening banquet at the Hyatt Lodge. Yankee pot roast. My dinner companions were the delightful Crescent Dragonwagon and Officer J. P. Little from Arden Hills, a Minneapolis suburb. Little was in uniform; he wore a gun. The year before, I was told, a band of Jesus Freaks had crashed the festival, stirring things up. 'Expecting trouble?' I asked.

'Naw. They seem like regular, ordinary people to me.'

'But you are on duty here?'

Officer Little lowered his eyes. Toying with his fork, he said, 'Well, helping out, sort of. My lieutenant's a witch. He has a coven of his own.'

There were two more cops, plainclothesmen, on duty inside the Gnostica Bookshop, guarding the door to the basement witchmeet. Fortunately, Carl Weschcke had issued me a pass.

There was no magic circle. The witches sat in rows, like the P.T.A., rising now and then to pluck a Coke from a machine thoughtfully placed in a corner. Once more the ladies favoured skirts slit to the thigh and many of the men wore hooded robes. Plump, middle-aged Lady Sheba rose to speak, flashing gold teeth. 'There has been bickering among the people of the wise,' she said, 'because an evil man, *you all know who I mean*, some of his followers may even be here, has cast a spell on some of you, attaching elementals to your back. If any of his innocent victims wish to come to me privately afterwards, I will cleanse you in Carl's temple.'

A young man, his face ashen, stood up to plead for the evil one. 'He is sick. He means well.'

Another witch shot defiantly out of his chair. 'His name is Eli.'

'*I didn't mention his name*,' Lady Sheba shot back, '*you did*.'

'I tried to return his elementals,' a man began falteringly, 'but he polarizes them.'

'He left me with sores on the soles of my feet.'

Lady Sheba's eyes widened. She held a hand to her cheek. 'Oh, he's a vampire, then. You've got real trouble!'

Witches began to murmur among themselves.

'Why don't we do a return-to-sender?' P. E. I. Bonewits suggested. 'The curse of the mirrored light. Until he disintegrates.'

But Tim Zell wouldn't have it. 'Oh, fine. A splendid start!

We're beginning with a witch-hunt. Paranoid pagans die of old age!'

'I am Sheba, queen of the witches. I published the *Book of Shadows* because the goddess so commanded me. I am meeting many of you here for the first time, but I tell you that she has asked me to gather all our rituals together – '

'Ours are secret – '

' – into revised temple books. The night I arrived here, the goddess took me into the astral to reveal to me thar that the star of knowledge hangs over St. Paul. Carl wanted me to announce it to the world, but I didn't want the publicity. But we are going to build a temple here, because this is the source, this is the centre.'

'I've never seen you before. How do I know you are queen?'

'I am the queen and I will publish the temple books. Thus I have been commanded and thus I will do – '

Bonewits interrupted again. 'This is the U.S.A. We don't want a monarchy but a congress of witches. We don't want a monarchy, regardless of your ancestry.'

'The fact remains I am queen and there is nothing any human being can do about it.'

Everybody began to talk at once.

'*If you don't follow me,*' Lady Sheba threatened, '*there are thousands who is.*'

'Why don't we lay our quarrels aside,' a witch interjected, 'and find out those things we can agree on?'

'Yes,' somebody else said. 'How would we describe ourselves, for instance?'

A robed man, unheard from until now, rose slowly from his chair. 'Let's say we are gods and goddesses in human form, and leave it at that.'

Everybody clapped for the first non-controversial remark of the witchmeet. And then suddenly, without warning, George Lincoln, a lecturer and consultant on witchcraft, clad in a black velvet robe with a red satin lining, stood up and pointed a stern, trembling finger at Lady Sheba. In a booming voice, he declaimed, 'Lady Sheba, I challenge you! In the name of the Great White Brotherhood, do you stand in the light?'

Lady Sheba glared. She snickered. 'You go into the astral,' she said, 'and the goddess will answer you thar.'

The next morning I managed to corner Lincoln in the coffee shop. 'I wouldn't have done it,' he said, 'but my contacts demanded it. I was commanded astrally.'

'Did you at least get the answer you wanted?'

'No. I saw the challenge go out astrally, but then she put up her shield, *deflecting it*.'

Gavin of Boskednan pointed out that there was rather a lot at stake. If Lady Sheba were recognized as queen, it could mean a fat publishing contract and a good deal of TV exposure. 'It's a ticket to the network talk shows.'

Finally, I caught up with Lady Sheba. 'It's for goddamn sure,' she said. 'I don't stand in his light and I don't goddamn want him standing in mine. I don't need him in my aura. But they can't pick on me any more than they could pick on Moses.'

In this life, Lady Sheba sprang from Knott County, Kentucky, and now lived in Florida. She was fifty-three years old and her legal name was Jessie Whicker Bell. Her husband worked for General Motors.

'Doing what?' I asked.

'Oh, he's a leader, or boss, or something. I'm reincarnated into my family every seven generations. Oh, I have such a beautiful memory of when I was queen of Camelot. Eleanora, you met her, she was my nurse then. She knowed it and I knowed it.'

There were other lives. In India, Lady Sheba was once a great queen, tall and majestic, and even now she returned to the River Ganges from time to time. On the inner plane, travelling astrally. She showed me her hand of power. 'Nancy becomes queen in two years. I'm going to step down for my daughter. I want a movie made of her crowning. I want it shown all around the world.' Rising, Lady Sheba smiled and said, 'I was a magnetic child. People used to flock to me like bees to honey. I used to have beautiful blonde hair. Now my hair is Lady Clairol "Moongold." '

Friday, I eschewed the public lectures in favour of private consultations with astrologers, palmists, graphologists and psychic and tarot readers. I was told, on the one hand, that I was untrustworthy and not particularly generous, but, on the other, that I was a big spender and absolutely incorruptible. One palmist proved her sagacity by confirming that I had royal blood, something she had detected on only 2 percent of the hands she read, and another endeared herself to me by saying I would live until ninety-three and, furthermore, could count on a creative revival at eighty. My tarot reader, distressed, observed that for a writer I had a singularly uncreative disposition, but an astrologer swore I was due for a big literary breakthrough. I was informed that I was both a fast and a slow thinker. Within two years, depending on which advisor I credited, I would leave my home in Montreal to live in England, Connecticut or Brazil. I was also told my finances were in both good and bad shape. I was diplomatic, yet a fault-finder. My next novel, an astrologer advised me, should be 'energized.' I ought to begin right now. 'Mars changed direction on September nineteenth,' he said, clinching it.

But my tarot reader pleaded with me not to begin for another six months if I wanted to make the New York *Times* best-seller list.

My first consultation, at 9:30 a.m., was with Noel Tyl, six feet nine inches tall and a Capricorn. Tyl, a charmer born, held a degree in psychology from Harvard and was an opera singer who had performed with the Vienna State and New York opera companies. He was writing a twelve-volume series on the principles and practice of astrology. He greeted me with a magnetic, all-embracing smile. 'I've been working on your chart since six o'clock this morning and, Mordecai, it's made my day. If I had never seen you and this chart had come in the mail from Iceland, I would have known immediately that here was a writer indeed. You're not the most brilliant of men, there are better minds – '

Prick.

' – but Mordecai, Mordecai, *you can hear the grass grow*.'

Consulting my chart, Tyl told me, 'You had a big sexual experience in 1947.'

'You're damn right.'

'You've yet to come into your full creative powers, but it is about to happen. Nineteen seventy-six will be a very big year for you.'

Later in the day I ran into a girl who had also consulted Tyl. 'Isn't he wonderful?' she asked.

'Very perceptive, I thought.'

'Yes. You know what he told me? He told me I could hear the grass grow.'

I got off to a bad start with the next astrologer I consulted, the venerable Marc Edmund Jones. 'You have an empty first house,' he said. 'Just like Richard Nixon.'

After having my palm read twice and visiting a tarot reader, I hurried off to meet with bouncy Prince L. Bokovoy, Jr., 'a leader and innovator in Twin City graphology circles.' Bokovoy, fifty-eight years old and out of North Dakota, was a construction inspector when he wasn't lecturing or entertaining at private parties. He told me I'd make a good detective. I hold grudges and think in bed a lot. Nudging me, he added, 'You're a smooth lover and a smooth operator. More greedy for sex than money. You know I can tell if a guy's a homosexual?'

'How?'

'If a guy makes a "g" like this,' he said, drawing a tangled letter for me, 'he jacks off, he's a fag. But me, I'd just tell him he had "unconventional sexual desires." Listen here, I can tell if a girl is over-sexed or dry-sexed. That's useful, don't you think?'

'And how.'

'Okay. You want a girl who's lots of fun?' Without waiting for my reply, Bokovoy drew yet another 'g,' this one with a generous oval tail. 'If she makes that kind of "g," she's hot stuff.'

Committing Bokovoy's salacious 'g' to memory, I entertained visions of myself going from bar to bar, cross-country, inviting girls to write 'gang, gringo, or garbage,' and if the tail of the 'g' was full-blown, taking matters from there. But, first of all, there was the evening banquet. Butter-baked one-half spring chicken. I sat with the Weschckes. Sandra, also a witch, turned to her husband. 'After the witchmeet, remind me to go to Super Valu to pick up some cat meat.'

Friday night's witchmeet was poorly attended but much more convivial to begin with, possibly because this time we sat in a magic circle, invoking the power. Lady Sheba, her mood conciliatory, even refreshingly republican, referred to the meet as no less than the first council of American witches, and then she called on the Wiccans to identify themselves and their 'trads.' The witches in the circle stood up one by one.

'I'm Avery, American Celtic. My training comes back many years in other lives.'

A pot-bellied man in a white sweater declared, 'I'm a wizard, unaffiliated with any trad.'

'I'm Lady Cybele. I've been practising in this life for twenty-four years.'

'George Lincoln. American eclectic.'

An attractive witch, slender, long-legged, with streaky blonde hair, who had practised the craft in three previous lives, identified herself as Celine. 'I am a solitary witch,' she said.

'I'm Lady Circe, from Toledo.'

Uneasily, I realized it would soon be my turn to stand up.

'My name is Charles Leach. We're Celtic reconstructionists. And I just want to say there seem to be very good vibes here tonight.'

'I am Jehovah,' another witch declared, his manner sour.

'I'm Morning Glory and I'm from Oregon. I was initiated in the Neo-Gardnerian fashion.'

Now it was my turn and there was no evading it. 'I am Mordecai,' I said 'and my trad is Jewish.'

Jehovah shot out of his seat, enraged. 'We were only supposed to be initiated witches here. He's from *Playboy*. And he described himself as a Jew. I used to be one and I know them and their ilk. If he's here tomorrow night, I'm not coming.'

Sunday's unrivalled attraction, for which more than a hundred of the curious turned up, was a demonstration of 'hypnosis, regression and past-life memory' by Jack and Mary Rowan. Three subjects, or astral trippers, were on hand, having their auras cleansed, when I slipped into the lecture room – two youngsters called Tom and Sharon, and a cross-eyed, middle-aged man called Jack. The only difference, incidentally, between dusting a person and cleansing the aura is that, in the latter case, you do not actually touch the person.

Astral travel, Jack Rowan assured everybody, 'is real fun and real easy.' His first subject, Jack, was already seated in a chair onstage. 'Go back into the depths of your mind . . . deeper and deeper . . . asleep . . . '

Within seconds, Jack was snoozing.

'Now we're going back to a life you lived before. Where are you?'

'Germany . . . My name is Heinrich.'

'Hiya, Heinrich. He's in Germany, folks. And what do you see?'

'Cathedral . . . '

'He sees a cathedral. Describe it.'

' . . . big, stones . . . '

'It's big and made of stone. Who is your most famous friend?'

'Johann Sebastian Bach.'

'Bach. Did he teach you to play the organ?'

'His son taught me . . . '

'His son, huh? Now say something in German for us, Heinrich.'

No answer.

'They can speak German. Now say something in German, Heinrich.'

Jack began to mutter softly.

'*Heinrich, will you please say something in German?*'

'*Guten Tag* . . . '

'*Guten Tag*,' Rowan said, beaming. 'Did you hear? He said *Guten Tag*.'

Next, Sharon was taken into the astral by Mary Rowan.

'We're going back to a life you had before. Way back in time . . . '

Egypt, 1221 B.C., and Sharon is a boy in a house with many slaves. The son of Orpheus.

'And what does your dad do for a living?' Mary asked.

'He's on the council. For the Pharaoh.'

Sharon went on to describe the temple, with its immense white pillars, and, my God, I recognized it. *Yes, yes, I knew that temple*. It was undoubtedly the temple featured in Cecil B. De Mille's *Ten Commandments*.

In another life, one squandered in the Dakota Territory circa 1863, Sharon was a saloon singer called Lola, and, filling that office, she sang a ballad for us, very poorly indeed. Afterward, Mary Rowan revealed, 'In that life, you know, we found out Lola was my granddaughter. I was her grand-*father*,' she added, tittering.

Finally, Jack Rowan guided Tom back through time and space to a previous life in Ireland, A.D. 413, where he was Sean O'Donnell, the renowned Kerry wizard. 'I can create or stop storms,' Tom declared, his affected Irish accent unconvincing. 'I can see into the future.'

'He can create or stop storms and see into the future,' Jack announced. 'Anybody want to ask him something?'

'Make rain,' some lout shouted out.

'Not today.'

'Not today, he says. Anybody else?'

'Can you see into the twentieth century?'

A hush fell over the assembly, as Tom, his eyes closed, obviously in a trance, struggled with words. Rowan, solicitous, offered him a sip of water and the wizard tried again.

He struggled, he winced. 'I see wars . . . many wars . . . trouble, trouble . . .'

'He sees wars and trouble. O.K., that's it. Cleanse his aura for him, will you, Mary? Sean, you're going into the astral again . . . You're dying, but it doesn't hurt . . . into the astral . . . and when I snap my fingers three times, you will wake up in 1974, at the Hyatt Lodge, in Minneapolis. One, two, three! Wake up, Tom.'

Only later did I discover that the intrusive oohs and aahs from the next lecture room, even as the Rowans guided subjects through the astral, had been evoked by Gavin of Boskednan's practical demonstration of sex power to which couples only (preferably robed, for easier mutual access) were admitted. The foreplay, however, was all in the good name of healing. All the sexual energy, or horniness, evoked was to be dispatched to a nine-year-old boy who was going blind.

'Did it work?' I asked.

'I don't know yet.'

'Something else, Gavin. If, as you say, nobody was allowed to come to a climax, weren't your subjects, um, frustrated?'

'Oh, once the energy was harnessed, we didn't care what they did with it in their rooms afterward.'

At the closing, sparsely attended witchmeet on Sunday night, Lady Sheba sang out, 'I'm going home the happiest woman in the world. I'm going home just glorified because of you.'

I saw the queen of the witches once more later that night, in the lobby of Hyatt Lodge, as I was hurrying to catch a late flight to Chicago.

'I expect to be on NBC television on Hallowe'en night,' she called after me. 'Don't forget to watch.'

MULRONEY

SHORTLY AFTER BRIAN Mulroney was elected prime minister, 'The Journal,' appropriately enough, surfaced with a jiffy profile. L. Ian MacDonald figured prominently in it. His voice charged with reverence, he revealed that when Brian was a mere boy in Baie Comeau he asked anybody who was taking the train to Montreal to please bring him some books. MacDonald, addressing us on CBC-TV, a family network, did not tell us if these were the seminal, character-forming books of your steamy adolescence and mine, say, Thorne Smith's *Topper Takes a Trip* or Kathleen Winsor's *Forever Amber*, or if they were the sort fancied by the school swot, say, John Gunther's *Inside South America* or H. G. Well's *History of the World*. But, obviously impressed, he did say that the young Mulroney not only read these books, but compiled a list of words he didn't understand and (wait for it) *actually looked them up in a dictionary*.

Well now, I have met Mulroney more than once. I have no reason to doubt his intelligence. I certainly did not expect that he looked up the meaning of words in a laundry hamper or dug for them in his garden. So, while MacDonald's inside information was reassuring, it hardly counted as an illumination. Even more worrying, it promised that when his biography of Mulroney appeared, it would not be a critical study so much as a fan's notes. *Mulroney: The Making of the Prime Minister* fulfils that promise.

To be fair, MacDonald – possibly anticipating that some might find his 1984 biography somewhat premature, no more than prologue – states in an afterword-cum-disclaimer that his book was not meant to be a critical biography, since there is still no record of achievement or disappointment in office. There was, however, that long climb up the greasy Tory pole. Or, as MacDonald puts it much more nicely, 'It is not too early to place the man in the context of places and events that shaped his life and brought him from Champlain Street in Baie Comeau to 24 Sussex Drive in Ottawa.'

The machinations that went into managing that change of address, surely the stuff of a novel by Trollope, MacDonald views with a generosity so large it ultimately rebounds unfairly on his subject, compromising him, if only because it portrays him as unbelievably squeaky clean at all times. We know better. So does Mulroney. No pol, certainly no Quebec pol, ever got from here to there without spilling some blood, in this case Joe Clark's. I'm not complaining. I count the unseating of that pathetic striver a service to the nation, but I never dreamt it was accomplished by heeding the Ten Golden Rules of the Baie Comeau Wolf Cubs. It involved, among other diversions, the support of the born-again Tories of Montreal's Old Brewery Mission, of whom Mulroney said with a straight face that many of them had served their country. He said this even as that perfect little ghost of bought-voters past, Frank Hanley, was waiting to reward them with beer, the sort of consciousness-raising ceremony that makes Montreal, our Montreal, such an endearing city. There was also the black comedy of Mulroney's endorsement of Joe Clark at the Ritz-Carlton Hotel, but more about that later.

Meanwhile, it should be said that in an early chapter Mac-Donald happily reveals the titles of some of the books Mulroney ordered from Montreal. A biography of Ben-Gurion. Edgar Snow on China. As a boy, he also had access to a swimming pool and tennis courts. There was a piano in the house. His sisters attended a private school in eastern Ontario and he was sent off to St. Francis Xavier University in Antigonish. Clearly, he was not as poor as he likes to make out. However, many self-made men, not only politicians, have exaggerated early hardships. It is a tolerable conceit.

At St. F.X., Mulroney met Sam Wakim and Pat MacAdam, who would become part of the Mulroney Mafia. 'Even in those days,' a university official has said, 'Brian was thinking big.' Obviously having outgrown his bookish Baie Comeau days, he recommended to the university president that Ed Sullivan be awarded an honorary degree. 'I had visions of us all on television,' he recalled later.

MacDonald's adoring biography celebrates Mulroney's rise from Baie Comeau, through St. F.X., to Laval, where Peter White, Michel Cogger and Jean Bazin were added to the Mulroney Mafia; his emergence as a public figure in the Cliche Commission hearings in 1974–75; his brash, heavily bankrolled run at the P.C. leadership in 1976; his fall from grace; his high-rolling Iron Ore Company of Canada days; his trouncing of Joe Clark in the Ottawa leadership convention; and, of course, his landslide election victory in 1984.

Months before Joe Clark stupidly pulled the trapdoor on himself at the Winnipeg convention, Mulroney, in a disconcerting ideological shift hardly noticed at the time, quietly broke with the grand Tory tradition established by Sir John A. Macdonald and enthusiastically pursued by Mulroney mentor Winston Churchill. He gave up booze. He chose ambition over solace, country over cognac. Or, as MacDonald puts it, sorely underestimating Mulroney's capacity for once, 'He was no longer having a cognac after dinner.' An urgent signal, I should have thought, for Joe Clark to no longer walk alone after dark, or certainly to change the locks at Stornoway.

The strongest chapter in *The Making of the Prime Minister* is the opening one, which captures the drama of the Ottawa leadership convention, a contest brilliantly managed by Mulroney and his men. For the rest, the editing is slovenly. Repetitions abound. There are double negatives here and there. The prose is at best functional; at worst, Hallmark cards. In one paragraph, for instance, we are told that when Mulroney graduated from F.X. his mother's 'smile [was] as wide as the St. Lawrence at Baie Comeau' and, in Mulroney's mind, 'his father would always be ten feet tall.' No wonder he left home.

MacDonald is not so much a writer's writer as a lawyer's lawyer. He had not taken on a subject, but a client. Which is to say, like Mulroney himself, he often protests too much. He would, for instance, have us believe that when the news story of Claude Wagner's sweetheart trust fund broke during the 1976 leadership convention, it was without Mulroney's approval or wink that pointman Peter White leaked the story to the Toronto *Star*. 'Peter, God love him,' Mulroney said, 'did that on his own accord. He didn't tell me, he didn't tell anybody. The facts revealed in the story I learned for the first time.' This, even though Mulroney and White were intimate friends and Mulroney, by his own account, had driven Fast Eddie Goodman to Wagner's house when the actual deal was set.

MacDonald would also have us believe that when Mulroney endorsed Clark as Tory leader at the Ritz-Carlton Hotel in 1982, it wasn't a calculated act of hypocrisy, a ruthless political ploy, but, instead, an honest gesture of support. He quotes Mulroney saying to properly suspicious, even bemused, reporters, 'I have no supporters of my own, only friends.' Formidable friends, he might have added. Among them Rodrigue Pageau, Guy Charbonneau, Frank Moores and Michel Cogger. Friends working full-time for Brian.

When MacDonald first met Mulroney in a Montreal bar in 1972, he felt that the future PM was a bit of an operator, but that it was impossible to dislike him, even when you realized he was trying to sell you a line. Dalton Camp, that most perspicacious of Tories, considered Mulroney charming, but too much of a pol, essentially shallow, until one night he heard him expound on the importance of trade unions and the responsibilities of enlightened management. Afterwards, Camp said, 'I think he can make it.' Donald MacSween, director of the National Arts Centre, who once toiled in the same law office as Mulroney, saw him as 'a main-chance guy, but you can't become a national leader unless you are,' which is very much to the point.

The Tories elected Mulroney leader, not because they took him for an innocent, like Joe, but because they desperately wanted a winner. Canadian voters thrust him into office, not because they considered him Simon Pure, but, as he was obviously street-smart, steely tough, a true professional: they wanted him to deal as well for Canada as he has for himself.

His first days in office earned him a mixed report card. Like any opposition leader who has ever come into power anywhere in the Western world, he has said, Sorry, fellas, his many promises will have to wait, because – who ever would have guessed? – the till is empty. My grandfather heard that story. So will my grandchildren. Then his government's first pronouncement was a cosmetic one. The Canadian forces, we were told, will no longer dress like German bus conductors, but will revert to individual service uniforms, which must have caused fear and trembling in the Kremlin. First the MX missile; then the B-1 bomber; now the Canadian Armed Forces going cutesy-poo.

On the other hand, Mulroney could be applauded in 1984 for his then seemingly consistent support of bilingualism and his courageous stand on minority language rights in Manitoba. There was also the inspired appointment of Stephen Lewis to the UN. Above all, Mulroney had our goodwill. Just about everybody in the country, myself included, wanted him to succeed. We wanted him to establish a more amiable relationship with the United States, so long as it wasn't that of the manager and the batboy. We needed him to put our economic house in order, as promised, which would have been sufficient to assure him office for years to come. Meanwhile, my fear, after reading MacDonald's book, is that at times Mulroney appears like a man who has been in such a hurry that he just doesn't understand his own life and, therefore, is always putting a gloss on it, burnishing it for the widest possible approval. MacDonald has served him well as a fan, but as a journalist, he has failed to keep the necessary distance. Such premature celebrations as *Mulroney: The*

Making of the Prime Minister can backfire. Mulroney should be warned. Those whom the press would destroy, they first exalt. Ask Trudeau.

WRITING OUT OF WASHINGTON, D.C., 'CITY OF DREAMS, GREAT AND SMALL, OF HOPES BOTH FOOLISH AND DARINGLY GRAND'

1

PATTI

BILLY GRAHAM, IF memory serves, found God on a golf course. I don't remember on which hole or I'd pass it on. But Patti Davis, the insufferably sincere daughter of Ronald and Nancy Reagan, lost Him when she was a teenager. Or at least her alter-ego, Beth Canfield, did, refusing to attend church one Sunday. 'I'm an agnostic,' she told her daddy, Robert Canfield, governor of California.

' "I see." There was a long pause. He picked up his pen, turned it in his hand, and put it down again. "Beth, this saddens me. Your mother and I tried to raise you with a respect for God and His teachings. Now God says in the Bible that we should gather together and worship Him."

' "God didn't write the Bible, Dad. Men did."

'He looked at me patiently. "No, Beth, that's not true. They may have put it down on paper, but they were delivering God's message . . ." '

Which just goes to show that in Hollywood even actors, never mind producers, have no respect for scriptwriters – but let it pass, let it pass.

I plucked this tidbit from *Home Front*, described by the

publishers as a 'candidly autobiographical novel' by Patti, with some help from novelist Maureen Strange Foster. The Californian Patti not only writes (or co-writes) but she also exercises, attending yoga classes that her husband, Paul Grilley, instructs, and she works as a stage and TV actress. *Ms.* magazine picked her as one of its Women of the Year in 1985 'for retaining her own identity, despite pressures of being a president's daughter and for writing honestly about honoring our families and principles at the same time.' This is nice, very nice, I think. Patti does write honestly, but, alas, not very well. Even so, *Home Front* is of some interest.

William Saroyan once wrote that he never threw out a book, because he learned something even from the bad ones, and it was in such a spirit of generosity that I picked up Patti's novel. I was not disappointed. Like the many readers out there who made *Home Front* a best-seller, I wasn't looking for literary quality, or even a page-turner, but for prurient gossip about the Prez and his First Lady, the best of which I now pass on, if only to spare you an otherwise tedious trip through 231 banal pages.

Here, for instance, is Patti/Beth on Governor Reagan/Canfield once he has decided to shoot for the presidency.

' "Beth," my father said, pausing as he usually did when he wanted to stitch together the fabric of his thoughts, "I may as well lay it on the line. There's been a lot of talk about my running for higher office, *and I'm not sure that isn't what the good Lord intended for me*" ' (Italics mine).

The possibility that God, between dictating scripts, actually fingered Ron for the Oval Office may be yet another rap against the Lord, but it does make me feel better about the Republican Party, which I had considered culpable until now. On the other hand, the fact that Ron might even entertain such a thought – a thought that some might consider blasphemous – does undermine his advertised modest posture. Something else. If God nominated Ron, who picked Walter Mondale to run against him? Beelzebub?

All this speculation, mind you, could be unfair. If Reagan/Canfield emerges from *Home Front* as a sketchy, poorly realized character, there is no disputing that he is a straight arrow. Once a year he and his wife receive a leather-bound collection of *Reader's Digest*, which I suspect he then files under 'Ideas.' Before going beddy-bye each night at eleven, the governor, as he then was, and his wife each drink a glass of milk.

Actually, the genial Reagan gets off lightly in *Home Front*, most of Patti's animus being directed at Mommie Dearest – that is to say Nancy, or Harriet, as she is called here. Her first day in the White House, Nancy/Harriet ducks in and out of rooms, inspecting furniture, drapes, walls.

' "There's just so much history here! Imagine all the people who have been within these walls. But, good grief, I just can't wait to redecorate." '

Harriet is described somewhat snidely as always looking perfectly put together, as though she'd just stepped out of *Town & Country*, 'and [she] managed to achieve that perfection in record time. One morning I clocked her from pillow to front door – in a navy-blue Chanel suit, matching shoes and pearl earrings – at twenty-nine minutes and thirty-six seconds.' Elsewhere we are told that Nancy/Harriet has about one drink a year, usually on New Year's Eve. In another descriptive passage, Patti writes, 'She took out her compact, touched up her lipstick and checked her hair for any misplaced strands, of which there were none. There never were. Her hair was always perfectly in place, framing her face in the most flattering way possible.' Not surprisingly, it also turns out that Mom is not a follower of the *Playboy* philosophy as expounded, in the absence of Aristotle, by H.M. Hefner, Esq. 'When I was twelve, my mother told me that there are three places a boy may put his hand: in your hand, around your shoulders, and around your waist.'

Oh, yes, there is also a story. Patti/Beth, a rebellious girl, determined – *pace Ms.* – to retain her identity, comes out strongly against the war in Vietnam, surfacing as a campus activist, much to the embarrassment of her father and the unflagging anger of her mother. Happily, Patti/Beth ultimately finds true love in the arms of an embittered marine *who has been changed* by what he has seen in Nam. Mind you, one of the first letters Greg, the marine, writes to Beth from Nam makes it clear he is a sensitive type. 'Getting to know a couple of nurses over here who are without a doubt some of the finest women I've ever met has taught me that there can be more to a relationship with a woman than getting it on. And I consider you to be a woman.' But when Greg flies home on leave, Beth discovers 'the hardness of his muscles and the smell of Old Spice around his face and neck.' And, good grief, once his hands wander south of the three areas designated A-OK by Mom, Beth's whole body shudders 'like waves cresting and breaking one after another.'

Home Front goes in for snappy chapter endings reminiscent of 'As The World Turns'. Take this last line, for instance, closing Chapter Three: ' "I think I'm pregnant." '

It is also a novel of ideas. Received ideas. War, for example, is adjudged ugly. Patti writes, 'After the assassinations of Martin Luther King Jr. and Robert Kennedy, I was tormented by thoughts that we were a country gone crazy.' The sentiment is legitimate, certainly, but while its expression in such a manner would satisfy in a letter home from summer camp, it reads decidedly inadequate when committed to print. Poor Patti's problem, I fear, is that if her parents think and talk in right-wing clichés, she responds with knee-jerk liberal bromides. On the evidence, she hasn't a fresh idea or sentence in her pretty little head.

Reagan/Canfield's concern, stated again and again in *Home Front*, is that his daughter has fallen into bad company on campus. Well, he's not only the prez, he's also right. But the trouble isn't the ruthless, yellow-bellied comsymps who are manipulating her. No, sir. The trouble is her bloody creative writing instructor, who has mischievously encouraged her to write poetry, several samples of which adorn the text. I will quote one poem in full:

>   i am afraid
>   ‾afraid my words,
>   hollow as matchbooks,

hobble to ashes.

i stumble,
heavy with memories
of days somersaulted past –
days swaddled in comfortable hands,
turning to your eyes for seasons.
hours lapped like ocean foam
on the shore of a rooted earth,
dreams were like plump sails
in syrupy sunsets.

but they sank
on my breasts and belly –
i bear their bruises.

accept these words,
born of a night
huddled in the milkweed distance
as dawn scrapes the lowest star.

Earlier critics of *Home Front*, obviously dastardly liberals, overeager to accuse Reagan of insensitivity, have made much of the fact that when Patti/Beth left this poem on her father's desk he never found the time to read it. Speaking for myself, I think he was lying, if only to be kind. I think he read the poem and that's when he encouraged his daughter to study the guitar.

Ms. magazine has got it wrong this time out. Patti has not retained her own identity in spite of the pressures of being a president's daughter. If she wasn't the president's daughter, this prosaic little novel would never have been published. A still dependent Patti is exploiting the family name and office.

2

MAUREEN

Why did President Bush appoint U.S. ambassadors to the United Nations and Britain so quickly? According to a senior U.S. diplomat, Maureen Reagan, the ambitious daughter of Bush's predecessor, was angling for one of the two prestigious posts. 'She is the ashtray-throwing type – loud, uncouth, undisciplined and vicious – everything that goes against Bush's grain,' says the official.

Time

Only a couple of years later, Patti's older step-sister, Maureen, was into the same game, which brings me to a packet I received by courier on January 12, 1989, from Little, Brown and Company, Publishers. Inside, there was a letter from the firm's publicity director.

Dear Mordecai Richler,

Through my error you have received a bound galley of Maureen Reagan's book, *First Father, First Daughter*, to be published on April 3, 1989.

My sending of this galley is in violation of our contract with Ms. Reagan. We are requesting no use of this galley in any form occur.

Please return the galley immediately to my attention at the following address: Little, Brown and Company, 205 Lexington Avenue, New York, N.Y. 100116. We will reimburse you for any costs you incur.

Our lawyers inform me that, under U.S. copyright law, the author controls the right to first publication. This will place you on formal notice that any publication by you of any portion of this material will be in violation of Ms. Reagan's rights.

Actually, the bound galleys of Ms. Reagan's book had yet to arrive. I found myself waiting for the postman every day, vacillating between two possibilities.

1. Once the galleys arrived, I would charter a plane and

deliver them to New York by hand, mindful of the publicist's generous offer to reimburse me for *any* costs incurred.

2. I would review the book in violation of Ms. Reagan's rights and then undergo plastic surgery and go into hiding under an assumed name.

And finally, there it was in my hot hands, *First Father, First Daughter*, by Maureen Reagan, who had some help from Dorothy Hermann in organizing the clichés. According to the blurb, *FF, FD* is the story of Ronnie's elder daughter and her loving – and candid – relationship with her famous dad. Well now, first daughter (a claim registered six times in the opening chapter) she may very well be, but she is also the second Reagan daughter to publish, proof of her determination – to quote the blurb – 'to become her own person.'

To judge from this memoir, the relationship between the half sisters – Maureen is the daughter of Ron's first marriage, to actress Jane Wyman, while Patti is Nancy and Ron's child – is more candid than loving. So it is in the fond hope of patching things up between the girls of the former First Family that I'm pleased to report, whatever their differences, the two do share at least one common characteristic: neither one can write worth a damn.

The first chapter of *FF, FD* deals with Ron's inauguration on January 20, 1981 ('The President. My father. The President's daughter. Me.'), an event Maureen prepared for, flying in from California, by losing herself 'in a big hardcover book.' She then goes on to describe the event for the ages: 'What a moment!' 'And what a brilliant day it was!' 'Twenty-one events in three days!' 'Thirty-two thousand people!' 'The Oval Office!'

Entering the Oval Office for the first time, Maureen promptly posed for photographs seated in her father's chair. 'This,' she writes with characteristic feeling, 'has got to be the biggest *wow!* in the history of big *wows*.'

The somewhat sappy prez and his iron lady come off better in *FF, FD* than do the 'fictional' governor and his forbiddingly icy missus in Patti's novel. That much said, the only revelation in Maureen's gabby, breathless memoir is that Reagan was more grievously wounded in the Hinckley assassination attempt than we were allowed to know. In fact, for some time it was really touch and go for the president, who had to be turned over regularly by nurses in order to breathe.

For the rest, Maureen babbles on and on about a hitherto mercifully unexamined life that would be of no interest were she not Reagan's daughter. Born on January 4, 1941, she grew up calling the ineffable Louella Parsons 'Aunt Lolly,' and tells us twice that by all accounts she was 'a precocious child.' Her first experience with death came when Bonzo of *Bedtime for Bonzo* perished in a fire, which is not exactly what Dylan Thomas had in mind, I think, when he wrote, 'After the first death there is no other.' Her parents were divorced in 1948, and three years later Ron was dating a small, slender actress named Nancy Davis. Maureen and Nancy got along fine because they had a lot in common. 'And – the biggest coincidence of all! – we both loved Dad.' In 1962, her father was almost fired as spokesman for General Electric. 'I've always suspected,' she writes, 'and I'm sure Dad agrees with me on this one, that Robert Kennedy had a hand in all this. I think the Kennedy administration saw in Dad's remarks a backhanded slur against their way of doing things, and their way of doing things wouldn't sit still for something like that.'

In 1959, Maureen, now living in Washington, D.C., entered the Miss Washington competition, a preliminary round for the Miss America pageant, and a year later she was licking envelopes on behalf of Vice-President Richard Nixon, with whom she agreed entirely 'on foreign policy and most domestic issues.' Her first marriage, at the age of twenty, in 1961, was to a cop who turned out to be a vicious wife-beater. They were divorced a year later, and Maureen mentions this sad episode only because there are thousands of women out there who 'need to hear the story of someone who survived her ordeal.' She married once more, in 1964, this time to a Marine lieutenant, only to be divorced again in 1967. 'Here I was, only twenty-six years old, on the losing end of two failed marriages. . . . I needed to get my act together.' Instead, she would lie awake in bed '*imagining* what it would be like to see Dad in the White House . . . I couldn't *imagine* a more forceful, *imaginative*, and sympathetic leader to take us into the next decade' (Italics mine).

Maureen tried acting, doing a Crisco commercial, but life continued to be difficult for our young heroine, the daughter of California's governor. A director once told her, 'Gee, kid, I like your work, but it's against my religion to do anything that might build up the name of Reagan.' And a producer, who had possibly seen the Crisco spot, said, 'Oh, yeah, I saw some film of you. You're good, but I hate your old man's politics.' Against the odds, she earned a place on a USO tour of Vietnam. 'What a beautiful country it was!' And soon she could boast an intimidating list of artistic credits, including appearances on 'The Partridge Family' and 'Marcus Welby, M.D.,' and a part in a movie called 'Death Takes a Holiday.' She also did turns on talk and variety shows, with Donald O'Connor, Art Linkletter and Merv Griffin. Then the big break – a television talk show of her own in Los Angeles. Gore Vidal submitted to an interview once: ' . . . he is really quite a character,' Maureen writes.

I could go on and on, but it would be cruel. Fate dealt Maureen a hard blow. Had she not been the bearer of a famous name, she would undoubtedly have become one of those officiously cheerful stewardesses or pushy cosmetic saleswomen, but, things breaking the way they did, she was compelled to try acting, politics, and now writing. Damn shame, that.

3

MO

There are natural peaks and valleys in the evolution of any society's literature. For instance, we had to wait fifty-seven years between the publication of *The Education of Henry Adams* and *"Mo": A Woman's View of Watergate*, published in 1975 and enjoying a cherished place in my library ever since. Plucking it off a shelf and opening it at random, I immediately came across the following passage:

> Before we went to sleep, John told me he had some good news and some bad news.
>
> The bad news first: we had to return to Washington the following day – Sunday, November 12. Brrr.
>
> Then the good news: we had been invited to fly back on Air Force One with President and Mrs. Nixon!
>
> I squealed with delight. If I could fly on the plane of the President of the United States, I didn't care if it was headed for Point Barrow, Alaska.
>
> That night I hardly slept a wink.
>
> Was I excited?
>
> Yes. I was excited.
>
> To fly with the President of the United States and the First Family in the presidential plane! It was a long way from Mar Vista for Sidney Charles Kane and Irene Kelly's little girl Mo, and she had to pinch herself a time or two to make sure she wasn't dreaming.

Her sensibility thus established, Maureen Dean has now struck again. This time out it's a novel, *Washington Wives*. Well, let's say the book of the miniseries at least. In a touching, if somewhat ambiguous author's note, Mar Vista's little Mo writes, ' . . . mostly I must thank my silent partner lurking behind every page of this book, the ghost who also lives in my bedroom.' I take it that the lurker is the Watergate snitch himself, who certainly lived to haunt Tricky Dick, but I had no idea that he now also spooked bedrooms. Never mind. Mo, in her gracious author's note, also thanks the editors who helped her 'refine' her manuscript (cleverly not naming names, for editors have been hanged for less) and 'the motion picture producer who conceived the project.' Uh-oh. Mo, born and bred in Los Angeles, should know that producers have lots of money, or access to it, but ideas – hardly ever. However, I must admit that in this case I'm the one who could be wrong, because I have a hunch it was the producer who came up with the idea for the opening pages. A real sizzler.

We are eavesdropping on an assignation in a suite in the Hay-Adams Hotel in Washington, D.C., 'city of dreams, great and small, of hopes both foolish and daringly grand.' There is a 'heart-stoppingly handsome' fella there, no less a personage than Bradford Barry, the prez's chief of staff, and a nameless beautiful woman who (confound her) seems to undress backwards. 'Her bra, garter belt, stockings, shoes, blouse and skirt, so carefully chosen, soon followed from the door to the edge of the tub.' And no wonder, for she is about to slip into the shower with a man whose black lashes are 'so thick they clumped.' And they are up to no good in there, you bet. 'Gently, he placed the soap between her legs and teasingly rubbed it back and forth until she thought she would scream.' Then there is trouble. Big trouble. Brad's head sinks lower but 'did not stop where she thought it would.' Holy cow, his face 'a mask of pain,' he's out of it. Heart attack. Even as the lady, still nameless, hurries back into her threads, getting the order right this time I hope, she thinks, 'Could this really be happening?'

The short answer is yes, and only one steamy page later, nice girl Jan Kirkland, deputy chief of protocol and a beauty, of course, has to cope with a sex conundrum of her own. Jan, I should point out, is married to Mark, a former *Newsweek* correspondent who is now the prez's press secretary. Her own secretary tells her that a Middle Eastern prince, presently visiting Blair House, wants a beautiful blonde transvestite sent over for tea.

Golly. Assuming this is something of a *roman-à-clef* as well as a novel of ideas, I immediately tried to figure out

121

who the dirty-minded wog was. Obviously it couldn't be Khomeini. But, good heavens, what if it was Yitzhak Shamir or Shimon Peres? – as if my people didn't have enough troubles. The mind boggles.

Washington Wives sets up a couple of riddles.

One of the wives, obviously a soap freak, is the nameless tart caught in that fatal shower with the heart-stoppingly handsome Brad. There are three candidates.

1. Nice girl, but obviously ambitious Jan Kirkland. Is she as sweet as she first appears? Visiting Mark at the White House, *during office hours*, she allows him to lock his door, close the shutters that face the West Portico *and lift her skirt*. Mo, who is awfully big on smalls, then tells us, 'She was wearing her little Miss Muffett pink garter belt with white stockings and black patent leather pumps. . . . It made him hotter than any porno flick ever could.'

The fiend has her right there, leaning her back on to the desk, teasing her by withdrawing even as she is moaning, asking her, 'Do you really want it?'

Mo writes: "Of course this is what she wanted. Getting laid in the White House was like joining the mile-high club, except the membership was far more exclusive. And Jan was excited by being in a special class of anything.'

2. Sinclare, yet another beauty, known to her friends and lovers (so help me God) as Sin, married to former Senator Eliot Ives, but having it off with another senator, whose crotch she is given to stroking whenever they meet.

Sin, when she was still a hatcheck girl, once endured a night of abandon with Danny Rankin, quarterback for the Washington Redskins. 'She was kissing a real man, not those wimps at school with the slobbering kisses and nervous weak hands.' Sociologists will be interested to note that Sin is the only one of the three Washington wives who wears panty hose rather than a garter belt, and these the beastly Rankin promptly tears off. Rankin himself, happily, wears neither garter belt nor panty hose: 'He was not wearing underwear and he was enormous.'

3. Caroline Riggs, also gorgeous, married to straight-arrow General Dalton Riggs, the national security advisor. Carol is a secret lush who doesn't yet appreciate that her daughter, Polly, a 'West Point second class-person with a straight A average, had been betrayed by the thing she could always count on – her own body. It was a wondrous machine – strong, lean and beautiful to boot. It could outrun, outjump, and outdo most boys in almost any competition, but the competition ended when it came to sex. She had lost.' Lost, mind you, to a Secret Service man who fondly calls her 'my kick-ass cadet.'

The second riddle posed by *Washington Wives* is which of the three husbands will be appointed the new chief of staff to the prez?

Since I am not a total swine, I refuse to reveal which wife was being soaped in the shower and whose hubby wins the big job. Suffice it to say that all the hubbies and wives – in fact just about everybody in Washington – is being manipulated by another beautiful lady, whose name is resonance itself: Echo Bourne. Echo, a nasty piece of work, provides shapely girls, and sometimes even her own beautiful bod, to senators, congressmen and visiting statesmen, taping the sessions for posterity. But Echo isn't all bad. She has also been known to service a journalist or two. A considerate touch, this.

Once a week, Echo visits the powerful William Buchanan Sumner, better known as Buck, a semi-retired diplomat who has carried the title ambassador-at-large for three presidents. And she isn't dropping in to discuss disarmament proposals or supply-side economics. 'As she reached up to his zipper her gold Piaget watch glinted in the morning sun. She unzipped the fly, resting her head against the trouser fabric of his Savile Row suit. He ordered five every year from his London tailor. Gently she reached inside his forty-dollar Egyptian broadcloth boxer shorts. . . .' Yes, you've guessed it, beyond pricing the haberdashery, Echo is there to give head, and afterward, as Mo delicately puts it, she will linger in the jakes to 'pleasure herself.' These epiphanies, graphically described, are certainly not there to titillate the reader. They are, I take it, an exceedingly clever metaphor, something that shows us – without ever saying as much – that hard-working Washingtonians suffer from a certain failure of communication. Only human, they don't always get it together.

Like Anthony Trollope, Mo sometimes pauses to reflect on the follies of man, or should I say womankind. Writing about a vicious gossip columnist called Deena, she observes that Deena knew that 'the real story at the heart of politics and male power was their wives and lady friends. Just ask Gary Hart. All the rest was tax policy, arms control, and international flimflam.'

Deena, incidentally, has been working on a novel about Washington politics for two years. Lowering her voice 'to a confidential purr,' she says, 'It's got everything – sex, glamour, power-fucking, intrigue, real inside Washington stuff that only I could know. Sally Quinn, Allen Drury, Barbara Howar – none of 'em could capture what's in here.' Then she says, 'I know I'm sitting on a gold mine here, hardcover, paperback, book clubs, miniseries, maybe a movie.'

Tell me no mo.

4

GARY

Gary Hart, once his political career was kaput, was rumoured to be pondering an alternative job, that of a working novelist. I am indebted to the proprietor of the fabled Too Hot Miami bikini boutique at Turnberry Isle, Ms. Lynn Armandt, for this information. Lynn was the other girl in that naughty foursome on board the now celebrated mini-ship of fools, *Monkey Business*, that docked overnight in Bimini. Something of a paid snitch, perhaps, but clearly in the admirable spirit of public service, Ms. Armandt revealed to *People* magazine, 'I awoke at 7 o'clock in the morning to the sound of engines, and I was alone. There were only three guest bedrooms, and I assume [Donna] didn't sleep with Broadhurst.' More important, Ms. Armandt also told *People* that 'we talked about books. Gary gave us a very detailed account of the novel he wrote – he's a great storyteller.'

Even earlier, Hart's campaign manager, William Dixon, told *Time* that Hart, with little accumulated wealth and two children in college, needed to begin work immediately. 'Like the rest of us he can't afford to interrupt that income stream. He just can't take a year off and write novels.' But the story went on to say that Hart, author of two novels already, hoped to start another *in his spare time*. (Italics mine.)

Hmm.

The fact that starting a novel would mean interrupting his income stream suggests that no publisher was willing to stake Hart to an advance against royalties anything like what former Phi Beta Kappa cheerleader Donna Rice was being offered to shed her tutu for *Playboy* in *her* spare time. This, mark you, did not prejudice me against either *The Strategies of Zeus*, by Gary Hart, or *The Double Man*, by William S. Cohen and Gary Hart, both of which I offer for consideration here.

According to that traditional master of understatement, the blurb writer, in *The Strategies of Zeus*, 'Gary Hart opens the door on to the clandestine world of international power politics to bring readers a captivating, tension-filled drama.' Actually, it is yet another pot-boiler about our world gone mad, on the brink of World War III, saved from the nuclear nuts on both sides by sexy Ekaterina Davydova, a translator from the Russian arms-control delegation, and lanky Frank Connaughton, of the U.S. delegation, who turns out (hello, hello) to be a lovable, straight-shooting fella out of Montana who favours cowboy boots. A singular man, Hart writes, whose 'aura of separateness made him seem, to those around him, strong but elusive.' Connaughton serves a president whom 'he considered little better than a fool, or perhaps a dunce.' The prez isn't 'accustomed to being confronted – to being spoken to so directly. His staff was superb at constructing a cocoon of euphoria all about him.' As for the vice-prez, well, he 'was a man who operated consistently so far beyond his limitations he had forgotten where they were.' All of this leads me, a moxie reader, to what Edmund Wilson would have called 'shocks of recognition.'

As political thrillers go, *The Strategies of Zeus* threatens neither John le Carré on one end of the scale nor Robert Ludlum on the other. It suffers from endless clunky runs of dialogue that read like liberal editorials or bits snatched from *Father Knows Best*. Here is Connaughton cooking dinner for his fifteen-year-old daughter, Frankie.

> "Let's go, Sis. My night to cook and yours to do dishes. Besides, you're never going to catch a husband if you don't learn the secrets of venison à la Connaughton.'
>
> 'I'm liberated, Dad, remember? I don't have to know how to cook. Besides, I don't intend to get married.'
>
> 'Sure, sure. I know. You can't ever hope to find anyone as great as good old Dad. Right?'

Connaughton, who is being trailed by CIA snoops, manages his assignations with Ekaterina better than the author did his monkey business with Donna. Put another way, it is a clear case of art improving on life. But, once they get it together, it's strictly Harlequin Books time.

> Without thought, he kissed her softly. During an eternity when time seemed suspended, his only realization was how long he had wanted to do this. They clung to each other, fearing even to move, fearing some magic might escape them forever. The fire crackled and blazed as the embrace went on. Neither wanted to separate or break the spell. Then finally they breathed, still holding each other. He touched her cheek, then her hair, marveling at its blackness. Her fingers roamed the rough lines of his face as if to memorize the contours for a long time to come.
>
> Then she said in a whisper. 'I want to love you, to make love with you. I want to more than anything right now.'

The Double Man is a thriller that answers two questions put to us by the blurb writer. 'Would the KGB ever plot terrorist attacks against high-ranking American officials – on American soil? Could a United States senator turn out to be a "mole" working for the Soviet Union?' In common with *The Strategies of Zeus*, it features wooden characters and prose that has the resonance of aluminum siding. This time our hero is the senator from Connecticut, Tom Chandler, whose marriage has gone bad.

> In the end not even political expediency could save the marriage. It had lasted for twenty-one years, though for the final few in name only. Love, if it had ever existed, had been replaced by indifference and increasingly empty displays of affection for the sake of appearances. In the end all that remained for Chandler was an emptiness and silent resignation.

Until the senator from Connecticut meets the fair Elaine Dunham, a curvy CIA op. Hell, all Tom does is touch her and 'it was as if a current of heat passed through his fingers and met an answering impulse deep within her.' Soon Tom and Elaine are truly plugged in, lacing fingers, giving themselves up completely to joy and possible short-circuits. Back at her pad, they do it, releasing all those locked-in currents – 'two rivers of energy rushing together, gloriously, powerfully.' Then they recharge, starting the touching business again, 'as if [*pace* Ekaterina] they were trying to memorize each other's bodies in the dark.' Only a few pages later they are at it again, in front of a fireplace, obviously big with Hart. 'Two people became one silhouette against the firelight. At that moment, if the flame had leaped out to consume them, they might not have noticed. Or cared.'

Oh, come on.

DIVORCE

'A LANDMARK BOOK,' say Erik and Joan Erikson. 'Deeply touching, impressively researched,' according to Judith Viorst, and, so far as T. Berry Brazelton, M.D., is concerned, it's great. All this in praise of *Second Chances: Men, Women and Children a Decade After Divorce*, by Judith Wallerstein, Ph.D., and Sandra Blakeslee.

This definitive book on divorce, based on a study of sixty middle-class families interviewed over five, ten and sometimes fifteen years, does answer some perplexing questions. But before serving up these answers, let me first assure you that they are grounded in solid research. Here, in the authors' very own translucent prose, are a few words about their methodology:

> The choice of research design, including measurement strategies and creation of variables from coding schemas, stems from decisions about which dimensions of the phenomena under study are of interest. This investigation was originally conceptualized as a hypothesis-generating study in which the goal was to explore and track the perceptions and experiences of individual family members, particularly children, following divorce.

Now for the questions.

1. If a child sees his hitherto adorable dad hurl a screaming mom into the hall closet and lock the door – or witnesses mom pitch a table lamp at dad's head – will this be disturbing to the child in future years?

a. Yes. b. No. c. Maybe.

The answer, *based on a fifteen-year study, the data fully analyzed, is – yes.*

2. Are there winners and losers in divorce? The answer is that the one who packs his bags, bound for a bimbo's apartment, tends to whistle while he works, but the other one, left behind with the dirty dishes, the N-to-Z half of the family dictionary and the resentful children, tends to feel rejected and maybe even vengeful.

Wallerstein and Blakeslee claim that *Second Chances* 'is the longest study tracking divorced families ever conducted, with no counterpart in the world,' and for this many of us will be grateful. To be fair, either this book resonates with astonishingly original perceptions or, on the other hand, there are no truths like received ones. Here are some of their conclusions:

> Divorce is a major turning-point for men and women.
> In families with children, divorce is rarely a mutual decision.
> Divorce has two purposes. The first is to escape the marriage, which has grown intolerable for at least one person. The second is to build a new life.
> In most families, divorce tends to benefit one of the adults more than the other.

I cannot quarrel with any of these wise pronouncements – or the authors'' credentials. Judith Wallerstein, Ph.D., is the founder and executive director of something called the Center for the Family in Transition, not surprisingly located in sunny Madera, California. Sandra Blakeslee is a free-lance science and medical writer who contributes regularly to the New York *Times* science department. By their admission, Judith and Sandra are also a lovable pair. 'The children remember us with startling clarity, providing tiny details of our first meeting a decade ago,' Judith says. After interviews, their adult subjects tend to stand tearfully on the sidewalk or to reach out and hug them. Ten years after the initial contact, 'some are absolutely delighted by my overture,' she reports. 'One woman, after driving three hours, sweeps into my office and throws her arms around me; a man kisses me impulsively on both cheeks and says, "What you are doing is wonderful." '

To the wonderful ladies, it is disconcerting that some adults (obviously churlish types, jealous of their privacy) find it difficult to discuss their divorces a decade later. Well now, the time has come for me to interject a personal note. I also happen to be an expert on divorce, with my own creation of variables from coding schemas. My parents parted acrimoniously when I was a sensitive, vulnerable thirteen-year-old, and my own first marriage came to a stormy end after three years. Yes, gentle reader, I am an open wound, lugging childhood traumas into my middle years. But had Judith and Sandra knocked on my door, armed with intrusive questionnaires, I would have told them to mind their own business and booted them down the stairs.

The ladies can be shockingly naive. 'I did not expect to discover that there are winners and losers in the years after divorce; and I certainly did not expect to find gross indiscrepancies [sic] within each couple.' They can also leap to wrong conclusions. 'A child who loses a parent through death does not go through life feeling a common bond with all other children who have lost parents the same way. But the children of divorce do feel a common bond. They carry the experience throughout their lives and feel a kinship with all other children of divorce, claiming an identity that sets them apart from their peers.'

As a surly, pimply, thirteen-year-old shoplifter, I was totally lacking in distinction of any kind. Happily, my parents'' divorce lent me a certain cachet. Suddenly, some girls found me more interesting than the airheads who had made the basketball team. I was somebody in need of affection, maybe even a little smooching.

'You must be going through hell at home.'

'You betcha.'

So I deeply resented other boys of divorced parents muscling in on my sympathy territory, as it were.

Even as an adult, at dinner parties, embellishing stories of my cruel childhood, I didn't care to have someone else trump me with lies about his own parents' bloody boring divorce.

The children of divorced parents, the authors write, may have trouble concentrating at school. Adolescents often act out and get into trouble.

Until now I thought *I* was to blame for my embarrassing report cards and for being in and out of trouble as a teenager. I am relieved to discover that it was actually the fault of my unhappy parents.

Growing up, Judith and Sandra suggest, is harder for the children of divorce, who feel deprived of the kind of support that children from happy, intact families take for granted. Furthermore, these children also suffer a lack of attention from relatives and family friends, people who tend to act as if divorce were contagious.

Possibly, I'm the exception that proves the rule. But in the months leading up to and immediately following my parents' divorce, I suddenly found myself the centre of attention of aunts and uncles who had hitherto treated me (justifiably, I'm afraid) as an all but intolerable smart-ass. 'Don't worry, kid. It's not your fault.' I also discovered that my parents' situation had economic value. All I had to do was mope and, presto, notoriously stingy relatives pelted me with quarters for Cokes and hot dogs, half-dollars for double features at the Rialto and, on two memorable occasions, a buck for a good time on a Saturday night. And I'm talking 1940s pre-inflation dollars and cents.

Then, when I became head of a family happily intact, father of five cherished children, I discovered that when the kids were younger they felt deprived. They envied the other brats at school, many of whom boasted four or even six parents, all of them trying to win their affection by buying them extravagantly expensive gifts. I think they found my wife and me boring.

BARBARA HUTTON

ONE MORNING, SITTING at the foot of Marjorie Merriweather Post's bed, Barbara Hutton complained about the collapse of her third marriage – this one to Cary Grant.

'You're too impetuous,' said Aunt Marjorie. 'You should try to patch things up with Cary.'

'Maybe I just haven't met the right man yet,' said the Woolworth heiress to the General Foods heiress.

'Nonsense,' replied Marjorie. 'You've already had too many husbands. You must be doing something wrong.'

'Like what?' asked Barbara.

Marjorie pondered just a little before she said, 'Have you tried rotating your hips? I'm told it makes it much better for the man.'

Noel Coward had already composed a song with her in mind:

> Poor little rich girl,
> You're a bewitched girl,
> Better beware!
> Better take care!

Young Barbara, according to David Niven, was 'a petite, snub-nosed blonde, very pretty American girl with the smallest feet I had ever seen . . . a gay and sparkling creature, full of life and laughter.'

From 1926 to 1933, not exactly vintage financial years for most people, her personal piggy bank increased in value from £26 million to $42 million. Even so, just like the perennial travelling salesman stuck for the night in a sleazy hotel in Buffalo, she always had to pay for her loving. Mind you, at a rate undreamed of by your average drummer. Take husband number five, for instance, the legendary Porfirio Rubirosa. He collected approximately $1 million in gifts and $2.5 million in cash before he would dissolve their seven-and-a-half-week marriage, which works out to more than $66,000 per diem. In her final days, an emaciated, toothless hag, adrift on drugs and booze, Barbara had to fork out $1,000 to California beach boys to come up to her Beverly Hills Hotel bedroom and shoot the breeze with her.

The family fortune was put together by Barbara's grandfather, Frank Winfield Woolworth. F.W. opened his first 'Woolworth's 5 and 10¢ store' in 1879. By 1917 his company had grossed $100 million and he opened his thousandth store – in New York, at Fifth Avenue and 40th Street. Woolworth employed thousands of young girls – many of them immigrants – and paid them notoriously low wages for long hours. He was, he said, providing a paid apprenticeship to unskilled workers. He was also, in the long run, providing for Barbara.

Barbara's world, as set out in *Poor Little Rich Girl*, by David C. Heymann, will not evoke your misspent youth any more than it did mine. Hers was a world of polo tournaments, chartered jets and Elsa Maxwell scavenger-hunt parties, the most talked about of which was held on Hallowe'en of 1933. 'Ninety-nine couples spent the night searching for a live goat, a hair from Kermit Roosevelt's moustache, and a pair of actress Marilyn Miller's underpants,' Heymann reports. No Venetian season, the author reminds us, was complete without Elsa's annual masquerade party, or the presence of that most boring and foolish couple of our times, the Duke and Duchess of Windsor.

Barbara, born in 1912, had her debutante ball in 1930, the year she acquired her first private railway car and also seduced a bodyguard hired by her father to protect her. 'He was,' she wrote, 'rampant as a bull, literally tearing himself out of his clothes, diving on top of me.'

There were seven husbands before she was done.

The first, a White Russian and self-proclaimed prince, was Alex Mdivani of 'the marrying Mdivanis' (one brother had wed actress Mae Murray and another movie vamp Pola Negri). Alex, once he had been accepted by Barbara on April 14, 1933, cabled his sister: 'HAVE WON THE PRIZE, ANNOUNCE BETROTHAL.' Barbara paid him a dowry of $1 million plus a substantial allowance and, for a wedding present, gave him a string of polo ponies. Not easily bought, however, Alex told his 148-pound bride on their wedding night, 'Barbara, you're too fat,' and thereby launched her on a lifetime of ruinously severe dieting. To begin with, her diet gave her a sleek, varnished look, and soon her photograph was featured in the pages of *Vogue* and *Harper's Bazaar*, and on the cover of *Life*.

Soon after her wedding, Barbara's personal fortune, held in trust by her father, was transferred to her name, so that at the age of twenty-one, Babs, taking all her holdings into consideration, was worth more than $50 million – approximately $800 million at today's market prices. Immediately, she tipped her prince another $1.25 million as well as contributing one thousand Christmas baskets to the New York poor. Ed Sullivan cheered in the pages of the *Daily News*: 'Princess Barbara is the tops. You're a swell person – just swell!' A year later she divorced Alex and was a free woman for only a few hours before it was announced that she was marrying husband number two – this one an authentic count.

Count Heinrich Eberhard Erdman Georg Haugwitz-Hardenberg-Reventlow was a Prussian-born Dane, then thirty-nine years old, with whom she was to have her one and only child, Lance Reventlow. By this time, Barbara was suffering from anorexia nervosa. The count, put off his appetite by her eating habits, found his own weight dropping from 200 to 160 pounds in four years of marriage. Sublimating, perhaps, he developed a taste for sex shows.

Which brings us to 1942 and husband number three, Cary Grant, the only Hutton husband who actually worked for a living and did not accept a dowry from Barbara. Reporters dubbed the pair 'Cash 'n' Cary.' Grant, according to his valet, 'was stingy as hell. He begrudged the help every bottle of Coke they took from the pantry. His rule was no soda between meals, only with your meal. If he caught you drinking a soda, he docked it out of your pay.'

Barbara tipped an Errol Flynn sidekick, Frederick Joseph McEvoy, $100,000 for introducing her to her Pixie, her dimpled husband number four, otherwise known as Prince Igor Nikolaiewitsch Troubetzkoy. Of their first dinner date, Igor later recalled, 'She called. We ate. And then – boom – to bed and new realities!' They were wed in 1947, by which time the dieting Barbara was not only heavily into booze but also into amphetamines. Once Barbara was done with Igor, she got rid of him cheaply. He was given a deed to a house in Gif-sur-Yvette, a car and a lifetime trust that yielded approximately $1,000 a month.

Husband number five, Porfirio Rubirosa, or *'Toujours Prêt'* as he was also known, had already wed another poor little rich girl, Doris Duke, and had enjoyed the favours of Zsa Zsa Gabor, Dolores Del Rio, Joan Crawford, Veronica Lake, Jayne Mansfield, Marilyn Monroe, Susan Hayward, Tina Onassis and Evita Peron. Understandably, he once told a reporter, 'Work? I have no time for work.' He was, Barbara said, 'Priapic, indefatigable, grotesquely proportioned.' His valet was even more enthusiastic: ' . . . a stallion, an absolute stallion. *E la uova, la uova!* They were so enormous that they bothered him and he usually wore a jockstrap.'

Husband number six, wed in 1955, was German tennis ace Gottfried Von Cramm, a confirmed homosexual. Seemingly, their marriage was never consummated. Ted Peckham, who had run a male escort service in Europe that catered to either sex, said Barbara 'had a kind of double standard about gays. She found her husband's homosexuality threatening to her femininity. Otherwise, she had this old lady's attitude toward gays, adoring them because they adored her.'

Von Cramm, his $2-million dowry in hand, was sent on his way to be replaced in 1963 by husband number seven, one Raymond Doan, for whom Barbara considerately purchased a title for $50,000 from the Laotian Embassy in

Rabat. Prince Raymond Doan Vinh Na Champassak lasted until 1971. He never disclosed the terms of his permanent separation from Barbara, but according to his son, it included a $2-million Swiss bank account to be turned over to Doan after Barbara's death on condition there was no intervening divorce.

From then on, it was a steady decline for Barbara, hastened by a diet of morphine, Quaaludes, cocaine and young blond men. She died on May 11, 1979.

In the endless spill of high society opportunists who crowded Barbara's life, there was not one you would want to have dinner with – except, perhaps, Barbara's cousin, the witty Jimmy Donahue. Donahue was the Duchess of Windsor's escort for many years. Once, when presenting a boyfriend to a fellow traveller on a world cruise, he declared, 'Let me introduce you to the boy who took the boy who took the girl who took the boy off the throne of merry old England.' Donahue couldn't have been all bad. 'It was common gossip,' writes Heymann, 'that Jimmy liked to cross-dress and entertain his mother's friends, including Cardinal Spellman, while attired in petticoats, a dress, wig, falsies and high heels.'

PAID LIARS

1

JOHN CHEEVER

'AND AT 3:00 a.m. I seem to be walking through Grand Central Station,' John Cheever wrote in his journal in 1956. 'And the latch on my suitcase gives, spilling onto the floor the contents of my life and what do we find there? A pint of gin and some contraceptives; the score for Handel's *Water Music* and a football; the plays of Shakespeare, *The Brothers Karamazov* and *Madame Bovary*; a sweater and a jockstrap and an old madder necktie; but also, to signify times of irresolution and loss about which I know plenty, a daisy for counting and a candle for impotence; but also a hairbrush and a love poem and a photo of happy times on the deck of the tern and a yellow leaf or some such – a stone from the beach to signify times of solid high spirits.'

According to his daughter, Cheever, who was forty-four years old at the time, had already spent a lot of energy trying not to drink before 4:00 p.m., and then before noon, and then before 10:00 a.m., and then before breakfast. But, she writes, the alcohol hadn't blurred his acuity or softened his critical vision in those days the way it did later. Years after, when the anguished Cheever gave in to his long-repressed homosexuality, he took on a series of younger male protégés, some of them overtly homosexual. 'I fell in love with Rip,' he wrote in his journal in 1978, 'in a motel room of unusual squalor. His air of seriousness and responsibility, the bridged

137

glasses he wore for his nearsightedness and his composed manner all excited my deepest love.' He also wrote of his dread, his self-loathing, and his fears of what the heterosexual community might say if they found out about him. 'Have you heard?' he wrote. 'Old Cheever, crowding 70, has gone Gay. Old Cheever has come out of the closet. Old Cheever has run off to Bessarabia with a hairy youth half his age.'

These and other painful revelations about a man who was surely one of the most gifted American writers of our time come in the form of a memoir, *Home Before Dark*, by his daughter Susan, a former *Newsweek* editor, who has published three novels of her own.

Certainly she is not the first child to write about a famous parent. One of Oscar Wilde's sons took a crack at it, and so did Hemingway's boy, Patrick. Arthur Marx wrote a nasty biography of Groucho. There was the notorious *Mommie Dearest* about Joan Crawford. Randolph Churchill pronounced on his big daddy and Anthony West had his considerable say about the perpetually horny H.G. Wells. These memoirs were written for a variety of motives ranging from greed, through a twisted need to belittle, to an honest attempt to set the record straight. Whatever, it is a form I have trouble with. I think authors, anyway, should be proof against their children interpreting them in print. I would rather they erred on the side of reticence.

In the autumn of 1981, when Susan Cheever discovered that her father, who had already endured a major heart attack, was dying of cancer, it seemed natural that she should write about it. She says she never intended to become her father's biographer. At first she thought her book 'would be a slim volume of anecdote and remembrance.' She wanted to tell a writer's story.

'I don't think I would have started this book,' she writes, 'if I had known where it was going to end, but having written it I know my father better than I ever did while he was alive.'

Yes, possibly, but this troubled memoir, however pure in intent, does raise larger questions.

'I write,' Cheever used to say, 'to make sense of my life.' And what he wrote he sent out to be judged and marketed. For the rest, the details of his private life, he might have appreciated a curtain of dignified silence – especially from his children. Surely he indicated as much in a discussion he once had with Susan about Saul Bellow's novel *Humboldt's Gift*. Susan, who had admired the novel, was fascinated to hear that the main character was drawn from the poet Delmore Schwartz. She couldn't wait to tell her father, but instead of being interested, he was indignant.

'That's the kind of speculation I abhor,' he said. 'The book is a great work of fiction; it cannot be reduced to gossip.'

Arguably, this memoir unintentionally – to give Susan Cheever the benefit of the doubt – does reduce Cheever's life to gossip, filled as it is with details about his sometimes rocky marriage, his dark moments, his infidelities both hetero- and homosexual, and his long struggle with alcoholism. Details, I should add, that are proffered in a manner that is sometimes irritating and the wrong side of generous. John Cheever's fiction, his daughter pronounces, 'focused on the surface and texture of life, not on the emotions and motives underneath,' which is to shockingly misunderstand a major writer and a body of work as enjoyable as it is important. Then, when Cheever notes in his journal, 'That was the summer that Joe Louis fought Harry Thomas and the Philadelphia Athletics won the pennant,' a reporter's picky footnote informs us, 'In fact, the Yankees played the Cubs in the 1938 World Series and it was the Yankees who won.'

John Cheever, it seems was fond of telling how his ancestor Ezekiel Cheever arrived in Boston Harbor on the *Arbella* in 1630, but his daughter's research has revealed that Ezekiel didn't really arrive until 1637 on board a ship called *Hector*. Her father, she states, wasn't, because of his writings, ostracized by the 'respectable' Cheevers, as he liked to boast, showing off in front of his kids. Furthermore, his aristocratic New England background was partly sham, and his patrician airs were mostly of his own invention. He never came from a fox-hunting gentleman's sort of world, as he encouraged people to believe.

John Cheever, as might be expected, put it all much better himself. 'I have been a storyteller since the beginning of my life,' he wrote in his journal in 1961, 'rearranging facts in order to make them more interesting and sometimes more significant. I have turned my eccentric old mother into a woman of wealth and position and made my father a captain at sea. I have improvised a background for myself – genteel, traditional – and it is generally accepted.' Or, put another way, Cheever, as gifted a liar or burnisher of tales as many a lesser writer, dealt in larger truths.

In his later years, Susan Cheever complains, success and celebrity took a toll on her father, and he became pompous about himself. Well, maybe, but he had certainly paid his literary dues, and he could also, on the evidence, be self-deprecating about his honours. When, a year after the publication of *The Wapshot Chronicle*, he was elected to the National Institute of Arts and Letters, he immediately composed a ditty for the occasion. 'Root tee toot, ahhh root tee toot, oh, we're the boys of the Institute. Oh we're not rough and we're not tough, we're *cul*tivated and that's enough.'

He was uncommonly generous to younger writers and answered every letter that was sent to him, whether from a graduate student or a reader in Idaho or Saul Bellow or John Updike. And far from being pompous about his own importance, he threw out or burned his old manuscripts; letters were set aflame too, even if they were from Bellow or Updike. He could barely be persuaded to keep copies of his own books, his daughter writes, and if he liked a new book he had read, he often gave it away.

John Cheever was an unwanted child, his conception a drunken accident between two people who no longer cared for each other. When his mother's pregnancy was discovered, his father argued for an abortion.

His first short story, 'Expelled,' was published in *The New Republic* in 1930, when he was eighteen years old. Later, his fiction appeared in *Collier's, Story* and *The Yale Review*. *The New Yorker* didn't buy a short story of his until 1935, but by the early fifties he had published more than seventy in that magazine. Although he was to prosper in his later years (*Falconer* was a best-seller, and so was his collection, *The Stories of John Cheever*), for most of his life his annual income was no more than $15,000. Only in 1960, when he was almost fifty years old, could he afford to buy his own house in Ossining, New York. He was now famous as well as prospering, featured on the covers of both *Time* and *Newsweek*. He won the National Book Award, the Howells Medal from the American Academy of Arts and Letters, the Pulitzer Prize, the National Book Critics Circle Award and the National Medal for Literature. He had also become a drunk.

'Back at the house I want a drink,' he wrote, describing a Sunday morning in the sixties. 'Nine o'clock. I read the *Times* book review section and the magazine. Mary is in the kitchen with a clear view of the bourbon bottle. The beds are unmade I know, but she lingers in the kitchen. Then she goes outside to sweep the porch but should I make a grab for the bourbon I might be seen through the pantry window. I hope she will go into the garden and pick some flowers but she does not. She returns to the dining room and rearranges some ashtrays. I go on reading the *Times*. Then she starts up the stairs but changes her mind and returns to the kitchen. Finally she climbs the stairs to the first landing and then the second and I sail into the pantry and gulp down two hookers of bourbon. At half past eleven I get out the ice and settle down to formal drinking. . . .'

In 1975, Cheever entered the Smithers Alcoholism Rehabilitation Unit in New York; he gave up drinking and remained an active and grateful member of AA until he died. Cheever's journals, his daughter writes, were the pages where he could improvise, experiment and refine. They were also 'the arena in which he wrestled with his personal demons – alcohol, sex and his acute sense of what he might have done wrong.' He had tried psychiatrists, but never had any respect for them. As she points out, 'most of them hadn't read much of anything, and certainly not *Les Faux-Monnayeurs* or *Il Gattopardo* or Goncharov or even Fielding. How could he be expected to communicate with men like that?' How indeed?

His journals were private, but I think Susan Cheever is absolutely right when she notes, 'Toward the end of his life, after he stopped drinking, my father realized what an extraordinary document his journals had become, and I think that he meant them to be read some day. He hauled them out of their boxes in the attic, or off the shelves at the top of his clothes closet, and encouraged us to read selected passages from them. He sent a section off to the Brandeis University library and promised another for a small printing at the University of Alabama.' When the journals, which I understand run to thirty volumes, hundreds of thousands of words, are finally edited, I do not doubt that it will be a major publishing event. Meanwhile, these memoirs, honestly troubled, somewhat self-serving, with rather too much of Susan Cheever intruding, at least offer tantalizing glimpses of the riches to come.

2

TRUMAN CAPOTE

I can't say that I knew Truman Capote, but I did meet him more than once, the last time in a bar on 49th Street in New York, maybe a year before he died. He was drunk, surprisingly hostile, and so we talked only briefly. At the time, the word on him was bad. He was drinking prodigiously and falling off lecture platforms, they said, because he was 'all written out,' or suffering from a terminal disease, or both. They also said his big novel-in-progress, *Answered Prayers*, was a bluff. Only scattered and disjointed chapters existed. Mind you, the people who passed on these stories with such obvious glee had also lit a vindictive candle for each of the latter-day flops of America's great playwright Tennessee Williams. New York sizzles with such small fry.

The first time I met Capote was at an A-list party in Beverly Hills. He was already obese, a sausage threatening to burst its casing, and he was also drunk. He settled into a chair in a far corner, and it immediately became the centre of the room. We talked about mutual friends in London and a recent trip he had made to Canada. It was all very pleasant. At that time, he was acting in a Neil Simon film, *Murder by Death*. Somebody asked him, as he was a writer of such stature, did he not find acting . . . well, degrading?

Capote smiled. He took his time. Finally he said, 'Norman had to pay to act in his films.' A reference to Mailer, who several years earlier had shot *Maidstone* out on Long Island, a venture he had largely financed himself.

Bellow, Capote went on to say, was America's premier novelist.

'Do you read him, Truman?'

'Oh, he's far too intelligent for me.'

The house we were at was high in the hills with dimly lit stone steps leading down to the road. When my wife and I left, we noticed Capote and Isherwood ahead of us. Isherwood long and lean, Capote rotund. They were holding hands, taking the steps very slowly. 'Careful, dear.'

Isherwood's career, like Capote's had begun with a blaze: *Goodbye to Berlin, Mr Norris Changes Trains*. Isherwood faded away, writing books hardly anybody read. The author of *Other Voices, Other Rooms* and *In Cold Blood* became the most celebrated poodle of the very, very rich.

John Malcolm Brinnin once said to Capote, 'You spend half your life these days – more, for all I know – with people who travel in their own sleek planes and their Silver Clouds, who keep empty villas around the Mediterranean, shooting boxes in Argyll, bank accounts in Zurich or Grand Cayman, people who own the earth, from which they're insulated as completely as though they lived in time capsules. What's in it for you?'

'Keep your shirt on,' Capote replied. 'I simply had to know what it was like. Years and years I wondered: What if you woke up in the morning, so rich you were famous for it, being rich. What if you had your orange juice, read your paper, all the while knowing that if there was anything to buy you could buy it, any place to go, you could go there, today. Would you make life into a game? Manipulate people like children with an ant farm? What would absolutely limitless means do to your appetites? Would you get a yen for experience per se? Sex? Food? Power? Would you buy all those things – Fabergé eggs, solid-gold putters, first folios, Marie Antoinette's bed and chamber pot, things that other people *couldn't*? Would you try a quiet little murder or two, a little indulgence in *acte gratuit*, just to see if you could get away with it?'

'So?'

'So, I've found out what I wanted to know.'

'Which is?'

'Which is that there's nothing much *to* find out. The rich are as bored with themselves as you are, as I am – children, without the imagination of children. That's the thing that's squelched first: imagination. It's bred out of them as carefully as manners and a taste for pheasant and truffles is bred into them. . . . '

In 1985, there was a definitive biography of Capote due from Gerald Clarke. There was also the sadly unfinished *Answered Prayers*, which would eventually be published. Meanwhile, we had the affectionate but fussy memoir, *Truman Capote, Dear Heart, Old Buddy*, by John Malcolm Brinnin, which was really no more than an expanded version of a portrait that first appeared in Brinnin's *Sextet: T.S. Eliot & Truman Capote & Others*. It's gossipy, something of an intelligent literary voyeur's guide to the life-styles of the rich and famous: Tennessee Williams, Peggy Guggenheim, Noel Coward, André Gide, Carson McCullers all make an appearance. It's readable, but somehow unsatisfying, even suspect. Brinnin is one of those writers who has made a habit of mining his betters in memoirs. If any of you remember an earlier book of his, *Dylan Thomas in America*, he is also naïve and a bit of a schoolmarmish scold. Thomas obviously enjoyed provoking his American keeper, often claiming to have drunk more than he did. Capote, it's clear, also teased Brinnin – as he did so many others – with tall tales. Once, for instance, he claimed to be having an affair with John Garfield.

'This thing between you and Golden Boy,' Brinnin asked, 'how serious is it?'

'He's sweet,' Capote allowed, 'and sort of teddy-bear cuddly, that's all.' But, Capote went on to complain, what he couldn't stand was that Garfield treated him like a girl.

'What does that mean?'

'It means . . . well, he's like all those others who can't face up to the fact they're with a man with balls as hairy as their own and so they have to pretend this man they're with is really some baby doll in disguise.'

Brinnin first met Capote at Yaddo, the residence for writers not far from Saratoga Springs, New York, when Capote was a most promising twenty-one-year-old who had published glittering stories in *Harper's* and *Mademoiselle*. Had he been to college, Brinnin asked?

'I've never set foot in one,' Capote said. 'With an IQ that runs off the chart, why should I?'

He already understood his talent.

'Maybe everyone has stories to tell. What I mean is I have something to say that hasn't been said, simply because no one else knows what I know the *way* I know it.'

Brinnin knew Capote on and off for four decades, their association, he writes, sometimes intimate. But when an interviewer, referring to Brinnin's initial memoir about Capote, asked the author how well he knew Brinnin, Capote replied, 'He's never been a close friend of mine; he never really *was* a close friend of mine.'

On the evidence, this seems hard. Obviously they were friends. The question is, what manner of friend was Brinnin? Twenty-five-year-old conversations evoked in Brinnin's memoir lean on the meticulous journal he kept over the years. My problem is that there seems something calculating, even unsavoury, about a friend who records conversations, however frivolous, and then banks them in memoirs. Entertaining memoirs, to be fair.

There is at least one illumination. One evening in Venice, the late Cyril Connolly, that most astute of critics, turned on Brinnin: 'Truman Capote. What are you Americans going to do about him?'

'Do?'

'It appears to me that you are going to kill him with kindness, the insidious kindness that masks contumely, the kindness that turns all your best writers into performing seals and drunken derelicts.'

'I don't follow. . . . *Why* are we going to kill him?'

'I'll tell you why. Because you despise him, because you aren't prepared to cope with that completely alien kind of perception into an even darker underside of your character than Henry James could face up to. It fits no category you tolerate, conforms to no image of yourself you can accept. . . .'

Connolly, this time out, was guilty of overstatement. America doesn't turn all of its best writers into performing seals or drunken derelicts. Saul Bellow, Walker Percy and John Updike, among others, manage to lead dignified lives, never caught out playing the fool in late-night talk shows. Capote, surely, was a willing partner in his own destruction.

3

J. D. SALINGER

"What really knocks me out,' says Holden Caulfield in *The Catcher in the Rye*, 'is a book that, when you're all done reading it, you wish the author that wrote it was a terrific friend of yours and you could call him up on the phone whenever you felt like it.' However, had Holden called his celebrated but reclusive creator, J. D. Salinger, the odds are he would have hung up on him. Mind you, that's certainly the sixty-nine-year-old author's prerogative. He is not obliged to chat with his many admirers, or reporters from newsweeklies, or gabby talk-show hosts, or even to sit still for serious biographers, however well intentioned.

Ian Hamilton's *In Search of Salinger*, published in 1988, raises many questions larger than the legal tangle that delayed the book's publication for two years.

For openers, beyond a taste for gossip (a taste I admittedly share), I fail to understand what I take to be a burgeoning curiosity about writers'' lives. I find the biographies of politicians, tycoons and other con men great fun because their art *is* their lives, but with a few exceptions (most recently Richard Ellmann's *Oscar Wilde*) the lives of writers strike me as boring. This, of course, is just as it should be, because it is their fiction that is charged with incident and invention while their lives, in the nature of things, tend to be uneventful. I wouldn't go quite so far as the publisher Colin Haycraft, who wrote in the London *Sunday Telegraph*, 'The world is a peculiar place, but it has nothing on the world of books. This is largely a fantasy world, in which the pecking order goes as follows: if you can't cope with life, write about it; if you can't write, publish.'

But the truth is that most novelists start out by retreating into a cave with a ream of blank paper, and when they totter out with a finished manuscript they are two, maybe three years older and have missed out on an awful lot. As a rule, embarrassingly little beyond the ordinary (marital messes, losing battles with booze and tobacco and the IRS, spats with other writers and publishers) has happened off the page. Take J. D. Salinger, for instance. According to a neighbour, he is said to rise at 5 or 6 a.m. in his home in Cornish, New Hampshire, and then walk 'down the hill to his studio, a tiny concrete shelter with a translucent roof,' and spend fifteen or sixteen hours at his typewriter. Later he may watch one of his vast collection of 1940s movies. Hardly the stuff of drama.

In the opening pages of his book, Ian Hamilton writes, 'I had it in mind to attempt not a conventional biography – that would have been impossible – but a kind of *Quest for Corvo*, with Salinger as quarry.' The analogy won't wash. A. J. A. Symons's book, a fine and original work, happens to be about a literary scoundrel, Frederick Rolfe, a bizarre character whose squalid life was more fascinating than anything he wrote, while the obverse is true of J. D. Salinger, of whom Hamilton justifiably observes, 'The action, for [him], was on the page.'

There is another problem. Symons undertook his quest in 1925, twelve years after Rolfe's death, but Salinger, happily, is still among the quick. At the risk of sounding stuffy, I think it indecently hasty to undertake a biography-cum-critical-study of a still-working writer, and in highly questionable taste to pronounce him a perfect subject because, in Hamilton's view, 'he was, in any real-life sense, invisible, as good as dead.' Invisible? Look here, we are talking about a writer whose only published novel, *The Catcher in the Rye*, which first appeared in 1951, was declared in 1968 to be one of America's twenty-five leading best-sellers since the year 1985 and still sells something like a quarter of a million copies annually worldwide.

Ian Hamilton, to be fair, is not a vulgarian; he has good credentials as a biographer, poet and critic. In the first chapter of *In Search of Salinger*, he announces that he will confine himself to the years the author's life was in the public domain, that is to say, until 1965, when he last published. But Salinger, in a court deposition made in an attempt to restrain publication of Hamilton's book, revealed that he has been hard at it all these years, still writing, and so he is far from as good as dead. If and when he does publish again, he could astound us as he once did with *The Catcher in the Rye*.

Ian Hamilton first read *The Catcher in the Rye* when he was seventeen years old. Discouraged from undertaking this biography by Salinger, Salinger's family and friends, he writes, 'When I really ask myself how this whole thing began, I have to confess that there is more to it than mere literary whimsy. There was more to it than mere scholarship. Although it would seem ludicrous, perhaps, to hear me say it now, I think the sharpest spur was infatuation, an infatuation that bowled me over at the age of seventeen and which it seems I never properly outgrew. Well, I've outgrown it now.'

Outgrown it by composing a biography that is at best unfriendly, at worst hostile. The twenty-one-year-old Salinger's letters to Whit Burnett of *Story* magazine are described, for example, as 'too garrulously self-promoting . . . mock-boastful, and, now and then, plain boastful.' In January 1940, once Burnett had accepted the young writer's first story, we are told that, for Salinger, this was a way of showing Them. 'To judge from his letters . . . he was fairly buzzing with self-admiration and not at all disposed to keep quiet about it.' But an examination of these letters, as quoted in the original version of *Salinger* but excised from the published book, shows no such thing. They are, in fact, exuberant, self-deprecating and charged with hope.

After Burnett had accepted Salinger's first short story, he wrote to the editor: 'I'm twenty-one, New York born, and I can draw a rejection slip with both hands tied behind me. Writing has been important to me since I was seventeen. I could show you a lot of nice faces I've stepped on to illustrate the point. Now that you've accepted the story I'll tell everyone to waste no pity on the unpublished short story writer, that his ego can cope with people and circumstance, that he is his own worst enemy. Oh, I'll be wisdom itself.'

In another unpublished letter, to a friend who had written to congratulate him on his first publication, Salinger replied: 'Truly, I'm unspeakably pleased that you liked my stories. I have of course an ardent admirer in myself, but mostly when I'm at work. When I'm finished with a piece, I'm embarrassed to look at it again, as though I were afraid I hadn't wiped its nose clean. Or to that effect.'

The letters are also, as Salinger noted with hindsight in

ourt, occasionally gauche or effusive. 'It's very difficult,' he said. 'I wish . . . you could read letters you wrote forty-six years ago. It's very painful reading.'

Yes, certainly. But Salinger would have been better served if he had allowed his letters to be quoted rather than described so vindictively. On the other hand, Hamilton's hostility is understandable. He has been through a good deal. The first judge to hear the case ruled in the biographer's favour: 'Hamilton's book cannot be dismissed as an act of commercial voyeurism or snooping into a private being's private life for commercial gain. It is a serious, well-researched history of a man who through his own literary accomplishments has become a figure of enormous public interest. This favors a finding of fair use.'

But on January 29, 1987, the United States Court of Appeals for the Second Circuit reversed the earlier judgment. Hamilton could not quote from the letters he had discovered in the Firestone Library at Princeton University and elsewhere.

The bald facts about J. D. Salinger are as follows:

He was born into New York affluence of a sort in 1919. His father, Sol Salinger, was Jewish, a cheese importer, and his mother, Marie Jillich, was a Scottish-born Gentile. At seventeen, he was enrolled in Valley Forge Military Academy, the model for the Pencey Prep in *The Catcher in the Rye*. His first fiction was published in *Story* in 1940. He went on to publish other stories of no great distinction in *Collier's*, *The Saturday Evening Post* and *Esquire*. He joined the army in 1942, landed at Utah Beach with the 12th Infantry Regiment on June 6, 1944, and was involved in heavy fighting in the Hürtgen Forest. His first marriage, to a French doctor in 1945, lasted only eight months. In the late 1940s, Salinger's stories continued to appear in *Collier's* and *The Saturday Evening Post* as well as in *Cosmopolitan* and *Good House-keeping*. But with the exception of one story ('A Slight Rebellion off Madison'), which appeared in 1946, *The New Yorker* had not yet 'taken him up.' Then, in 1948, after several rejections, he finally gained acceptance from the magazine. His next two published stories in *The New Yorker* were 'A Perfect Day for Bananafish' and 'Uncle Wiggily in Connecticut.' Three years later came *The Catcher in the Rye*, which was turned down by Harcourt, Brace before being published by Little, Brown. He retreated to a ninety-acre estate in Cornish, New Hampshire, in 1953 and is still resident there. His second marriage, to Claire Douglas in 1954, ended in divorce in 1967. They have a son, Matthew, and a daughter, Margaret Ann.

J. D. Salinger's other books are *Nine Stories, Franny and Zooey, Raise High the Roof Beam, Carpenters* and *Seymour: An Introduction*. He published his last story, 'Hapworth 16, 1924,' in *The New Yorker* in 1965. According to rumour, reported by Hamilton, he has since then completed at least two full-length manuscripts, which are locked in a safe.

In its present unfortunately truncated form, Ian Hamilton's biography does not turn up much that is new and does turn up a good deal that is neither here nor there. We are told, for instance, that the name Holden Caulfield probably came from joining the name of a boyhood friend called Holden to that of the movie actress Joan Caulfield, on whom Salinger once had a crush. J. D., we also learn, was bad at arithmetic. 'A private for most of his time at Valley Forge,' Hamilton tells us, 'he was promoted in time to appear as a corporal in the yearbook. Academically, he did enough to graduate: 88 in English, 84 in German, 83 in French, and 79 in modern European history.'

Hamilton's biography is tainted by nastiness, born of frustration, perhaps, but hardly excused by it. Salinger is never given the benefit of the doubt. He is described as a 'callow self-advancer.' Aged twenty-two, we are told, 'the Salinger we were on the track of was surely getting less and less lovably Holdenish each day. So far, our eavesdropping had yielded almost nothing in the way of human frailty or warmth. The first-person voice we'd been so pleased to come across had spent most of its time boasting or pushing its career.'

This vengeful book is also marred by Hamilton's coy tiresome device of splitting himself in two, as it were, referring to Salinger's biographer in the third person. ('I was already thinking of "him" as somehow separate from "me." ') This, in turn, allows the use of the royal we, as in the opening of chapter three: 'We traveled back from Valley Forge to New York feeling triumphant. Look at what had been amassed, so far: Salinger's school records, some telling items of juvenilia. . . . And, sure enough, my companion now had a smug, workmanlike look about him. . . . He'd done his job. He had his Chapter 1.' But when the first version of his book was completed in 1985, Hamilton already had his doubts. It was, he writes, *all right*, but 'whatever its merits, the book had by no means solved the mystery of Salinger.' He tells his friends, 'It isn't much. Don't get the idea that it's a *biography*, because it isn't. But it's not too bad.'

Starting out with his sleuthing other self, Hamilton set himself admirable ground rules. He would not attempt to seek out Salinger's ex-wife, his children, his sister, or surprise his friends on the telephone. In 1961, a less fastidious *Time* researcher waylaid Salinger's sister Doris at Bloomingdale's, where she worked. Ms. Salinger told him, 'I wouldn't do anything in the world my brother didn't approve of, I don't want to be rude, but you put me in a very difficult position. Why don't you leave us alone? *Hundreds* of people want to write stories about him.'

Anything I might add to this cry from the heart would obviously be redundant.

4

ERNEST HEMINGWAY

Forget traditional, elegantly written literary biographies, years in making, like Leon Edel on Henry James or Richard Ellmann on James Joyce. Something is happening out there, something more appropriate to our fast-food culture. A new style. It is the oral biography, or the-book-of-the-radio-documentary-that-never-was. These gabby books are not written in longhand or on a typewriter or even on a word processor. In fact, they are not written at all. Instead, they are recorded. The book of the tape. A case in point is *Mailer: His Life and Times*, recorded by Peter Manso, wherein we learn from Arnold (Eppie) Epstein, who sailed through fifth grade with Norman, that the future novelist was not much taken with sports. 'He was busy building his model airplanes, and built some of the best models any of us had ever seen. . . . Other kids made models, but Norman always did the best ones, and this more or less set him apart.' A condition Mailer's mother appreciated much earlier. 'Even in the first grade,' she recalls, 'his teacher recognized his talent and let him write whatever he wanted to.'

Manso's book of the tape tells us more than we needed to know about the quality of cultural high life in America, as well as how an ambitious literary man should not plan a party. It reveals, among other things, why Mailer, having assured his friend Norman Podhoretz how much he liked his autobiography *Making It*, then turned around and wrote a pejorative review of the book.

Mailer explained, 'Now, there was some background to my shift in the review. Norman P. had a dinner party for Jackie Kennedy about a year or two before. It had been very, very important to him, and one of the little conditions Jackie Kennedy made was I not be invited. . . . ' His review of *Making It*, he allowed, had been a bitter disappointment to Norman P., but what the hell, Mailer probably had to watch TV and send out for pizza that night. 'From [Podhoretz's] point of view I had betrayed him,' Mailer said. 'And from my point of view I did betray him to a degree. Yet I also felt, this is fair – he betrayed me with the Jackie Kennedy party. Because not only had he not invited me, he invited Bill Styron, who was then my dire rival. Betraying Podhoretz, therefore, wasn't the world's worst thing to me. Maybe it was my way of saying, "Fuck you" back.'

Then in 1988, along came *The True Gen: An Intimate Portrait of Ernest Hemingway by Those Who Knew Him*, taped by Denis Brian, in which just about everybody who knew Hemingway or has written about him has hardly a good word to say about anybody else who knew him or who has also tried to market the friendship in a memoir.

Hemingway's brother, Leicester, for instance, didn't care for A.E. Hotchner, author of *Papa Hemingway: The Ecstasy and Sorrow*. 'Anybody who will hold a tape recorder on a man when he's drunk is not a friend.'

'I never had a tape recorder and he wasn't drunk,' Hotchner says.

Brian then says to Hotchner, 'Some people imply that Hemingway treated you less as a friend and more like a servant.' To which Hotchner replies, 'That you get from Jeffrey Meyer's [sic] biography of Hemingway. His nose was out of joint because I wouldn't see him and I knew he was going to smear me.'

But Hemingway's last wife, Mary, was also upset with Hotchner. She protests to Brian, 'At no time ever did Hotchner give the slightest hint to Ernest or to me that he was making notes with the idea of producing a book about Ernest.'

Brian then points out that he thought Hotchner was very fond of Hemingway.

'I guess,' Mary replies, 'you're always fond of someone who can make you a million dollars. He wrote this book and made a great deal of money on it, as a totally traitorous thing to Ernest.'

Yes, maybe, but, following Hemingway's death, Mary arranged to publish his letters, although he had left behind a written request not to make them public. She released his private correspondence in spite of once having told Oriana Fallaci, ' . . . a writer doesn't belong to the public, only his writing does. Unlike a prima donna or an actress, he has the right to privacy if he wants it. No one should be authorized to tell the dissolution of a man, even less to tell it for money or sensationalism.'

Hemingway was a grudgy type.

Denis Brian, babbling into his own tape recorder, says, 'Hemingway broke poet Wallace Stevens's jaw with one punch for denigrating his writing and making his sister, Sunny, cry; he knocked magazine publisher Joseph Knapp cold – sending him to the hospital; threatened to beat up Charles Fenton, H.L. Mencken, Irwin Shaw; taunted William Saroyan and Charles Boyer, among others. And wrestled in Max Perkins's office with Max Eastman, who had called his manliness into question.'

In *The True Gen*, Hemingway is variously described as charming, a sadistic son of a bitch, brave, a coward, a womanizer, a closet homosexual, a liar, a truth teller and both a loyal and a treacherous friend.

Nathan Asch, Sholem Asch's son and a literary hanger-on, says, 'I hated the son-of-a-bitch and I loved him.'

'He wanted to be more than Superman,' Leicester Hemingway says. 'He wanted to be Superman's older brother.'

Truman Capote didn't care for him. 'I never met Hemingway,' he says, 'but I hated him. . . . He was a total hypocrite and mean.'

But according to Morley Callaghan, 'He was a strange, warm, beguiling man.'

Hemingway's first wife, Hadley Mowrer, has a different story to tell. 'Ernest was very interested in art,' she says. 'He bought Jean Miro's [*sic*] The Farm and presented it to me. I could say things about it that show up Ernest's character. This was a present to me. Later, he suggested that we share it – for so long. "You have it for so long, and I'll have it for so long." He took it and I've never seen it since. That's one of his little tricks. The last I heard it was valued at $185,000. It's in the Museum of Modern Art.'

'My wife used to say of Hemingway,' George Seldes says, 'forgive him everything – he writes like an angel.'

Hemingway's mother, a real charmer, sent him the gun with which his father had killed himself.

'It was strange, wasn't it?' Hadley observed. 'It was a

shock to him when he got it. It was almost like suggesting Ernest do the same thing – shoot himself.'

In the end, that's exactly what he did. Like his father before him. Like his brother Leicester later on.

Poor Ernest.

Only sixty pages into *The True Gen* we find ourselves embroiled in a controversy that is obviously crucial to our continued appreciation of some of the finest short stories in our language. The question, put plainly, is what were the true dimensions of Papa's weenie? Was it inadequate? So-so? Or Nobel Prize size?

Those of you who have read Hemingway's evocative but mean-minded memoir of Paris in the twenties, *A Movable Feast*, will recall that, according to Hemingway, Zelda Fitzgerald had complained that Scott's prick was undersized. Ernest told Scott, after scrutinizing his schlong, that he was endowed with the right stuff, and then reassured him by taking him to a museum and showing him the cock on a statue – obviously not Michelangelo's *David*. But now Barnaby Conrad says, 'Hemingway's bullfighter friend Sidney Franklin told me that *Hemingway's* sexual organ was undersized – about the size of a thirty-thirty shell. I wrote about it in my book *Fun While It Lasted*, as a retaliation for Hemingway's cavalier treatment of Fitzgerald in *A Movable Feast*. On the other hand, Franklin was full of bull. . . . He didn't have to exaggerate and lie the way he did in his book *A Bullfighter from Brooklyn*. Just about every third page of that is true, I think.'

But according to Jeffrey Meyers, a Hemingway biographer, Franklin was a far from disinterested reporter on the size of Papa's joystick. Professor Meyers reveals that, unknown to Hemingway – and despite Franklin's rugged appearance and daring – the saucy bullfighter from Brooklyn was actually a secret homosexual and child molester.

Arnold Gingrich, the former publisher of *Esquire*, also pronounces on the vital question. 'I happen to be in a position to give firsthand eyewitness observations in both instances, of Hemingway's and Fitzgerald's sexual equipment. It's true in neither case that they were undersized. I swam with them and fished with them *and all that*.' (Italics mine.)

At this point I began to worry about just how penetrating an interviewer we had in Denis Brian. What I want to know is, how often did Gingrich skinny-dip with Scott and Ernie, and just what does he mean by 'and all that'?

'The true gen' is RAF World War II slang for accurate information as distinct from rumour and speculation – 'gen' being short for 'general' or 'genuine.' Hemingway used the expression frequently. According to Brian, he wanted the true gen to be told about him, but – possibly anticipating gossipy books such as this one – he dreaded 'the shit' that would be written about him after his death. 'Why?' Brian asks in his introduction. 'What had he to hide?'

Plenty, according to Brian.

John Miller, who was a Red Cross volunteer in World War I, just like Hemingway, describes the Ernest of those days as a heartless wit, a garrulous nut. But he does allow that he was one of the first Americans wounded in World War I and was awarded the Italian Silver Medal for heroism, ostensibly for dragging a wounded soldier to safety after being shot himself.

Yes, but Agnes von Kurowsky Stanfield, the nurse who took care of Hemingway in the Milan hospital and became one of several models for Catherine Barkley in *A Farewell to Arms*, says, 'Oh, for heaven's sake, he was no hero. He got the injuries because he was just a boy giving out cigarettes and stuff like that. He went right up to where the fighting was to hand out chocolates to some of his friends. There was a big explosion and he saw the soldier who took care of his things fall, and he jumped over a fence and got a lot of shrapnel in his legs. But I never heard about him carrying a wounded man to safety.'

Henry Villard, a World War I ambulance driver who was in the hospital with Hemingway, claims to have been both astonished and shocked when he read *A Farewell to Arms* eleven years later. 'Much of the novel covered the overwhelming Italian defeat by the Austrians at the battle of Caporetto. I knew Hemingway had not even been in Italy when that took place. . . . '

In *A Farewell to Arms*, Frederic Henry, despite the handicap of a wound resembling Hemingway's, makes love to his nurse, Catherine Barkley, in his hospital bed. Villard says, 'The most I witnessed of any romance between Ernest and Agnes was their brief hand-holding under the cover of her taking his temperature. . . . When I read the book I was U.S. vice consul in Teheran, Iran. I corresponded with Agnes and made several attempts at a reunion, intending to ask to what extent Hemingway's portrayal of the romance had been wishful thinking. I finally met her again in 1975, when she welcomed me to her Gulfport, Florida, home. Now eighty-three, she told me she was the wife of a widower with three children, William Stanfield, Jr. I told Agnes I suspected the love scenes in *A Farewell to Arms* were simply how Hemingway would like things to have been. She said I was right, that she had never been Hemingway's mistress and that they had never made love.'

Good grief! This is really sensational stuff! Hemingway had never taken part in the battle of Caporetto. That sleazebag *imagined* the battle, just like larger liars before him, say Tolstoy or Stendhal, imagined other battles. And maybe, just maybe, he never enjoyed Agnes von Kurowsky Stanfield between the sheets. Or rescued a wounded soldier in World War I. Or shot 122 Krauts in World War II, as he once bragged in a letter. That son of a bitch wasn't just one more honest reporter. He embellished stories, enlarging his own role in them. *He had wishful thoughts. He made things up. He invented.* Hey, I've got it. Cat's out of the bag. Ernest Hemingway was a writer.

Martha Gellhorn, Hemingway's third wife, is entitled to the last word. 'He was a genius,' she once said in *The Paris Review*, 'that uneasy word, not so much in what he wrote as in how he wrote; he liberated our written language.'

HOLLYWOOD

1

GOLDWYN

THESE DAYS GOD forbid an independent producer in Beverly Hills should be caught actually strolling down from his *dacha* on the heights to take his meeting in the Polo Lounge or dine at Spago. The morning jog aside, bankables don't stir without benefit of a Rolls-Royce, Mercedes or Jaguar. But the original independent, the behemoth who produced the first feature-length film made in Hollywood, walked. I speak of Schmuel Gelbfisz, a.k.a. Sam Goldfish, but celebrated as Samuel Goldwyn. In 1895, this tall, skinny, virtually penniless sixteen-year-old, the first-born son of Hasidic Jews, walked out of Warsaw three hundred miles to the Oder River, crossed, and then hiked another two hundred miles to Hamburg, where a kindly glovemaker named Liebglid raised the eighteen shillings required to put him on the boat train to London.

From there Schmuel tramped on to Birmingham, and in 1898 sailed steerage to Halifax, Nova Scotia, continuing on to Gloversville, New York, where he found work as a glovemaker. Only a year later, Goldfish, who would be a compulsive gambler all his life, cheating at the poker table and croquet, was sufficiently at home to bet two dollars that Harvard would beat Yale in a football game. He had also absorbed the copybook maxims that would pepper his speech for the rest of his days – 'Haste makes waste,' 'Early to bed and early to rise.' Then, in 1923, clipping the 'wyn' off a former partner's name, he was born again as Goldwyn, with Judge Learned Hand ordaining, 'A self-made man may prefer a self-made name.'

Samuel Goldwyn was a coarse man of daunting drive and appetite, a wayward husband and sadly inadequate father. But he was also one of a truly astonishing generation – the inspired ruffians who put the *shtetls* behind them to become czars of a sort. Seizing the day. Inventing Hollywood. 'Between 1880 and 1910,' A. Scott Berg writes in *Goldwyn*, a highly entertaining biography, 'one and a half million Jews joined wagon trains of pushcarts leaving Eastern Europe. In the 1880s alone, the family of Louis B. Mayer left Demre, near Vilna, in Lithuania; Lewis Zeleznick (later Selznick) ran away from Kiev; William Fox (formerly Fuchs) emigrated from Tulcheva, Hungary; the Warner family uprooted itself from Krasnashiltz, Poland, near the Russian border; Adolph Zukor abandoned Ricse, Hungary, and Carl Laemmle left Wurtemberg, Germany – gamblers with nothing to lose, all from within a five-hundred-mile radius of Warsaw.'

To each his own eureka.

One day Goldwyn, now thirty-four years old, the star drummer for Elite Fitwell Gloves, slipped out of the sales office on Fifth Avenue and drifted into the Herald Square Theatre on 34th Street to catch a 'flicker.' He saw a cowboy on horseback, Bronco Billy, jump on to a moving train, and within months Goldwyn was in the saddle himself. He formed a partnership with his brother-in-law, Jesse Lasky, a former vaudevillian, and hired one Cecil B. DeMille to write and direct the film version of *The Squaw Man*, a hit play of a few seasons back. DeMille was to shoot the film in Flagstaff, Arizona, but didn't care for what he saw and continued west on the train, finally cabling Lasky: 'FLAGSTAFF NO GOOD FOR OUR PURPOSE. HAVE PROCEEDED TO CALIFORNIA. WANT AUTHORITY TO RENT BARN IN A PLACE CALLED HOLLYWOOD FOR $75 A MONTH. REGARDS TO SAM.'

When Goldwyn saw the print of the film that would become a Hollywood legend, as well as his first success, he adjudged the lighting awful. The people wouldn't be able to see what was going on. 'Tell them it's Rembrandt lighting,' DeMille said.

'For Rembrandt lighting,' Goldwyn said, 'they pay double.'

Goldwyn's short-lived marriage to Blanche Lasky, which would yield a shamefully neglected child named Ruth, ended acrimoniously in 1915, and Goldwyn, who had many affairs throughout his long life, became known as a 'chaser.' A producer with a casting couch. The model for Ivor Llewellyn in P.G. Wodehouse's *Luck of the Bodkins*.

The early Hollywood moguls, almost all Jewish, had problems. Rabbi Edgar F. Magnin, who presided for seventy years over the spiritual life of the Beverly Hills *yeshiva* – where *Variety* took precedence over the Talmud and Louella Parsons rather than Rashi was read for subtexts – once said, 'They were men who made all that money and realized that they were still a bunch of Goddamned Jews . . . Sleeping with a pretty Gentile girl made them feel, if only for a few minutes, "I'm half Gentile." No wonder they made idols out of *shiksa* goddesses.' One of them, Mary Pickford, would not let her husband, Douglas Fairbanks, forget that he had Jewish blood. When he defended one of the moguls, she reproached him: 'That's the Jew in you saying that.' She called Goldwyn 'Shylock.'[1]

The insecure moguls not only anglicized their names. The

---

1. Two years would pass before Hollywood marched to war itself. Beginning in 1942, working under the all-seeing eye of the Office of War Information, the studios submitted to directives such as 'Suppose there was a love scene in a café. The girl could say to the boy, "I want half a spoonful of sugar. It's not only patriotic – it's good for the figure too." ' Then came the real crunch. The Hays Office limited the number of bullets and blanks that could be fired on a set. Baddies in westerns had to fall after a single shot. Bank robbers were ordered to accelerate slowly, so as not to set a bad example of tire wasting. Early refugees from Hitler had to register as enemy aliens, Thomas Mann now obliged to leave Aldous Huxley's dinner table by the 8 p.m. curfew.

wife of one of them, Berg writes, used to wash her daughter's hair with eggs and lemon to brighten it, and scrub her skin with bleach. Goldwyn's second and enduring wife, Frances Howard, a slim redhead out of Nebraska and a Roman Catholic, was the daughter of a lady who could not even bring herself to say the word 'Jew.' She called them 'Orientals.' When Sam flew into a rage, Frances learned to silence him in Yiddish: 'Schmuel, *shveig!*' ("Shut up!") She had their only son baptized and, according to Sam Goldwyn, Jr., she was more than a tad disconcerted when she discovered in 1938 that, so far as the rest of the world was concerned, she was considered a Jew.[2]

Then, in 1940, Joseph P. Kennedy, having survived a few months of the Blitz in London, descended on Hollywood, addressing fifty power brokers at lunch, among them Goldwyn. 'Stop making anti-Nazi pictures,' he said, 'or using the film medium to promote or show sympathy to the cause of the "democracies" versus the "dictators." ' Instead of pounding Kennedy over the head with the nearest blunt instrument to hand, the moguls continued to sit there, mute. Kennedy went on to say that the Jews were already being blamed for the war. Hitler liked movies, he observed, and

2. It is worth noting that Cecil B. DeMille introduced to films in the first place, was also capable of anti-Semitic outbursts.

During the McCarthy years, DeMille, initially opposed by Joseph L. Mankiewicz (*A Letter to Three Wives, All About Eve*) and thirteen others, tried to have those directors who wouldn't sign a loyalty oath denounced to studio heads in a letter from the Screen Directors Guild of America. Addressing a highly charged meeting of the guild, he denounced some twenty-five directors. 'Let me just read you the names,' he said, 'of those who are Mr. Mankiewicz's champions,' and he proceeded to list them, pronouncing their names with an offensive Yiddish accent. 'Villie Vyler.'

DeMille was roundly booed. Billy Wilder stood up and said, 'I heard my name spoken with a certain intonation. The reason I am sitting in the front row is because I'm deaf in one ear. It got blown out over Berlin in a bombing mission for the air force, and I'm tired of being called a Communist because at one time I belonged to a leftist organization.'

would want America to go on producing them, but 'you're going to have to get those Jewish names off the screen.'

On the other hand, *Yiddishkeit* had its own rewards. Barred from the most exclusive country clubs in Los Angeles, the moguls founded one of their own, Hillcrest, and shortly thereafter struck oil on the fairways. Years later Goldwyn came out of the closet, as it were, becoming president of the United Jewish Welfare Fund. He was an enthusiastic supporter of Israel, but he was dismayed when Edward G. Robinson asked him to help Israel start its own film industry. 'My God,' he said, 'there are enough rotten Jews in Hollywood.'

Possibly he had the notorious Harry Cohn, who ran Columbia Pictures, in mind. When Cohn died in 1958, a member of the Wilshire Boulevard Temple asked Rabbi Magnin if he could think of one good thing to say about the deceased. The rabbi paused and said, 'He's dead.'

Ah, Hollywood.

Frances Goldwyn, after attending the premier of *The Jazz Singer*, the first talkie, in 1927, called that night 'the most important event in cultural history since Martin Luther nailed his thesis to the church door.' A point of view, certainly, but one that overlooked, among other cultural ripples, Einstein doodling E $= mc^2$ on his pad, Freud thinking twice about our dream life, and the price we are still paying for Marx sitting on his piles in the British Museum.

Goldwynisms abound in A. Scott Berg's biography. Yes, stomping out of a producers' meeting, he did shout, 'Include me out!' Reminiscing about dire financial straits, he recalled, 'I was on the brink of an abscess.' He wanted to shoot *Whoopie!*, a western, in Arizona because 'you need Indians and there you can get 'em right from the reservoir.' In a quarrel with Joel McCrea during the making of *These Three*, he protested, 'I'm having more trouble with you stars than Mussolini is with Utopia!' Appearing at the head of a staircase in his bathrobe for a meeting at his house with Gershwin and George Balanchine, he called down, 'Hold on, fellas, I'll be right down. And then we'll get into a cuddle.' Warned by his story editor that *The Little Foxes* was a caustic play, he shot back, 'I don't care how much it costs. Buy it!' And he once invited somebody to his house to see his '*Toujours* Lautrec.'

Goldwyn, who never churned out more films than he could handle personally (among his productions were *The Squaw Man*, two versions of *Stella Dallas*, the Eddie Cantor musicals, *Wuthering Heights, The Little Foxes, Pride of the Yankees, The Best Years of Our Lives, Up in Arms* and *Guys and Dolls*), picked up the concept of 'making fewer, better' as the star salesman for Elite Fitwell Gloves. He worked with some of the best talent of his time: DeMille, William Wyler again and again, Billy Wilder, Gregg Toland, Ben Hecht and Charles MacArthur, Robert Sherwood and the immortal Busby Berkeley. He signed the first of his contract players, Mabel Normand, to a five-year deal after she fled Mack Sennett. Over the years his other contract players included Ronald Colman (one of the few to manage the leap from silents to talkies), Eddie Cantor, a disgruntled Gary Cooper (who resented the quality of the scripts imposed on him), David Niven, Dana Andrews and Danny Kaye. But his quest for another Garbo yielded only the long-forgotten Vilma Banky and Anna Sten, whom Goldwyn took to saying 'had the face of a spink.'

Following enormous difficulties, Goldwyn signed Laurence Olivier for what he unfailingly called 'Withering Heights,' which was to be shot by Gregg Toland and directed by William Wyler. Olivier never got on with his co-star, Merle Oberon, whom he considered 'a little pick-up by [Alexander] Korda.' The animosity was mutual. Oberon protested once too often that drops of Olivier's saliva were hitting her in the face during the shooting of a tense scene. Olivier shouted, 'Why you amateur little bitch, what's a spit for Christsake between actors.'

After three weeks of shooting, with the movie badly behind schedule, Goldwyn appeared on the set. 'Willy,' Goldwyn said to Wyler, 'if this – this actor goes on playing the way he is, I close up the picture. Will you look at that actor's ugly face. He's dirty, his performance is rotten, it's stagey, it's just nothing . . . I won't have it and if he doesn't improve, I'm gonna close up the picture.'

'Right, Mr. Goldwyn,' Wyler said, and from that moment, Olivier later allowed, 'I was obedience itself.'

Goldwyn, an appalling father, alternately wrote his daughter Ruth maudlin letters and ignored her brutally. Sammy Junior does not recall ever eating a single meal with his parents in their elegant dining room. Instead, he took his meals in the kitchen, alone with the cook. When he was about to complete his boarding school education his father wrote him, 'Your graduation means everything to me, as I have only one son and I love him very much,' but of course he didn't show up. 'While I am not present,' he wrote, 'I am with you in spirit and pray for you every minute.'

Goldwyn finally won the Academy Award he coveted in 1947 for *The Best Years of Our Lives*. After the ceremonies, Frances found him sitting on a couch in the living room, holding his Oscar, his head bowed, sobbing.

He lived to the age of ninety-four, confined to his bed in his house on Laurel Lane for several years. In 1971, three years before Goldwyn died, President Richard Nixon came to visit the ailing mogul.

Berg writes, 'He had come to present Samuel Goldwyn with the Medal of Freedom, the nation's highest civilian honor. The President made a speech before hanging the medal around Goldwyn's neck, and the hollow rhetoric about the wholesomeness of the recipient's films made Sam Junior suspicious. It rang of an old speech written for the late Walt Disney, and he guessed that Nixon was just doing some early electioneering, trying to win the support of the motion picture industry. Goldwyn's head nodded forward. In raising it, he tugged at the President's coat. The President bowed, putting his ear close enough to Goldwyn to hear him whisper, "You'll have to do better than that if you want to carry California.'

'The President jerked upright, hastily closed the ceremonies, and exited. In the foyer, Nixon asked, "Did you hear what your father said?" Sammy had, but to avoid any embarrassment, said he had not. The President's shoulders dropped in relief. "He said," Nixon boomed, "I want you to go out there and beat those bastards!" '

Happily, A. Scott Berg's absorbing biography, thick with amusing anecdotes, is largely nonjudgmental and eschews psychobabble. It has the uncommon good sense to trust in the tale of the skinny boy who hiked five hundred miles and then some to freedom and fame and fortune. This story of a grabby but imaginative man would make a more telling movie about America, America than Goldwyn ever produced himself.

2

ZANUCK

Hard to be a Jew, but in Hollywood, in any event, even harder to be a goy. Take the case of Darryl F. Zanuck, as set out in Leonard Mosley's knowledgeable biography, *Zanuck*. In 1925, the twenty-three-year-old Zanuck literally saved the overextended, sinking Warner brothers (Jack, Harry, Sam and Albert) from ruin, doing the screenplays for the Rin Tin Tin films for them. As head of production, he saw the first talkie, *The Jazz Singer*, through all its complicated stages for Warner's. An obliging goy, he also rendered more personal services. On at least one occasion, when Jack Warner sat on his private toilet having his daily dump, Zanuck stood by with his hand on the chain, ready to yank it at the appropriate moment. For all that, he never got to be a partner. Possibly the fact that the five foot six inch Zanuck had already begun to dress like Mussolini, favouring tight breeches, riding boots and a swagger stick, didn't help. But there was something else involved. Something dark, something tribal.

'You stay with me, kid, and I'll have your name up there as a Warner partner,' Jack told him, and then he looked the short young goy over and sighed, 'If only you were one of us. That would make it so much easier.'

'What do you want me to do, Jack?' Zanuck asked. 'Circumcise myself?'

Not quite, but when Zanuck quit Warner's, going on to try harder, triumphing over racial adversity – *overcoming*, as it were – to found Twentieth Century Films, he had learned enough about Hollywood bigotry to swallow the unspeakable and maintain silence when partner Joe Schenck put his arm around him and said, 'We Jews stick together. It's us against the schmucks.'

Zanuck, who was born in Wahoo, Nebraska, did not enjoy a serendipitous childhood. His father, a hotel night clerk, favoured boozing and gambling above all, even as his poker-playing cronies, out-of-town drummers, regularly slipped away to screw his wife in the family apartment, a rough-and-tumble witnessed more than once by the young Darryl. Abandoned by his parents at the age of twelve, Darryl was raised by Grandpa Torpin, a self-proclaimed descendant of legendary British highwayman Dick Turpin. Darryl was only fifteen years old when he joined the army and was shipped off to France. Too late 'to kill a Hun,' he was still good enough with his fists to represent the U.S. Army as a fly-weight. Demobilized, it was inevitable that this descendant of a highwayman should drift to Hollywood, where he was hired as a $150-a-week gag writer by Mack Sennett. 'Sennett taught me two things about moviemaking that I never forgot,' he said later. 'One was that no matter how serious your picture is . . . the moment you forget to keep the action going, you've lost them. Put in anything, any old gag, a girl's leg, a big explosion, a sudden scream, rather than let the audience's mind wander, and that goes for any kind of film, whether you are making *Heartbreak House* or *Charley's Aunt*. As for comedy, Sennett taught me that using words to get a laugh is a confession of defeat. . . . Sennett knew that comedy is not words but action, and action is what movies are all about.'

Many years later, his son, Richard D. Zanuck (producer of *The Sting*, *M*A*S*H* and *Jaws*), learned an even more basic Hollywood lesson. 'This is a town,' he said, 'where only success counts. You can get away with anything except murder so long as your pictures are successful. And if they are supersuccessful, maybe even with murder too.'

Darryl Zanuck was of course supersuccessful until, in his declining years, he became obsessed with thrusting a bevy of lovely young friends into his movies: Bella Darvi, Juliette Greco, Geneviève Gilles.

Reminiscing about Zanuck in his prime, when the thirty-three-year-old wonder boy was running Twentieth Century Fox, executive Milton Sperling said: 'You know that Darryl was mad about women. Everybody talked about it in Hollywood and the rumor was that his prowess as a cocksman was just unbelievable. . . . Even I knew that every day at four o'clock in the afternoon some girl on the lot would visit Zanuck in his office. The doors would be locked after she went in, no calls were taken, and for the next half hour nothing happened – headquarters shut down. Around the office work came to a halt for the sex siesta. It was an understood thing. While the girl was with Zanuck, everything stopped, and anyone who had the same proclivities as Zanuck, and had a girl to do it with, would go off somewhere and do what he was doing. I honestly think that from four to four-thirty every day at Fox, if you could have harnessed the power from all the fucking that was going on, you could have turned the tides at Malibu.'

'It was usually a starlet who was chosen for this daily assignation,' Mosley writes, and it was rarely the same one twice. 'The only one who ever seems to have been called in more than once was a Fox contract feature player named Carole Landis, who was casually referred to as "the studio hooker." '

Between his daily four o'clockers, zipping up, Zanuck did manage to produce some of the best damn westerns ever made: *Jesse James*, *Drums Along the Mohawk*, *My Darling Clementine* and *The Gunfighter*. He also made *Little Caesar*,

I Am a Fugitive From a Chain Gang, Laura, The Snake Pit, Gentleman's Agreement, All About Eve, Viva Zapata! and, above all, *The Grapes of Wrath*. Irascible, hard-drinking John Ford, who worked with him again and again, once said: 'He knew I hated to go into the projection room, so I had this tacit agreement that he would cut the picture. If it was up to me, I'd cut everything out. He'd say, "What do you think of it?" and I'd say, "It's just another picture." He was a great cutter, a great editor.'

As a young man, he was also an obsessive polo player and a vicious croquet player, having picked up the latter game playing with Noel Coward and Ralph Richardson on a sojourn to England. Doubtless, it was on the playing fields of Beverly Hills that Zanuck encountered the stalwarts of the British film colony, most of whom also quit work at four in the afternoon, but in their case merely for tea and bickies. If Zanuck was surprised that Leslie Howard, for many years the quintessential Englishman in Hollywood, was in fact yet another Jew of Hungarian descent, there is no record of his reaction either in *Zanuck* or in Sheridan Morley's wry but, alas, somewhat pedestrian history of the colony, *Tales From the Hollywood Raj: The British, the Movies, and Tinseltown.*

'I had anticipated,' Sir Cedric Hardwicke once wrote, 'that Hollywood would be an actors' Eden: it proved to be a paradise only for the medical profession.... This was the only place on earth where man had attempted to build an industrial society in a sparsely irrigated and subtropical climate where the weather, being immutable, was denied him as a subject for conversation.'

Ronald Colman was even more cynical about his good California fortune. 'Before God,' he once told his agent, 'I am worth $35 a week; before the motion picture industry I'm worth anything you can get.'

And, for all their snide or patronizing remarks, anything they could get was what they were after. The longer they stayed in Hollywood, the more British they became, especially C. Aubrey Smith, who used to stroll down Santa Monica Boulevard in a blazer and straw boater on his way to the cricket club. George Jean Nathan, among others, was not impressed. 'They are not Englishmen,' he wrote, 'but burlesques of Englishmen; they are not actors, but burlesques of actors. There was a time when the inexperience and cheap snobbery of American audiences combined to work for an acceptance of such mountebanks as the real and rather correct thing. But that time is now past. I have seen a number of English actors on the London stage who know how to speak their language beautifully. But we do not often see that kind over here. They stay at home and what we get in their stead are a pack of acting pretenders suitable only for the roles of English butlers in American farces.' True, certainly, of Nigel Bruce, Arthur Treacher, Basil Rathbone and Brian Aherne, but not of Charlie Chaplin, Stan Laurel, and Cary Grant, or of the generation of Olivier, Richardson and Gielgud, who also worked in Hollywood from time to time.

Writers, of course, were something else again. P.G. Wodehouse, who didn't arrive until 1929, wrote: 'If motion picture magnates must have authors they should keep them in hutches. In every studio in Hollywood there are rows and rows of hutches, each containing an author on a long contract or weekly salary. You see their anxious little faces peering through the bars. You hear them whining piteously to be taken for a walk. . . . '

One of them, R.C. Sherriff, did indeed take a walk. Sheridan Morley writes:

His assignment [the screenplay for H.G. Wells's *The Invisible Man*] duly, rapidly, and happily completed, Sherriff was packing up to return with Mother to England and his mature studentship at Oxford when to his amazement he was sent for by the head of the script department at Universal. The offer was a twelve-month contract to write three screenplays at $25,000 each, and this in 1936; Sherriff politely explained about his studentship at New College, Oxford. The Americans looked at him in amazement and sent him to see Uncle Carl Laemmle (who had started Universal Studios) in person; again, and carefully, Sherriff explained about the place that had been held open for him at New College during his Californian sabbatical. "What do you do there?" asked Laemmle suspiciously. "I write essays for my tutor," explained Sherriff. "And how much does he pay you for them?" asked Laemmle, determined not to be outbid by some goddamn English tutor. Sherriff explained carefully that he was paid nothing; on the contrary, he pointed out, he paid New College for the privilege of being allowed to study there. Laemmle was still more confused. He explained slowly and clearly to Sherriff that Universal was offering $75,000 for three of Sherriff's screenplays, and that he, Sherriff, would have to pay nothing in return. Sherriff still refused, and Laemmle bade him a sad and confused farewell. . . .

3

BEGELMAN

What was to become one of Hollywood's juiciest boardroom scandals of the seventies – rendered into high drama by David McClintock (*Indecent Exposure, A True Story of Hollywood and Wall Street*) – began innocuously enough. On February 25, 1977, Oscar-winning actor Cliff Robertson's secretary presented him with a form from the IRS indicating that he had been paid $10,000 the previous year by Columbia Pictures. Unfortunately, there had been no such payment. There was, however, a real cheque for $10,000, endorsed 'Cliff Robertson,' that had been cashed at a Wells Fargo bank in Beverly Hills. What appeared to be a forgery, unabashed studio head David Begelman told the police, was actually an accounting booboo that needn't trouble them. He also told Robertson's accountant that 'we've looked into this very carefully and it turns out that a young man who was employed here in the studio last summer somehow managed to embezzle the money.'

But so far as others at the studio were concerned – most prominent among them an increasingly frenetic president and chief executive officer, Alan Hirshfield – the handwriting on the cheque was clearly Begelman's. Presented with the evidence, Begelman said, 'I swear to you on the life of my child that this is not my handwriting and I have done nothing wrong – nothing which merits the attention of the Beverly Hills Police Department.'

Then another dubious cheque was uncovered, this one for $35,000, payable to a man named Choate, that had been personally requested from the accounting department by Begelman.

Begelman had once been the hottest agent in town, representing Paul Newman, Steve McQueen, Robert Redford and (yes) Cliff Robertson, as well as Barbra Streisand and Judy Garland. He was, McClintock writes in his day-to-day recreation of the boardroom brawls at Columbia, ashamed of his Bronx background. Always faultlessly dressed, he was fond of saying that he was a graduate of Yale Law School, which was a fib.

'Are we going to find other things when we look?' a board member asked him. 'Other cheques, other fake contracts?'

'No.'

Then a third embezzlement surfaced, another cheque with a forged endorsement by Begelman, this one for $25,000. It was made out to Pierre Groleau, the maitre d' at Ma Maison, which suggests that, however murky Begelman's morals, he was – at least in his mind's eye – one helluva tipper. Unfortunately, Groleau never saw the cheque. Questioned by a board now more than somewhat concerned about a possible SEC investigation into what was after all a public company, Begelman broke down. He wept. 'I know I've betrayed you, but you just can't take everything away from me now. I'll be finished as a man, as a husband, as a father . . . I'm pleading for my life.'

Begelman came up with a nifty psychological explanation for his behaviour, a rationale later to be endorsed by none other than Dr. Judd Marmor, 'psychiatrist to the stars.'

'I have a compulsion to destroy myself. I have no self-respect. That's why I committed these acts. I was trying to punish, defeat, and destroy myself.'

Members of the Columbia board, flitting between New York and L.A., were now raging at each other. Alan Hirschfield, supported by President Leo Jaffe, who had been with the studio since 1930, was determined that Begelman must go. But Herbert Allen and Matthew Rosenhaus, the largest shareholders in the company, were equally set on retaining Begelman, whom they regarded as Columbia's saviour – the man who had brought them *Taxi Driver* and had fought for *Close Encounters of the Third Kind*, an enormous hit.

Then another cheque was found, this one for a mere $5,000, made out to director Marty Ritt, also with a forged endorsement by Begelman – but what the hell – in Hollywood *everybody* thinks he's a writer. Expense irregularities were uncovered – $6,000 here, $4,145 for Begelman's honeymoon trip to the French Riviera, charged as a business expense.

Begelman was fired, or so the sometimes vacillating, often indecisive Hirshfield thought, but the resentful board did not issue the promised press release. In the opinion of Dan Melnick, Columbia's head of production, the studio had a problem. 'Our press manipulation isn't up to snuff. We don't have people sufficiently schooled *in that sleazy world*.' (Italics mine.)

In December, Hirshfield – his authority in the company now badly eroded, his relationship with the slippery Herbert Allen and the maudlin Rosenhaus increasingly acrimonious – turned full circle and agreed to reinstate Begelman. Riding the elevator back to his studio office, Begelman, not without a sense of humour, joined in the jokes with his old colleagues. 'How,' he asked, 'would the Polish government have handled the Begelman problem?'

'Just like Columbia Pictures,' somebody shot back.

'Well, it looks from now on like Columbia Pictures will be *forging* ahead with David Begelman,' somebody else said.

Begelman, according to McClintock, roared with laughter, truly appreciative of all the jokes at his own expense. So it is in the hope of adding to his fund of fun that I pass on one story, probably apocryphal but still going the rounds, that he may not have heard.

Seemingly, in the days when Begelman was still a talent agent, running Creative Management Associates in partnership with Freddie Fields, his little boy came to him and asked, 'What is integrity, father?'

Inviting the lad to sit on his lap, Begelman replied, 'I will tell you, my son. I am Paul Newman's agent. I sign him to a picture for a million dollars and he sends me a cheque for a hundred thousand. That is not integrity, it is my proper commission. But a month later, lo and behold, Newman forgets and sends me another cheque for a hundred thousand. Integrity, my son, is not do I return the second cheque to Paul Newman, but do I tell Freddie Fields?'

Begelman's reinstatement led to such a public uproar (just as Hirshfield had predicted) that it was very brief indeed. It was decided that Begelman should resign for the good of the company's already tainted image. So, on Sunday, February 5, in the windowless Columbia boardroom at Seven-eleven Fifth Avenue, Alan Hirshfield offered a haggard, near tearful Begelman the Hollywood Embezzler's Award, an independent producer's contract with the studio. Begelman sniffed at the terms and found them wanting. 'I hear what you're saying, Alan, but I just can't accept anything less than a full settlement of my contract plus an independent production deal that is competitive with my position and record in the industry. Look, Alan, I'm broke. The only thing standing between my sanity and putting a gun in my mouth is the prospect of a financial arrangement that will leave me whole and give me security for the future.'

Hirshfield, his own days with the studio numbered, now began to secretly seek buyers for the company. Time Inc., Philip Morris Inc., British financier Jimmy Goldsmith. All unavailingly. Five months later the Columbia board voted five to two to terminate Hirshfield's contract, Leo Jaffe denouncing the firing as 'a disaster and a disgrace.'

Begelman moved on to MGM, where his slate of films bombed at the box office. Released by that studio, he was hired by yet another production company. Alan Hirshfield became chairman and CEO at Twentieth Century-Fox.

*

'The radical singularity of Beverly Hills, California,' McClintock writes in *Indecent Exposure*, 'is evident not so much in its famous residents and lavish homes as in certain of its statistics. Within an area of less than 6 square miles and a population barely exceeding 30,000 – only 20,000 of whom are old enough to vote – Beverly Hills supports 35 banks, 20 savings and loan associations, 711 lawyers, 299 beauty salons, 651 medical doctors and psychoanalysts, and 761 gardeners. The banks and savings and loans hold deposits of more than $7 billion.'

In this climate, stealing, far from being an aberration, is a happy rule of the game, time-honoured. One of the best stories I know about it involves that cherished old star of so many westerns, Joel McCrea.

Some years ago, I'm assured, a young cousin of McCrea's knocked on his door and said he was now a graduate accountant looking for work. McCrea had just the thing for him. He had made his last two westerns at one of the major studios on a profit-sharing basis and suspected that he had been given a sticky-fingered account. Would his cousin go through the books? He did just that, and then McCrea called the studio head and asked to meet him for lunch. The studio head obliged. After all, McCrea was now one of Hollywood's grand old-timers. At lunch, McCrea allowed he felt that he had not seen his legitimate share of the profits on the last two films he had made at the studio. Not likely, the studio head countered, aghast.

'Well,' McCrea ventured, 'there's one item here, for instance, charged against both films: $280,000 for colour prints.'

'Oh, that,' the studio head said, 'well you know how sloppy the labs are these days. It sounds steep but the truth is with you in it we would settle for nothing less than top quality colour.'

'As it happens,' McCrea said drily, 'both were filmed in black-and-white.'

The studio head didn't blink. 'I'll tell you what,' he said, 'come back to my office, I'll write you a cheque for $250,000, and we'll call it quits on both films.'

If any defence can be mustered for Begelman, it is that cheating is even more important in Beverly Hills than proficiency at tennis. To begin with, outrageous studio overheads are charged against each production, as well as, among other things, the bill for a new chinchilla coat for the producer's wife, the redecoration of his mistress's Malibu pad and his son's scream therapy. If, after all that, a film stubbornly manages to show a profit, the magicians are sent for. The real masters of magic in Beverly Hills, I should point out, are not the so-called 'creative' folks but the studio accountants. Present them with a film that has cost $10 million and grossed $80 million, throw in a couple of felt-tip pens, and they will prove to the dolts who directed, acted and wrote the film that it never earned a profit. On the other hand, there is also cheating on the so-called creative side, which brings me to another Hollywood story.

Once, after the mass firings of executives in a major studio, the new bunch of bandits running the place found out that the dim second cousin of the former studio head was employed as a writer for ten big ones a week, with a year to run on his contract. They tried everything to insult him. They took out his office phone. When that didn't work, they removed his desk. Then they changed the lock on his office door. But he wouldn't quit, for the good reason that he was unemployable elsewhere. And so, finally, the studio head called him in, handed him a multi-coloured cap and a funny jacket and said, 'All right, Harry, if you insist on staying, from now on you're working as a studio guide.'

'Okay,' Harry said, accepting his cap.

Three months later the eastern bankers came out to look over their studio. They treated their wives to a tour of the lot, drawing the deposed writer as their guide. When they were done, one of the bankers offered Harry a twenty-dollar tip. 'Oh, no,' he protested, 'I never accept gratuities.'

'Aw, come on,' the banker said, 'I mean, what the hell, how much can you earn as a guide?'

'Oh, me, I earn $10,000 a week.'

The appalled bankers hurried into the executive offices and, as a consequence, more heads rolled.

Hollywood larceny ranges from the endearingly trivial to the grand. If a car, even a camera or a soft drink, is seen close enough for the brand name to be revealed, you can bet your life that the producer has made out on the deal. Men who earn as much as a million for producing a film will also find a way of charging their son's Bar Mitzvah to the production – or, as in Begelman's case, a honeymoon trip. However, even in Hollywood there is such a thing as bad form. There are limits. '*The man forged checks*,' Andrew Tobias wrote in *Esquire*. 'Not once, in a drunken stupor, but at least three times.'

Indecent Exposure sometimes suffers from an overload of documentary detail, as when McClintock writes: 'David [Begelman] and Ray [Stark] decided to walk. They strolled over to Park, down Park to Fifty-sixth, across Fifty-sixth to Lexington, up Lexington to Fifty-seventh, back across Fifty-seventh to Park, back down Park to Fifty-sixth, around the block again and again – seven or eight times in all.' Occasionally, in his attempt to be novelistic, he is driven to present conjecture as fact, as in 'Eventually, however, [Hirshfield] came to regret that Friday deeply and would continue to regret it for the rest of his life.' And there are times, not many, when the language jars: 'As she had suspicioned . . . ' But, for all these admittedly small quibbles, David McClintock has written a fascinating book about Hollywood, informed by taste and intelligence. I know some of the people involved, and he has got their voices exactly right.

Finally, taking into account that Hollywood is a town where the only unbreakable commandment is the bottom line, it is worth noting that Begelman, who only swindled Columbia out of something less than $100,000, might have saved them millions. He was against buying *Annie*. Had he been president of the studio, McClintock writes, 'through the autumn when the *Annie* deal was negotiated, he would have opposed the purchase and conceivably might have talked Hirshfield out of it.'

Go know.

4

WELLES

Had Orson Welles, that great master of entrances and exits, died at the age of twenty-four, after completing *Citizen Kane*, he would undoubtedly be mourned today as the ultimate American filmmaker, a man who would certainly have gone on to create a body of classics if only . . .

Instead there was no bang, but a good deal of embarrassing whimpering. Welles lingered on, Hollywood's ancient mariner, telling and retelling his sad tales at Ma Maison, almost all his projects incomplete for one convoluted cry-baby reason or another, his outsize life reduced to self-serving anecdotes. For all that, on the spurious Hollywood standard, many still grieve for him as an unfulfilled genius. Some genius. Imagine, if you will, the twenty-six-year-old Chekhov, unable to finance his next play, sitting still for a vodka commercial. Or Bach, his fridge running low on Dom Perignon, phoning his agent to see what he could set on the table.

'Well, Johann baby, what would you say to banging out a jingle for Coca-Cola? Big bucks and resids. Or I could get you a guest spot on "Hollywood Squares" or "The Love Boat". Terrific exposure!'

Orson Welles, seventy years old in 1985 – a compulsive eater, weighing some three hundred pounds – is probably best known to the younger generation as a TV huckster for Paul Masson wines.

The one-time compellingly handsome *enfant terrible* and uncompromising artist reduced to 'reading a book at a pebble-glass table on a sunlit patio,' saying, 'Margaret Mitchell began writing *Gone With the Wind* in 1926 and she finished it ten years later. The writing of a great book, or' – a pregnant pause here – 'the making of a fine wine takes time. What was true nearly a century ago is true today. Paul Masson will sell no wine before its time.'

Mind you, even degrading himself for his grocery money, he could still be the irascible Welles. Once, for instance, he refused to say, 'Stradivarius took three years to make one of his violins; Paul Masson took . . . ' Balking at the vulgarity of such a pitch, he protested, 'Come on, gentlemen, now really! You have a nice, pleasant little cheap wine here. You haven't got the presumption to compare it to a Stradivarius. It's odious.'

'Another time, while shooting a champagne commercial,' writes his biographer Barbara Leaming in *Orson Welles*, 'Welles found himself posed in a living room with a particularly plastic collection of extras.

' "Who in the hell are these people?" he asked Hamburg (the director).

' "They're at a party, Orson," Hamburg explained.

' "A party at *my* house?" Orson asked.

' "Yeah."

' "I wouldn't have these people at a party. I mean, this is really lousy. I wouldn't have these people at a party at my house. [This looks] like a party that Robert Young would have." '

In an even more acrimonious shooting session with the same director, Welles challenged the man to make him feel piqued. 'Now, you're the director. I'm the talent. You create this emotion. . . . Do some directing with me. Get me in the mood.'

Provoked, the director ventured, 'Well, you're a fat slob.'

'No, that doesn't do it. You're just going to make me laugh.'

'You're a has-been,' the director continued.

'Nah, nah, that doesn't do it either. You have some pretty weak acid you're throwing in my face. . . . Say something to me that will make me piqued.'

'Well,' the director said, 'how come you screwed Mankiewicz out of the credit on *Citizen Kane* when he actually wrote it?'

'Orson,' writes Barbara Leaming, 'went blood red.'

We all know who wrote *Anna Karenina* or painted *Guernica* or composed *The Magic Flute*, but filmmaking is a group activity unlike any other and, success or failure, it has always been difficult to establish who was responsible for what. Given a film like, say, *Porky's* or *Caddyshack*, the astonishing thing is that those who are guilty will scratch and scream to ensure that their names are included in the credits or charge sheet, when you'd think, assuming they are grown men who intend to be seen in public afterward, they would do anything short of murder to have their names kept out of it. But given something unique, like *Citizen Kane*, it is understandable, if not exactly endearing, that somebody would claim something like sole credit. Orson Welles undoubtedly directed the film and played Kane brilliantly, but, such was his appetite for praise, he would make even larger claims for himself. He had a problem. Like Roger Maris, he would know only one fabled season. He wasn't going to hit sixty-one home runs twice.

The enduring reputation of Orson Welles rests largely on three achievements that illuminate his undisputed talents as showman, filmmaker and performer: his Mercury Theatre radio adaptation of H.G. Wells's *The War of the Worlds*, *Citizen Kane* and his role as Harry Lime in *The Third Man*. Only his role in *The Third Man* was entirely his own, but such was his ego that he continued to go out of his way – unnecessarily – to claim total credit for *The War of the Worlds* as well as *Kane*. Actually, the script for *The War of the Worlds* was written by Howard Koch (who went on to write the film *The Letter* in 1940 and to win an Academy Award for his share of the screenplay for *Casablanca*), but it was certainly Orson Welles who contributed the crucial idea to do the Martian play in the form of news bulletins. 'Some years later,' Pauline Kael writes in 'Raising Kane,' from *The Citizen Kane Book*, 'when CBS did a program about the broadcast and the panic it had caused, the network re-created parts of the original broadcast and paid Koch $300 for the use of his material. Welles sued CBS for $375,000, claiming that he was the author and the material had been used without his permission. He lost, of course, but he may still think he wrote it.'

More importantly, Welles insisted that the script for *Citizen Kane* was essentially his, a claim vigorously endorsed by his adoring biographer, Barbara Leaming. But the evidence, such as it is, strongly supports Pauline Kael's case that the script was in fact written by Herman J. Mankiewicz. Mankiewicz, the celebrated Hollywood wit, drinker and gambler, also produced two Marx Brothers classics, *Monkey Business* and *Horse Feathers*. Before he went to Hollywood, he was a regular contributor to *Vanity Fair* and the first regular drama critic on *The New Yorker*. Once, when Welles walked by on the set of *Citizen Kane*, Mankiewicz was heard to say, 'There, but for the grace of God, goes God.' One of the best stories about Mankiewicz can be found in Ezra Goodman's *The Fifty Year Decline and Fall of Hollywood*. It seems that one night, at a formal dinner party given by Arthur Hornblow, Jr., one of the town's more pretentious producers, Mankiewicz threw up at the table. 'A deadly hush descended over the assembled guests. . . . Mankiewicz broke the silence himself: "It's all right, Arthur; the white wine came up with the fish." '

Barbara Leaming, a professor of theatre and film at Hunter College, New York, seems to have been totally conned by Welles and, consequently, emerges not so much even-handed biographer as uncritical fan, always accepting Welles's version of why so many of his latter-day films remained unfinished. Her narrative, however, is rich in rewarding Hollywood detail. Here, for instance, is the unspeakable Harry Cohn, who used to run Columbia Pictures. 'The mogul was known to poke his letter opener into the mouths of aspiring starlets to pull down their jaws so he could inspect their teeth; and would quickly use the same opener, now moist with saliva, to lift their skirts for a glimpse of their thighs.' She also seems to have all the goods on Welles's affair with

Dolores Del Rio and his turbulent marriage to Rita Hayworth. Welles was a celebrated womanizer. 'He had not just one-night stands,' said his former private secretary, 'but afternoon stands, before-dinner stands and after-dinner stands. Quickies by the thousand!' Or, as Welles himself once put it, 'You see, I have been blessed by some kind of interior sexual mechanism, where if a girl is not ever going to say yes, something clicks, and I don't want it. This has given me the impression that no woman in the world would refuse me if I tried hard enough.'

If he had a larger and more enduring appetite, it was for food. 'He's like a heap of Jell-O,' actor-producer Martin Gabel has said, and director Henry Hathaway once observed, 'There is no *reason* to be that gross.' Even when Welles was a young man, three steaks for dinner, consumed in swift succession, was not unusual, and over the years, the star of *Citizen Kane* ballooned from 210 to 300 pounds.

Leaming's prose, adequate for the most part, sometimes smacks of Harlequin Romance, as when she writes of Rita Hayworth's first meeting with Aly Khan. 'Behind the public persona of the relentless womanizer there was a loneliness and a genuine need for love that Rita found immensely appealing.' The author is also guilty of accepting many of Welles's chestnuts as original stories. Take this, for instance:

> At that time, Orson tended to run into [George Jean] Nathan at '21,' where both of them were regulars. To illustrate how cheap Nathan really was, Orson liked to tell the following wicked and outrageous joke about him: Nathan resided across the street from the famed Algonquin at the Hotel Royalton because it was cheaper. After years of not being tipped, a disgruntled room-service waiter would piss a bit in Nathan's tea each morning. Day by day – Orson says – the waiter increased the amount till finally he was serving Nathan *all* piss. Once, when Nathan was dining at '21' – Orson recalls – the critic exploded over the tea they were served, 'Why can't anybody else make tea like they do at the Royalton?' – at which everyone else dissolved into laughter, because

Nathan was perhaps the only person left in New York who hadn't heard about the waiter's revenge.

Alas, I have read this story at least twice before, the last time in Michael Korda's *Charmed Lives*, wherein it was a miserly Rothschild who suffered the same indignity. For all that, Barbara Leaming's book is blessedly free of film jargon, the most complete study we have yet about a man who once made a film that was truly great, but it is not nearly as closely observed as Pauline Kael's essay.

The film of *Citizen Kane*, Pauline Kael has written, 'is a shallow work, a shallow masterpiece.' Orson Welles had help – the crucial help of Herman Mankiewicz and cinematographer Gregg Toland, among others – but he did bring forth a miracle.

THE SCREENWRITER'S
LOT

'Why you can hire anyone!' exclaimed his visitor in surprise.

'Oh, we hire them, but when they work out here they're not good writers – so we have to work with the material we have.'

'Such as what?'

'Anybody that'll accept the system and stay decently sober.'

From *The Last Tycoon*, by F. Scott Fitzgerald.

OVER THE YEARS, lecturing on campuses here and there and making the occasional raid on Hollywood, I have finally grasped that things are seldom what they are supposed to be. Surprisingly, in the groves of academe, the tenured clerks of our cultural weights-and-measures offices are more interested in talking about money than ideas. They want to know how much you were overpaid for your last novel (frankly speaking, a disappointment) or film script (don't bother to apologize, obviously you needed the money) or perfectly silly little article. Your social status soars if you have ever met Goldie Hawn, not Doris Lessing. Feed the academics an anecdote about Gunter Grass and their eyes will cloud over, but tease them about the time you were actually in the same room as Dustin Hoffman or Kathleen Turner, lying if necessary, and they or their wives will instantly demand more details. Then, with some pride, they will guide you through the room where they maintain their collection of Bogart and Ritz Brothers film posters. If their son pops in, cross-eyed drunk, he is bound to be sporting a Mohawk hairdo and will be the lead guitarist in a group he has put together called the Menstrual Flow.

But out there among the parvenus in disgustingly rich Beverly Hills, where money-grubbing is the happy rule, it is considered gross for the 'real' writer, whom they have flown out there first-class, to even wonder aloud about his script fee. They want to know if you have ever read Peter Handke and what you think of the minimalists. Then, with some pride, they will guide you through the room where they keep their first editions of Henry James, their burgeoning Library of America collection and a poster from the original production of *Death of a Salesman*. If their well-groomed son pops in from the kitchen, where the naughty devil has just fixed himself a yogurt nightcap, he is bound to be studying atonal music at Julliard or deconstructivism with a little Eurotrash creep at Harvard.

The two worlds do collide. Once, Mike Todd, contemplating a production of *War and Peace* (possibly starring his then wife, Elizabeth Taylor), went to visit Sir Isaiah Berlin to discuss his book on Tolstoy, *The Hedgehog and the Fox*. Todd was so impressed by Sir Isaiah that he finally blurted out, 'Damn it, Issy, how did a guy as intelligent as you are end up at Oxford?'

The two worlds, seemingly incompatible, do share at least one certitude. Living writers – those shameless peddlers out there working the street with their portable typewriters, cadging drinks whenever they can, propositioning your wife or daughter no sooner than you turn your back – are an intolerable nuisance. At an English department cocktail party ostensibly tendered in my honour (on offer, the traditional plonk in plastic glasses and all the pretzels you could eat), I was told, 'There are some eighty thousand books being published this year. Do you really think it's necessary?' While in Hollywood, writers – or 'the boys,' as they are called, even when in their sixties – are just another film production hazard, worse than the Teamster chauffeurs, if only because they expect to be invited to sit down at the big table rather than wait outside behind the wheel of the limo, scanning the market pages in *The Wall Street Journal*.

I was reminded of the sorry status of the writer in Hollywood when I came across *Film Flam: Essays on Hollywood*, by that fine novelist (*The Last Picture Show, Terms of Endearment*), Larry McMurtry. McMurtry, who also wrote the most entertaining western I have ever read, *Lonesome Dove*, has stitched together on uncommonly sensible collection, largely based on his own experiences in Hollywood. For decades, as he sees it, 'writers have drifted around Hollywood more or less like unloved wives.' On the other hand, he justifiably notes: 'So much has been written about the miseries of screenwriting, or, more precisely, about the miseries of the screenwriter's lot, that I, for one, am sick of reading it. I think it's time to redress the balance, to treat Hollywood fairly, and to suggest that screenwriting, far from being hard work, might actually be considered a form of creative play.'

I agree. But if you look closely at my typing fingers, you will notice that the pads are calloused. If Roger Clemens suffered from the same ailment, he would be put on the twenty-one-day disabled list, but not a writer. We are expected to play with pain, giving 110 percent all the time. I think McMurtry has done his colleagues a disservice, airing the literary laundry in public, as it were. His seemingly amiable book could fall into the wrong hands – say, those of a producer.

Snitch that he is, McMurtry lets it slip that screenwriting 'happens to pay well[1] – like, say, professional football' –

---

1. In 1938 Aldous Huxley, newly-arrived in Hollywood, signed his first screen contract – $1,800 a week for eight weeks, more than he had earned on his last two books. The contract, with MGM, was for a screen treatment of *Madame Curie*, a treatment that would certainly not mention that Madame Curie chose her lab assistants partly on their looks and made love to them in a bed over which hung a picture of her husband Pierre. A quick Hollywood learner, Huxley – writes David King Dunaway in *Huxley in Hollywood* – fantasized about trips, at MGM's expense, to places where uranium could be found, say, the Belgian Congo. His script, intended for Garbo, was actually a 145-page novel.

Christopher Isherwood was not totally happy to see Huxley in Hollywood. 'I don't know what in the hell you imagine you're doing here. Selling your soul, I suppose? All you writers have such a bloody romantic without exposing the practitioner to bodily danger or hard work. This, I must say, while not quite calumny, is certainly a half-truth. Surely McMurtry, who has put up at the Beverly Wilshire more than once, must know that any lonely writer who descends to the bar for a drink at 5 p.m. risks bodily danger of a kind. On assignment in Hollywood, he is also exposed to producers and, God help us, the story conference.

On firmer ground, McMurtry observes that producers 'don't really like to think of themselves as glorified personnel managers, though that's what they usually are; they want to be allowed to participate in the creative act. Keeping a writer handy to talk to every few days convinces them that they are, in fact, participating – it may, at the same time, drive the writer crazy.'

Once, labouring hard on a film out there – that is to say, putting in an arduous two hours on my trusty portable, then turning to room service and whatever game was available on the sports channel – I shrewdly waited until 4 p.m. before passing on ten immortal pages to my director. They began:

EXT. DAY. MAIN STREET.
Car pulls up in front of apartment building.
EXT. DAY. CLOSER SHOT.
Irving, looking anxious, gets out of car.
EXT. DAY. APARTMENT BUILDING.
He enters, lighting a cigarette.
INT. DAY. APARTMENT BUILDING.
He seems somewhat more anxious as elevator doors slide open for him.
INT. DAY ELEVATOR.
Irving going up.

My director was reasonably pleased with my efforts, but that wasn't the case with the producer. The producer in question, I should point out, was blessed with an uncanny eye for detail, the small things that render a scene utterly convincing;

---

attitude. You think you're too good for the movies. Don't believe it. The movies are too good for you. We don't need any romantic nineteenth century whores. We need technicians.'

his wife's favourite colour was blue, and he had a contract with one of the hottest ad agencies in town. So, after a creative conference, I rewrote the scene to read:

> EXT. DAY. MAIN STREET.
> Shiny blue Volvo pulls up in front of apartment building.
> CLOSER SHOT.
> Irving, looking immensely pleased at its performance, gets out of Volvo, closing door with a satisfying clunk.
> EXT. DAY. APARTMENT BUILDING.
> He enters, lighting a cigarette.
> CLOSER SHOT.
> Reveals it's a Parliament, low on tar.
> INT. DAY. APARTMENT BUILDING.
> He seems somewhat anxious as elevator doors slide open for him.
> INT. DAY. ELEVATOR.
> Going up, he takes out a pen to make a note.
> CLOSER SHOT.
> Reveals it's a Cross pen.

Once, a screenwriter I know was rebuked by his producer for only one shot in a 160-page script. It showed a character's luggage going round and round on an airport carousel. The character's name was Jimmy Hardwick. The shot read:

> INT. DAY. CLOSE ON AIRPORT CAROUSEL.
> Hardwick's Gucci luggage, initials J. H. prominent, going round and round.

"You don't have to give me a quick yes or no on this,' the producer said, 'but I think it would be more believable if the character's initials were L. S.'

'You mean your initials, Lou?'

'That just happens to be a coincidence. I'm talking visuals here.'

McMurtry, spilling the beans yet again, writes that screenwriting doesn't call for art but craftsmanship. 'It is a form of piecework, generally done in collaboration with other people, so that even the labor of conception is shared. Take the best screenplay ever written – if you can find it – and compare it, say, with *Middlemarch* or with *The Origins of Totalitarianism*, to use a couple of admittedly disparate examples. Which looks like hard work, which like fun and games?'

Right.

JOURNALS

April 18, 1988

Select Books
Organization for
   Publishing and
   Trade of Books
Director General:
   Nicos G. Hatzievangelou
Head Office:
   Stadiou Street 3
   Athens – Greece

To:
His excellency
Mr. Nordecai Richler
c/o McCeland and Stewart
25 Hollinger Rd.,
Toronto, Ontario
M4B 3G2
CANADA

Your Excellency,

The large and difficult preparatory work of the most *significant* Edition of our epoch, of our century, on *high intellectual level*, which will contain the Reflections, the inferences, the conclusions and the settlings of the Thought, of Great Personalities of Universal weight and brilliancy, all over the world, has already been completed.

These texts of the most eminent personalities of our Century, will be a great luminous lighthouse of the Thought, as well for our epoch, our Century, as for the coming Centuries, because we don't accept that the evolution will bring also alteration of the human reflection bases, which are established and unshakable from thousand years, as well as of the creative exaltation, penetration, search and evaluation.

We deem that the particular setting of your texts is indispensable to our Volume, because they will surely be considerable and so the readers of today, as well as those of the future centuries will give their full attention to their study with great intellectual benefit, from the high field of Reflection, given that this work will remain *eternal*, as it will represent the genious of our Century.

Your enormous experience from life, with your very significant successful promotion, your rare talent and your work of great brilliancy, are rendering really valuable the profusion, the wealth of your knowledge. For this reason, we warmly ask you to make us the great honor to answer our enclosed questions.

The space for the formulation of your Reflections is *unlimited*, for the welfare of all the readers.

A warm, a very warm request that all your answers be handwritten and signed, if this doesn't tire you too much, in order that they have the token and incontestability for the reading public.

In case that this is tiring or troubling you too much, then we warmly ask that all your typed answers have your signature.

Anyway, we warmly ask you to be so kind and answer at least one question or more, by hand, because the readers and we, will be very touched.

Allow us to require your autobiography, which will surely move the reading public, because it will be authentic.

We kindly ask you to honour our Edition, with a photo of yours, at your choice.

I will consider it as a great honor, if you will have the kindness to write on your photo a dedication to the author, who has worked hard since fifty years and works hard till *now* for this work of so high intellectual importance.

With the occasion, I am mentioning that great personalities, have already in the past, answered in writing, the answers of whom, will come to light for the first time *now* with this Edition of ours. These eminent personalities are: Winston Churchill, Charles de Gaulle, John Kennedy, Nicos Kazantzakis, Kostis Palamas, K.P. Kavafis, Angelos Sekelianos, Gamal Abdel Nasser, Tito and others.

191

The Edition which will be *de luxe* and *perfect* will circulate in seven languages, for the time being: GREEK, ENGLISH, FRENCH, GERMAN, ITALIAN, SPANISH and JAPANEESE, with the title:

THE PHILOSOPHY OF LIFE
The Most Eminent Personalities of the World are
speaking and writing
UNIVERSAL EDITION

With the warm request that you honor us with your texts, in order that our significant Edition be enriched and completed, we thank you in advance, and remain,

Sincerely Yours,
The Director General.
signed Nicos Hatzievangelou
Stadiou Street 3 – Athens
REQUEST: I warmly ask you to send your reply by REGISTERED MAIL LETTER, for safety sake, due to its valuable content.
NOTE: Please don't speak about the present to third persons, due to professional secret.
Encl.

The Mail. Today's batch yielded the usual requests for funds to stop acid rain, fight apartheid, support abortion-on-demand and to send a personal item, however modest, for auction at the hard-pressed public library in Regina. However, it has been months since I had a registered letter from the reader in Tulsa whose dentist, a CIA agent wise in tradecraft, has implanted a transistor in one of her molars, which enables her to monitor every telephone call out of Jupiter to the Russian embassy in Washington. This spring I haven't heard from the Reading Glasses Hall of Fame, somewhere in Tennessee, requesting a pair of my specs, and there has been no further word from the English major at Indiana U., who was writing a thesis on 'The Second Rate in Contemporary Fiction.' More to my taste was the following letter from the Nigerian Society for the Advancement of Management &

Business Studies (NSAMBS), P.O. Box 426, Owerri – Nigeria, W/A.

Dear Professor Richler,

REQUEST FOR YOUR ACADEMIC TREASURES/ PUBLICATIONS

We are very happy to write you for the first time today and perhaps not the last, this humble and friendly letter which we sincerely believe would receive your gracious blessings.

First and foremost, we wish to express through this medium our appreciation, immeasurable gratitude and great admiration for your remarkable, highly exemplary and fruitfully inspiring contributions towards the rapid advancement of higher learning in the world today.

Unfortunately, we only read about your wonderfully motivating and practically rewarding academic works from some Overseas Academic and Book-review journals, as we have not been lucky to find your nice publications in any of our local bookshops and libraries. As a result therefore, we have decided to approach you as a world great writer and publisher for immediate assistance. We therefore, strongly request you to help us by sending to us some of your brilliantly authoritative academic treasures/publications such as:

'JOSHUA THEN AND NOW' 'IMAGES OF SPAIN' 'THE STREET'
'SHOVELLING TROUBLE' AND 'CANADIAN WRITING NOW'

We should in addition to above, graciously welcome any other book(s), journals, posters or even reprints you may wish to send us in any field.

As we optimistically and anxiously look forward to hearing favourably from you soon, we pray God to guide and bless you in your wonderful academic works. We wish you the best!

Yours sincerely,
P. ABANGWEL OSUAGWU
Secretary (NSAMBS)

April 21

Dentistry, my Uncle Myer said to me years ago, chewing on a White Owl, that's the ticket. 'People won't bother you at all hours of the day and night, like you were a doctor, and I just happen to know where you can pick up the equipment second-hand.'

I opted for writing instead, the essential capital equipment – a portable typewriter, a desk, a chair, a dictionary, a bottle of a decent single malt Scotch – coming considerably cheaper than the dentist's chair and drill that rested in a corner of Uncle Myer's junk yard.

I made a bad mistake. My dentist works four days a week, not seven, and he doesn't have to autograph yanked molars for customers.

'I want you to write,' I was once told at a book signing, ' "Happy anniversary, Nate and Sadie, you're the greatest. I wish I could be with you this weekend. Love, Mordecai." '

'But I've never met Nate or Sadie.'

'They don't mind.'

My dentist drives a Jaguar. He skis in Vail, where he owns a condo. He flies on the Concorde. I was seated in his chair one day, sweaty, helpless, my mouth filled with clasps, when he thrust a typewritten short story at me. 'Read this and give me your honest opinion.' Something that had earned his daughter an A in Creative Writing 101. 'She's got a book in her, that kid, but she hasn't got your connections. Be frank. But open wider, please. I'll try not to hurt.'

Too late I have grasped that, being a novelist– unlike the butcher, zipper manufacturer or junk bond guru– I produce nothing anybody really needs, and just about everybody I've ever met thinks they could do better, if only they were sufficiently childish or had the spare time.

May 15

Abandon your wife and children, do some crack before breakfast, convert all your savings into South African rand, but don't redo your kitchen. If it's dark, with a rippling floor, a malfunctioning stove, a veritable cockroach heaven, count yourself blessed. Don't touch it. But if you simply must redo your kitchen, go for broke, as we did. Tear the whole room apart. The roof, the walls, the floors, everything. 'And furthermore,' I said to my wife, 'we're not going to overpay some snot-nosed architect to tell us where the sink goes or how high we can raise the roof. We can manage everything ourselves.'

The kitchen in question is in our country cottage in Quebec's Eastern Townships, hard by the Vermont border. Our cottage sits on a leafy hill on the shores of Lake Memphremagog, but our kitchen, where my wife – a splendid cook – spends a good deal of her time, is in the rear. The only dark room in the house. It seemed unfair. So one afternoon I repaired to the Owl's Nest, a ramshackle bar on the 243 where I drink with other craftsmen (housepainters, self-taught carpenters, gravel pit operators), and consulted with two cronies, Sweet Pea and Buzz. 'How long,' I asked, 'would it take you guys to tear apart our kitchen and do it up again with skylights, ceiling-to-floor glass doors, the works?'

'Oh, six weeks at the most,' Pea said, squelching laughter. 'Let's go.'

They arrived early one morning armed with crowbars. The kitchen was emptied. Drawers and shelves and cupboard doors we might use again were stacked high in the library, rendering it unusable. Pots, pans, dishes and canned goods were stored in the dining room, making it all but impassable. My wife, no fool, left for Italy.

Reducing the kitchen to nothing took a week. Pea and Buzz, considerate fellows, did leave me a functioning gas stove, but then the rains came. In order to prepare a modest breakfast, I first had to get into my raincoat and rubber boots. Ignoring the shambles around me, I looked for inspiration in Mary Gilliatt's *Setting Up Home*. 'Lighting,' I read, 'can change a room beyond recognition. Properly controlled, arranged and directed light can produce dramatic effects.' Oh, my God, I thought, we've got to rewire. 'Hey, Pea, what are we going to do for an electrician?'

'You're not going to be stuck with thirty bucks an hour. We got a guy, he's retired, he runs a worm farm now, he'll work for eighteen, but you've got to pay him cash.'

I phoned my wife in Rome, drew up a new light-location plan according to her specifications and the next morning explained it at length to the worm farmer.

'Oh, shit,' Pea said. 'I should'a told you. It's no use explaining things to him. He's deaf.'

'Should I write it out then?'

'Well I'm afraid he don't read too good. TRY SHOUTING.'

In the evening – bats swooping down on me, attracted by the one working light in my roofless kitchen – I heated my baked beans, reading *The Mary Gilliatt Book of Color*. 'Black and white are natural accents, delineators, outliners. The Egyptians outlined their frescoes in black vegetable dyes or in a black pigment made from crushed bones.'

Florence was long back from Italy by the time the new roof, skylights and ceiling-to-floor glass doors were in place. 'You want to cook in here,' Pea told her, 'you're going to have to wear sunglasses.'

The scheduled six weeks for the job had come and gone long before the plastering and sanding had even started. We were drunk on dust and a kind of euphoria set in. Where we had once been intent on economies, we now opted for a binge. No ordinary cooker, we decided, would do for *our* kitchen. It had to be the legendary Aga. 'More than an extraordinary cooker. It's a way of life.' A way of life, mark you, that cost $9,000 plus delivery and installation charges. But, what the hell, John Updike had one, so did Princess Anne, David Ogilvy, Paul McCartney, André Previn, Billy Joel and that celebrated cook, Princess Diana.

This unique cooker was the brainchild of Dr. Gustaf Dalen, a Swedish physicist and Nobel Prize winner, who built it for his wife in 1922. To quote the Aga brochure, what he was after was 'one cooker capable of every culinary technique . . . one that could cook a variety of dishes simultaneously, and one that delivered perfect results consistently. Eureka! The AGA!'

The handcrafted Aga, flawlessly engineered, made of cast iron in a foundry in Coalbrookdale, England, weighs some 1,500 pounds. Once set in place, the burner ("famous for providing a lifetime of trouble-free service") is constantly lit. It heats four ovens at different temperatures as well as two surface hot plates, one for boiling, the other for simmering, but covered by insulated lids when not in use. Friends in England swore by it. Without a doubt it is a beautiful object.

The Aga, however, is comparatively new to North America. Ours was being trucked in from Toronto by an expert at installing the cooker, the amiable Ernie. Ernie was joined at our cottage by a man I'll call Harry, another expert, who drove in from Stowe, Vermont. It took the better part of a day to assemble the cooker, and then Harry left, leaving Ernie to finish the job the following day. Problems. The chimney pipe didn't fit properly – it bent dangerously at the elbow – and had to be kept in place by a wedge of wood. Once lit, the flame in the burner seemed to be firing erratically. Ernie, perplexed, got on the phone to Toronto. He called Harry in Stowe. In fact, every time there was a hitch he had to phone somebody.

'Hey, Ernie,' I asked, 'have you ever had any trouble with one of these before?'

'Only once.'

'How many have you installed?'

'One.'

Hours after Ernie had left to spend the night in a nearby inn, our kitchen had turned into a sauna. The Aga was too hot to touch, the mercury heat gauge on the front registering far too high. Hell, I thought, I'm not babysitting a cooker at my age, and so at one a.m. I turned it off.

Four days later Harry drove in from Vermont, this time with his apologetic boss. They removed our burner unit and replaced it with another one famous for a lifetime of trouble-free service. They also came bearing gifts. An Aga apron, an Aga dish towel and Aga oven gloves. 'But don't use the gloves on anything really hot,' we were warned, 'they're not properly insulated.'

May 16

Can't hack it today, so I decided to sift through a stack of unread magazines and discover that John Leonard, the notorious Canada-basher, has been at it again. Reviewing *The Bourne Identity* in his television column in *New York* magazine, he wrote, 'Only a Ludlum could be so paranoid as to imagine Canadian killers, which is sort of like imagining killer koalas or killer daffodils.'

Hogwash. Obviously Leonard is ignorant of the true nature of the northern beast. Not so R. Thurston Hopkins, author of *Life and Death at the Old Bailey* who in 1935 wrote of a Canadian, taking him as a prototype: 'There are men in the world who are not of this world. They seem to be creatures who have strayed from some land beyond human ken. They may look like us, walk about like us, and speak our language . . . But we know, somehow, that they live in some other secret world: sometimes a world of sinister alleys. . . . Always we feel in their presence that we are out of step and out of time.'

Hopkins was describing Thomas Neill Cream, an 1876 graduate of McGill University medical school, who some still believe was Jack the Ripper. When Cream, a.k.a. the Lambeth Murderer, was hurled into eternity, the hangman thought he heard him say, 'I am Jack the Ripper!'

Had an American made such a claim before taking his last leap, it could be dismissed as typically boastful, but coming as it did from a self-effacing Canadian, it was possibly true.

Cream, in any event, was no koala or daffodil but in those days McGill's most successful serial murderer. His, the appreciative Hopkins wrote, was 'a tale of diablerie and death in twilight streets.' Cream, adjudged an excellent worker, a brilliant boy, by one of his McGill profs, was, in fact, a morphia fiend, bent on poisoning hookers, or what the more poetic Hopkins called 'the frail sisters of the London streets.' He did in several of these girls, among them one

Matilda Clover, 'who for some months had been entertaining furtive seekers after love in her room.' He poisoned Matilda with a 'long pill.' As Hopkins wrote, Cream was such a clever fellow that 'if [he] had remained in Canada after his 1891 killings, no suspicion would have fallen on him.'

But had he remained in Canada, hardly anybody – certainly not John Leonard – would ever have heard of him. Why, as late as the 1930s, Canadian thugs with their eye on celebrity still had to quit the country to make their name, leaving us with something of a crime drain. Take the case of Alvin Karpis, or Old Creepy, who certified J. Edgar Hoover's reputation for personal machismo, or as Old Creepy himself put it in the parlance of his set, 'I made that son of a bitch.'

When the Associated Press ran a sort of all-star team of hoodlums, listing such greats as Bonnie and Clyde, Dillinger, Ma Barker, and Nelson and Floyd, the name at the very top of the list was a Canadian one: Alvin Karpis, né Karpowicz in Montreal. 'My profession,' Karpis once told writer Bill Trent, after he had been released from prison and repatriated in 1969, 'was robbing banks, knocking off payrolls, and kidnapping rich men. I was good at it.'

The Karpis-Barker gang thrived in the early thirties. According to FBI-nurtured legend, Karpis, the head of the gang, was personally captured by an intrepid Hoover in 1936, the FBI director jerking open the door of a car and grabbing Karpis even as he made a move for a rifle lying on the back seat. All this was supposed to have happened, conveniently enough, at a time when the fledgling FBI, as well as Hoover's own courage, was under attack in Congress. But according to Old Creepy that's not the way it was that day in New Orleans. The story of Hoover as hero, he maintained, was false. Karpis insisted that he was surrounded by a couple of dozen FBI agents armed with pistols, rifles and machine guns, and that they rounded a corner and one of them shouted, 'We've got him. It's all clear, Chief.'

'A couple of others shouted the same thing,' Karpis told Trent. 'I turned my head in the direction they were looking. Two men came out from behind the apartment. They'd apparently been waiting in the shelter of the building, out of sight. . . . They walked closer, and I recognized the dark, heavy man. I'd seen pictures of him. Anyone would have known him. He was J. Edgar Hoover.'

Far from being koalas or daffodils, we are fighting fools, sufficiently fierce to have repelled dastardly American invaders more than once. Or, looked at another way, Antietam, Harper's Ferry, Bull Run and Gettysburg are mere skirmishes to those who remember the glory of Pigeon Hill in 1866, on that day of infamy when the hand that held the dagger stabbed it into its northern neighbour's back.

Pigeon Hill lies on the Vermont border not far from where I live in the Eastern Townships. In the mid-1860s, Irish veterans of the Union army began to mount sneak attacks on us, marching on Canada, singing:

> We are the Fenian Brotherhood,
> skilled in the arts of war,
> And we're going to fight for Ireland,
> the land that we adore.
> Many battles we have won,
> along with the boys in blue,
> And we'll go and capture Canada –
> for we've nothing else to do!

The Fenians, gathered in St. Albans, Vermont, in 1866, were led by General Spear, a graduate of West Point who had served thirty years in the American army. A General Mahon, formerly of the 9th Massachusetts, was his chief of staff, and the Third (Fenian) Cavalry was headed by Colonel Coutri, who claimed to be a veteran of John Singleton Mosby's Confederate guerrillas.

According to a local historian, Bernard Epps, author of *Tales of the Townships*, once Townshippers learned of the Fenian presence in St. Albans, a few of them crossed the border to seek out the enemy. There they exchanged insults with and bought rifles from the parched and impecunious

Fenians. The Fenians, the infiltrators discovered, had been issued only two bullets each and had already begun to desert. General Spear, who had expected 16,800 warriors at the front, had to settle for some 1,500 louts and a war chest that contained $20.15, a pittance, even allowing for inflation. There was only one thing for it: to gather together the stragglers and deserters and attack immediately. 'On to Canada,' he cried.

So on June 7, 1866, the hollering Fenians scrambled across the international border. 'You are on British soil,' Spear proclaimed. 'I charge you to spare the women and children. I leave in your hands the enemies of your country. . . . On to Montreal!'

Headquarters were established in a farmhouse, the flag of the Republic of Ireland, a golden harp on a green field, flying from the roof. Horseless cavalrymen roamed the fields, searching for mounts, and bored foot soldiers wandered into Frelighsburg and Pigeon Hill, where they stole sheep to roast over open fires. The first engagement was indecisive. A Fenian scouting party, having advanced two and a half miles into Canada, espied three mounted British soldiers in red coats at a distance of three hundred yards. They promptly opened fire, hitting nobody. The alarmed redcoats fled in one direction, the Fenians in another.

Inevitably there were incidents. Some Fenians burst into a tavern in Pigeon Hill, ordered drinks at gunpoint and robbed the Canadian patrons, taking one of them prisoner. Elsewhere a respectable citizen of Pigeon Hill was arrested by members of Coutri's cavalry, still without horses. According to his testimony, the ruffians 'placed a guard over me and took off my clothes and searched them, kept all my papers and offered Fenian bonds (which looked too green) for my horse and when I refused to take them they seized it and took me into camp. . . . '

Meanwhile the Canadian forces were camped in faraway St. Jean, pondering the best strategy. But even so there was already a casualty. Jerry Sullivan of Boston was wounded in the leg by the accidental discharge of his own revolver. Next, the regular American forces took umbrage. Major General G. Meade, commander of the Military Division of the Atlantic, rounded up besotted Fenians on his side of the border, rooting them out of taverns and hotel beds and locking them up in the Burlington jail.

So many Fenians entrenched in Canada began to desert, drifting back across the border with their booty, that suddenly General Spear found he was able to muster no more than two hundred men. He inquired how many of them were willing to fight on with him. Only sixteen volunteered. So General Spear ordered a retreat. This emboldened the wildcats who made up Canada's thin red line, the men of the Royal Artillery, and they now charged, striking out with the flats of their swords and treating the Irish rabble to a taste of hot Dominion steel. No sooner did the fleeing Fenians stagger across the border than Major General Meade's men arrested them.

'They came,' the *Stratford Beacon* crowed the next morning, 'they saw, but they skedaddled.'

May 20

A letter from Yaroslav Sokolyk.

Dear Sir,

This year, men women and children of Ukrainian heritage living in Canada are marking the Millenium of Christianity in the Ukraine.

In honour of this momentous occasion, the Ukrainian Canadian Committee – Toronto branch has issued a set of commemorative stamps. On behalf of the U.C.C., we enclose a complete set of these commemorative stamps for your personal collection.

We hope they make an interesting addition to your existing collection.

No sooner had I unlocked my toy box, plucked out my stamp album and slipped the U.C.C. first day issue right in there next to my U.S. stamp showing Lindy's Spirit of St. Louis flying upside down (worth a cool million, I'm told) than I was hit with an even more mind-boggling letter. This one from the considerate Ruth Danys of Toronto.

> Dear Mr. Richler,
>   I am writing a book about housing the elderly and including a round-up of opinions on whether a Canadian writers" retirement residence would be a good or terrible idea. What do you think?

Blowing on the whistle I now wear around my neck brought my loving wife on the trot. She wiped my chin clean of breakfast remnants and changed my Pampers, reproaching me only a little. 'Mordecai's been naughty again!' Then she adjusted my pacifier and wheeled me over to my large-print typewriter.

> Dear Ms. Danys,
>   I've had to give up prowling through singles" bars because my wife won't let me out of the house any more without pinning a card to my jacket lapel, listing my name, address and blood type. My children are plotting to murder me for my royalties. Therefore your idea strikes me as inspired.
>   I'm willing to book a room right now providing:
>   a. the writers" retirement home is located in a decent climate, say Cap Ferrat or Dubrovnik or Ibiza.
>   b. there is a handsomely appointed bar.
>   c. and we are allowed to stay up late to watch dirty movies every night.
>   I can't include a self-addressed envelope, because I don't remember my address, but I am enclosing four stamps commemorating the Millenium of Christianity in the Ukraine. Write soon.

May 24

Recently came across a paperback reprint of *Native Tongues* by Charles Berlitz. The author, grandson of Maximilian Delphinius Berlitz, who founded the Berlitz schools, is a most engaging eccentric. Though he takes pains to state that he has no connection with the Berlitz schools, he has written more than a hundred language-teaching books. He is also the author of *Atlantis, The Eighth Continent*, a seductive if somewhat less than closely reasoned case for the real rather than mythological existence of the forgotten civilization of Atlantis, where Shirley MacLaine, bless her, once enjoyed another life, horsing around with her brother Ramtha.

One of the earliest advocates of the lost continent was Plato. In his *Critias* and *Timaeus* dialogues, he left a convincing description of the powerful empire, noting that it came to a sudden end while engaged in a war, the central island or islands sinking 'in a terrible night and day' to the bottom of the ocean that bears its name. 'The island,' Plato wrote, 'was larger than Libya and Asia put together ... and ... maybe most truly called a continent.' However, one of Plato's brighter students, Aristotle, pronounced his teacher a fibber. Atlantis, Aristotle wrote, was a myth: 'He who invented it destroyed it.'

Berlitz, convinced that his continent of golden cities drowned 11,500 years ago and has since lain at the bottom of the sea, lost and almost forgotten, understandably falls back on his prodigious knowledge of language as primary proof. Berber tribes of North Africa have their legend of Attala, now under the ocean and the Basques believe that they are the descendants of the people of Atlaintika. Furthermore, Berlitz writes, 'The ancient Gauls, as well as the Irish, Welsh, and British Celts, believed that their ancestors came from a continent that sank into the Western Sea, the latter two naming this lost paradise Avalon.'

Having written a fanciful book about the mysteries of the sea, Berlitz, in his preface to *Native Tongues*, ventures that language itself is one of the world's greatest mysteries. Happily, though he claims to be fluent in more than two dozen languages himself, we needn't be too intimidated by Berlitz. Taking the larger view, he is a mere beginner. According to the Académie Française there are at least 2,796 languages spoken on our troubled planet. If importance is measured by the number of speakers, then Chinese, with a billion practitioners, is the most important. English comes second with approximately 300 million native speakers, if you include politicians and TV talk-show hosts. It is generally accepted that language first evolved from a series of sound signals such as are used by birds, fish and marine animals, but nobody knows what the first language was or how it all began. How it will end, at least in the English-speaking world, is, however, abundantly clear. It will end with movies featuring the dialogue of Sylvester Stallone and the offerings of such heavy metal groups as Def Leppard, AC/DC, Ozzy Osbourne and KISS.

The principal languages spread by colonization are English, French, Spanish, Dutch, Portuguese and, increasingly, Russian. Swahili, a trade language in Africa's interior, has borrowed a good deal from English. English words in Swahili include *eropleni* (aeroplane), *lori* (truck) and *motokaa* (motorcar). Yiddish, originally derived from medieval German, continues to borrow here, there and everywhere. My grandmother, for instance, did not call a window, a *fenster* but, instead, a *vinda*. The English, however, are even more notorious pilferers. More than half of our English vocabulary is of French-Norman and Latin-via-French origin.

Most European languages have a built-in grammatical preoccupation with the gender of nouns, which also influences the adjectives used with them. In the Romance languages all nouns are either masculine or feminine. In English, as we all know, male chauvinist prejudice has recently been subject to revision by our most militant feminists: hence, herstory, chairperson, herkind and so on. This unseemly distortion of our language, taken to its logical extreme, may yet lead to a revised feminist edition of Shakespeare, where we may look forward to Hamlet musing, 'What a piece of work is personhood,' or Antony, mourning the slain Brutus, saying, 'He was a humanoid, take one for all in all.'

The Spaniards, as might be expected, have no patience with feminist feeling. 'In Spanish,' Berlitz writes, 'if only one man and twenty women passengers were on a bus, the group would be referred to as *pasajeros* (masculine), not *pasajeras* (feminine), and would become *pasajeras* only after the male passenger had gotten off the bus.'

In his chapter on swear-words and cursing and how they vary from nation to nation, Berlitz fails to take account of a charming French-Canadian custom. Too fastidious to stoop to gutter language, the Québecois utilize religious articles as curse words: *tabernâcle* (tabernacle), *ostie* (the host), *sacrement* (sacrament).

In Chinese, *Fuking* means 'Happiness Capital,' certainly not always the case in English. In Japanese, *fukkyu* is the word for 'restitution,' *fuko* means 'bad luck' and *fugu* is the name of a delicious fish, poisonous if not cleaned by an expert.

Further facts.

Shakespeare produced all his works with nineteen thousand words, the King James version of the Bible required only six thousand, but the Sunday edition of the New York *Times* requires more than either, averaging out at twenty-five thousand.

Surnames, always a source of fascination to me, come in for a good deal of attention from Berlitz. 'Many of the rulers of principalities, dukedoms, and kingdoms of medieval Germany,' he writes, 'devised a system of taxing Jews by requiring that they adopt German names and pay for them, on a sliding scale. The most expensive names in this medieval shakedown were pleasant, beautiful or poetic: Rosenberg ("mountain of roses"), Himmelblau ("the blue of heaven"), Blumenthal ("valley of flowers"). Occupations were less expensive: Schneider ("tailor"), Goldschmidt ("goldsmith"), Kaufmann ("merchant").

There is also a chapter on the meanings of the names of countries. Argentina is literally 'the silver republic,' and Ecuador is named for the equator, which passes through it, just like the CIA. Israel means 'the wrestler with God' and Tanganyika 'Land of Many Tribes.' I wish Berlitz had added a favourite legend of mine about the origin of the name of my own country. Many years ago, it seems, on a Spanish explorer's map of North America, all that was marked on the undiscovered land above the St. Lawrence River was '*aqui esta nada*.' Eventually this was corrupted to read 'Canada.'

May 25

For the past year my wife and I have been rooted in our country cottage, where I continue to struggle with a long and convoluted novel. Given the opportunity I could shaft it right now with a more scathing review than any I'm likely to see when I finish it. I've always suspected that every novelist writes one too many, and now that I'm fifty-seven all those luminous brain cells I once counted on seem extinguished by Remy Martin or Glenlivet. I wonder if my turn has come.

Originally Florence and I only came out here for two months of summer and weekends in winter, but now that we are no longer tied to the school year (our five children are grown up) we are thinking of giving up our Montreal apartment and making this our home. It's a wrench. It means finally disposing of books (bought maybe thirty years ago, crated and carted from continent to continent) that I now have to admit I'll never get round to reading. Florence is being difficult. She won't let me discard novels she has read years ago and will probably never turn to again. 'I am what I have read,' she says, settling matters. And me, I won't part with my three-volume *History of Ferdinand and Isabella*, by W.H. Prescott, not that I'm ever going to read it but because it reminds me of the sunny afternoon I bought the set at a stall alongside the Seine. From there I went on to meet Mason Hoffenberg at The Old Navy on Boulevard St.-Germain. We were joined briefly by Terry Southern. Then Mason and I strolled down to the Ile St.-Louis, talking about Céline and Duke Snider's season and the incomparable view from that hilltop overlooking Toledo.

Poor Mason.

A couple of years ago I took my wife and daughter out to dinner at our favourite restaurant in New York, Carolina, on West 46th Street. An hour after we had settled in, a party of ten took the adjoining table. One of the group turned out to be an old Hollywood friend whom I hadn't seen in years. We exchanged pleasantries and then he said, 'Have you heard that Mason Hoffenberg died a few weeks ago?'

Mason was in his early sixties.

I tried my best to join my wife and daughter in conversation for the rest of the dinner, but I was drifting for the most part, returning in my mind's eye to Paris, 1951, when we had all been young and promising, but none so much as Mason Hoffenberg, easily the most inventive of our bunch. A short, brooding man with protuberant blue eyes, Mason was disposed to long silences, which were redeemed by sudden explosions of corrosive wit. He had already begun to experiment with drugs.

I can't remember when I first met Mason, whether it was at the Café Royal or on Boulevard St.-Germain, at The Old Navy or La Coupole, in Montparnasse. Wherever it was, he was bound to have had a dog-eared paperback sticking out of the ripped pocket of a crumpled jacket, and probably Terry Southern was with him. Mason was, at the time, writing poetry, but so far as I knew he had been published only once, in *Zero*, a little magazine that Paul Bowles was editing in Tangier. Mason and Terry were part of the *New-Story* crowd. *New-Story* was edited by Eric Protter and David Burnett. Burnett, who died young, reportedly of a drug overdose, was the son of Whit Burnett and Martha Foley, who had published the legendary *Story* magazine.

Mason tolerated my drinking, but grudgingly. 'If I can put up with your Rotarian habits,' he once said, 'why do you find my drugs such a bore?' But he did warn me against heroin. 'Don't let anybody turn you on, whatever they say.'

A few years later, ensconced in Tourettes-sur-Loup, a village in the Alpes-Maritimes, I found flats for Mason and Terry and their wives. Mason soon discovered that the proprietor of an inn off the village square, an old Indo-China hand, had an opium pipe he was willing to share. Many an evening, settled at a café table on the square, Terry, Mason and I tried to develop the absolutely perfect *Reader's Digest* story, something that magazine's editors couldn't possibly reject, but the more we improvised, the more obscene it became.

I moved on to London, and Mason and Terry returned to Paris, where they wrote *Candy* together. Initially the novel was published in Paris by Maurice Girodias, just another item in his porn collection, the Traveller's Companion series, which also included two other celebrated novels: *Lolita*, by Vladimir Nabokov, and *The Ginger Man*, by J.P. Donleavy. Later, as puritanical standards eased at home, Putnam's published the American edition of *Candy*. It was critically acclaimed. It was also a best-seller. Unfortunately, however, its success led to the estrangement of Mason Hoffenberg and Terry Southern. When Terry seemed to attract most of the praise, a resentful Mason began to complain that he had been betrayed, unfairly thrust aside. But Terry had already published *Flash and Filigree* and went on to write that satiric gem, *The Magic Christian*, as well as writing the screenplay for *Dr. Strangelove* with Stanley Kubrick. A fulminating Mason wrote two porn novels under pseudonyms. Reading *Candy*, I felt that the style was unmistakably Terry's, but a good many of the comic inventions sounded like Mason. Some years later, long after most people lost interest, Mason was still brooding about the division of *Candy*'s critical spoils. It was a very sad business.

I continued to see Terry, whenever he was in London, and Mason, whenever I visited Paris. Mason was heavily into heroin and was now a prodigious vodka drinker as well. Then, after a gap of something like five years, Mason suddenly turned up in London. His marriage had fallen apart. He was staying in the luxurious Eaton Square flat of a famous pop star, pursuing a girl who was going out with one of the Rolling Stones. It was, he said, like a utility shortstop trying to make out with the same girl as Babe Ruth. He wanted to kick heroin, he added, something he had managed before, and he asked me if I could get him some methadone. I made the necessary connection and we arranged to meet for lunch. 'But not anywhere too far from home,' Mason said. 'I might have to get back in a hurry.'

I took him to The White Elephant on Curzon Street. Mason's arm was bandaged and he wore a sling, the aftermath of a dirty needle. We were barely into our first drink when Sean Connery wandered over to say hello. I introduced Mason. 'What did you do to your arm?' Sean asked.

Mason giggled.

'He fell,' I said.

Our main course had just arrived when Mason broke into a sweat. 'You've got to get me back to the flat right now,' he said.

Once in his bedroom, he began to rotate his arm, like a windmill softball pitcher warming up. The instant he stopped I knotted my tie around his forearm. Even so, he couldn't hit a vein. 'They know better than me,' he said. 'They keep sliding away from the needle. Next thing you know, I'll have to start shooting up my tongue.'

We tried again.

'I hardly ever go to the toilet any more,' he said, 'and when I do, you'd need a stick to break my shit.'

Finally, he made it. We packed his bag. I drove Mason out to our home on Kingston Hill, where he would sweat it out, trying to kick the habit. Mason had enough with him for one more shot and he needed it urgently by the time we got to my place. Florence, however, was still preparing one of the children's rooms for Mason. She knew he was a cherished old friend of mine and she wanted everything to be just so for him. Mason shot me a desperate look. I rudely hurried Florence out of the room, saying I had to have a private word with Mason. Mason quickly heated up his last hit in a Coca-Cola bottle top; he shot up and went to sleep. I left the methadone on the bedside table.

I had, of course, told Florence and the children many stories over the years about the fine times Mason and I and some others had once had together, broke but incomparably happy in Paris. They were looking forward to meeting him. But Mason emerged from his room only once, joining us for a half hour in the garden – silent – lost in a reverie of his own. For the next forty-eight hours I was constantly in and out of his room, bringing him bananas or soft-boiled eggs. Then, late in his second night in our house, Mason appeared at the head of the stairs. 'I can't make it,' he said. 'You've got to get me to Leicester Square.'

I should explain that registered addicts in England get a drug ration on National Health. In London, many of them tend to congregate outside an all-night drugstore off Leicester Square at 11:30 p.m., their daily prescription coming due at one minute past midnight. Those who have managed to wangle a larger drug ration than they actually require then sell off the surplus in the Leicester Square tube station.

I waved goodbye to Mason at Leicester Square.

Over the years I heard rumours and reports. Mason was travelling with Bob Dylan. Mason was working on a novel. Mason was in Israel. Mason was back in Paris. Late one night, in 1976, when I was staying at a friend's house in New York, I was told that while I had been out to dinner 'somebody named Mason Hoffenberg' had phoned. His telephone number was written on a small slip of paper. The next morning I was off very early for LaGuardia, and by the time I returned to New York three weeks later I had lost the little slip of paper. So the last time I saw Mason was when I dropped him off at Leicester Square to deal for what he needed to get him through the night. Then, in the summer of 1986, I ran into my old Hollywood friend at the Carolina 'Have you heard,' he asked, 'that Mason Hoffenberg died a few weeks ago?'

Florence and I have come to terms. We agree to begin simplifying our lives, as they say, by disposing of two shelves full of *National Geographics*, possibly the first move in any serious house-cleaning since the children have gone.

We like it on Lake Memphremagog. As I write, it has been weeks since the winter ice finally began to rot in the bay and we could see more open water each morning, the earth still hard, the trees bare. We have survived another seemingly endless Quebec winter. Florence now spends most of her day in the garden and her evenings contemplating garden catalogues and reference books. And I, lying without shame again, promise once more to help establish the vegetable garden. Then I stretch out on the sofa before the TV set, a prisoner to the Stanley Cup play-offs that will last a month.

May 27

In the nature of things, I fly down to New York every third Tuesday for the meeting of the Book-of-the-Month Club's editorial board. Usually Florence and I drive into Montreal the night before, and then I rise resentfully at 5:30 a.m. to catch Eastern's Flight 153 at 7:00. It's a flight I've come to think of as the '*Shmatte* Special,' because it is usually choked with mavins of the needle trade, metaphysicians of style, who argue the comparative merits of different lines of bras, sweaters and double-knits all the way to LaGuardia. An earlier generation of needle trade mavins, familiar to me as a boy, tended to be gruff and pear-shaped, favouring snappy fedoras with a brush that looked like a fishing fly jutting out of the band, glittering pinkies and hand-painted ties depicting palm trees blowing in the wind, moonlight blessing Miami Beach. No sooner did they sit down than out came *The Daily Racing Form* and a pencil or a deck of cards, and they settled into picking nags or playing pinochle. But this is the second generation. They don't bet on horses but ride them. Trim of figure they are, favouring Gucci loafers, designer jeans, necklaces, bracelets and silk shirts, a biscuit-thin pocket calculator or a *Woman's Wear Daily* riding their knees. As a rule, they don't chew on cigars, as their fathers did, and they decline the breakfast of damp, lukewarm scrambled eggs and sausages, because before leaving their homes they had their yogurt and crunchy granola and probably a pre-dawn jog as well. All the same, they are an amiable bunch, touchingly concerned about my welfare. 'How much do you get paid for writing that shit for *GQ*?'

'Thousands.'

'Atta boy.'

This time out, however, I overslept and had to take Eastern's 11:00 a.m. flight instead, which I figured would still get me to New York in time for lunch. Before boarding, I stopped, as is my habit, for an espresso at the coffee counter alongside Gate 16.

'Have you heard?' the counterman whispered.

'What?'

'Eastern's cut back again. They used to have twenty-one mechanics to service the planes, but now there are only ten.'

Eastern personnel tend to be an adorable lot. The stews always introduce themselves. Hi, my name is Dawn or Mary Lou or April. Once, I pointed out to one of them that the man who had been seated next to me, rather chalky in the face, had been in the toilet for half an hour. Possibly, she should check him out. He could be having a heart attack. 'Not me,' she said, and then she told me how one day she had gone in after a Japanese businessman, also in there for half an hour, and had found him masturbating, having scotch-taped a *Playboy* centrefold to the mirror.

On one flight, as we bounced into LaGuardia, the pilot announced, 'Captain Ginsburg, your intrepid birdman, has done it again.'

Another time the pilot told us, 'It seems that our landing-gear is not coming down, but I think it's really the warning light that's on the blink. Hey, better safe than sorry. We'll fly past the tower so they can have a look.'

Then, in this age of microchips, lasers and spaceships to the moon, the co-pilot came out carrying a flashlight; he rolled back the aisle carpet and peered into the baggage section.

'What do you think?' I asked him.

'The pilot will make an announcement.'

So far this time, our one-hour flight had been uneventful and on schedule. That is, until our pilot announced that we would be going into a holding pattern. We now skittered through thick traffic in soupy clouds, visibility zero, for another worrisome hour. Then the pilot, his voice far from calm, announced, 'We're running short of fuel so we will be going to Philadelphia. Everybody sit down. *I said everybody sit down.*'

The stew blessed us with a smile. 'It's nothing. We'll just refuel and head right back to New York.'

But after we landed in Philadelphia a half hour later, several Eastern officials came on board to confer with our captain. 'I don't give a damn,' he said, reaching for his attaché case, 'I'm not going up in that stuff again.'

I did the only sensible thing. I yanked my case out of the overhead compartment, fled, took a taxi to the station and caught a train to Penn Station. It was pouring when I arrived and there was a long wait for taxis. The man in charge of the lineup tried to reason with us. 'It's always like this on Wednesdays.'

'It's Tuesday,' I said.

Finally, I got my taxi.

'Where are you from?' the driver asked.

'Montreal.'

'Must be snowing.'

They always say that, even in July.

'But at least,' he went on to say, 'you haven't got too many niggers up there.'

'My wife is black.'

That shut him up until we pulled alongside a car with a 'NO RADIO' sticker pasted on the rear windshield. 'Aw,' the driver said, 'my brother-in-law stuck one of those in his window. They broke in just the same and left a note on the seat saying, "Just checking." '

May 28

Six p.m. Brooding over a Remy Martin in the bar at La Guardia, waiting to fly home, I glanced surreptitiously at the man on the next stool, sizing him up. He was in his mid-forties, portly, with blow-dried hair, a suede jacket, chunky rings swelling on both hands. Beside him on the floor rested an expensive leather attaché case with one of those important-looking combination locks. I didn't like him one bit and was about to reach for my drink and drift away to a table when he introduced himself, professing to be an admirer of my work. Once more I reproached myself for making glib snap judgments. Obviously he was a good fellow who just happened to look like the ingratiating maître d'' in a third-rate but upwardly mobile Italian restaurant. He was, at the very least, a discerning reader. His name, let's say, was Morrie. Morrie Kaufman.

'And what do you do, Morrie?' I asked.

'Me, I'm a creative printer.'

'What's that?'

'I do scratch games. You know, for gas stations. The New York *Post*. I do lotteries. I'm also in publishing.'

'No kidding?'

'Yeah, I'm into special offers. Like for *Reader's Digest*.'

'What kind of special offers?'

'Ah, you know, they fill in a coupon, they get a book. You ought to see how those books are packaged. I mean you gotta be a fucking genius to rewrap it and send it back. So they put it in their library and send a cheque. Boy, are those *Digest* guys ever smart! Hey,' he added, lowering his voice, 'about your novels . . . like there's something you ought to know.'

'Oh, really?'

'What if I could spell out for you how to double your sales?'

'Shoot, Morrie.'

'*Hot stamping.*'

That is to say, paperback covers that have embossed silver or gold lettering to catch the light.

'I do work for Harlequin, you know. We've researched it. Hot stamping on the jacket outsells everything else. The other thing is that you've got to get the bookstores to display your stuff *at eye-level*. Too high, too low, forget it. You want the impulse buyers. Take it from me, eye-level outsells everything else with them.'

The phone is ringing when I get back to our apartment in Montreal. It's a reporter from Canadian Press. He wants to know, assuming that I was shipwrecked on a desert island, what ten books would I like to have with me. I tell him to go to hell.

Once, after editing an anthology of modern humour, I was interviewed in Ottawa by a fellow from CP. I should explain that two types of reporters labour for CP. They are either young and bushy-tailed, clearly on their way to better things, or old, burnt-out cases. My interviewer was of the latter breed.

'I am familiar with your work,' he said, 'and just can't understand why anybody in New York would ask somebody like you to edit a humour anthology.'

'Well, I guess a lot of other writers turned down the job.'

Grudgingly, he flipped open the anthology. 'Mind you,' he said, 'I'm glad to see that you've discovered some new writers here.'

'Oh? Like who?'

'Ring Lardner.'

'Ah.'

'Now tell me,' he said, consulting his pad, 'would this Evelyn Waugh be the sister of the famous novelist?'

Alec Waugh he meant. *The Loom of Youth*. 'Yes,' I said. 'That's right.'

He wrote that down.

'Do you mind if I ask you a question?' I said.

'Go ahead.'

'When you're not interviewing writers, what do you actually do for CP? What's your regular beat?'

'Why,' he said, affronted, 'I'm their cultural correspondent.'

Not being utterly without vanity, I have submitted to more than one interview in my day. Interviewers, in my experience, range from morning-TV-show hosts, a pernicious breed, insufferably jolly at 8:00 a.m., to solemn academics who want to know why you traffic only in received ideas and when, if ever, will you write something seminal? Correspondents from the Jewish press unfailingly demand, 'Do you consider yourself a Jewish author or a writer who just happens to be of our faith?'

If we must have interviews with writers, none could be

more consistently intelligent than those that have been running in the *Paris Review* for years. In his introduction to the sixth collection to be put together in book form, *Writers at Work*, Frank Kermode writes: 'The interview is not a medium that is natural to writers: it requires of the script-bound a venture into naked orality. I remember from my own experience how difficult it was to get Graham Greene to say anything at all; what he did say was so unexpected (he would like to be able to write a novel like *Tom Jones*) that one wondered how much should be discounted as the involuntary product of boredom and embarrassment. Iris Murdoch, on the other hand, talked seriously but carefully rewrote everything she said before publication. Other writers prepare for the ordeal by deciding in advance what they will say, and again the sense of privileged talk is lost, and it becomes impossible for conversation to produce discoveries, as it should.' On the evidence, however, it certainly does produce malice. Here, for instance, is Rebecca West on a colleague.

INTERVIEWER: Are you interested in T.S. Eliot's writing?
WEST: Goodness! T.S. Eliot, whom I didn't like a bit? He was a poseur. He was married to this woman who was very pretty. My husband and I were asked to see them, and my husband roamed around the flat and there were endless photographs of T.S. Eliot and bits of his poetry done in embroidery by pious American ladies, and only one picture of his wife, and that was when she was getting married. Henry pointed it out to me and said, 'I don't think I like that man.'

June 4

Certain of my soul foods are unavailable out on the lake. Pickled herring. Rye bread. Smoked meat. The nearby town of Magog also lacks a decent butcher or fishmonger. So once a week we drive into town to shop and to see our youngest son, Jake, who still lives in Montreal.

Five o'clock in the afternoon I pop into Winnie's for a drink. Julian is the only one of my friends standing at the bar. He has just returned from a trip to Toronto, where he found what appeared to be a French restaurant, sat down, and looked at the menu. 'What's the soup du jour?' he asked the waiter.

'One moment, please, sir,' the waiter said.

He drifted off to the kitchen and came right back. 'It's the soup of the day,' he said.

I laugh and make a mental note to remember that. I can use it somewhere. I should keep a notebook, but I'm far too lazy. Besides, I don't trust writers who keep notebooks, suspecting they also make copies of their personal letters and keep scrapbooks and write smarmy thank-you notes to reviewers.

June 7

Son-of-a-bitch, I've got to think of something – anything – because Harry Pincus is threatening to come out for the weekend.

Much, possibly too much, has been written about the unjustly neglected writer, the hounded by bailiffs, but over-looked or even scorned by critics during his sour lifetime, buried in a pauper's grave but now considered seminal stuff, a classic, indispensible to our understanding of Western man. Very little, however, has been written about a much more commonplace literary animal, the justifiably neglected writer who has sacrificed his health and family to a decidedly capricious and unobliging muse. The man who has totally dedicated his life to art – unavailingly, alas.

Such is my friend and burden of some thirty years, a man I shall call Harry Pincus. Not that I'm worried that a seething Harry might recognize himself in these pages and sue for an unspeakable sum. On the contrary. Over the years, Harry has pleaded with me again and again. 'Put me into one of your superficial, derivative novels. Make me look awful. I'll sue you and we'll split the take fifty-fifty. Say, sixty-forty.'

Future biographers, should they be interested, will discover that Harry Pincus, bless him, has done everything to qualify as what, in more innocent days, we used to describe fondly as bohemian. For thirty years, rather than compromise his art, churning out an article here or a book review there,

Harry has endured cold-water flats ridden with cockroaches or mice, preferably both, in Paris, London, New York and, most recently, Montreal. He was a squatter long before it became fashionable. More than once, escaping a philistine landlord, he has packed up his wife and children and done a midnight flit. He drinks prodigiously. He is unfaithful, as often as he can manage it, to the wife who has been just about his sole means of support all these years. Gloria understands. 'Harry's a furnace. A force of nature,' she says. 'It would be selfish of me if I were unwilling to share him.'

Harry never repays a loan. Invited into the homes of old college friends who have settled for middle-aged respect-ability, he will steal whatever he needs or can redeem for cash in a pawnshop. Table cigarette lighters, bathroom towels, cuff-links, candlesticks. He will also search the children's bedrooms for unattended piggy banks, transistor radios and alarm clocks. If he needs a new winter coat, he repairs to a pricey restaurant, orders a drink at the bar and walks out with somebody else's coat. He is also inventive. On his return from Paris, in desperate need of furniture, he borrowed a truck from a cousin and went door-to-door in affluent suburbs, claiming to be collecting furniture for the Salvation Army.

I know of no writer more dedicated than Harry. He works at his craft possibly six hours a day and is deficient in only one thing: talent.

I first met Harry at college, where he was easily the most entertaining member of our crowd, a voracious reader, a brilliant conversationalist. Even in those days he revealed a rare gift for survival. Employed during the Christmas holi-days by the post office, he quickly recognized those long brown envelopes that contained pension or welfare cheques that he could put to better use than the intended recipients, who, unlike Harry, were merely mortal. Another Christmas, working at the shirt counter in a Montreal department store, he was considerate enough to phone me his first day on the job. 'Mr. Richler, your shirts are wrapped and ready. If you'd be kind enough to pick them up this afternoon.'

Rather than risk being denounced as a coward or – still worse – a bourgeois, I hurried over to the department store and accepted a bundle. To my immense relief, I was not arrested on the way out, but Harry was at my door immediately after work, demanding $25 for the six shirts. Still a bargain, he insisted, inquiring after my suit size.

Harry, even as a young man, was not physically blessed. He was short and chubby, his glasses thick, his fingernails black, his feet smelly. Even so, the best-looking girls swarmed around him in the bar where he held court, seemingly eager to be insulted, obviously glad to encounter a horny young man who was refreshingly honest and explicit about his sexual needs. Harry also composed scorching love letters, but was never so irresponsible or blinded by passion as to send, to what we used to call coeds, a first copy. Instead – mindful of his debt to generations as yet unborn – he mailed the girl a carbon copy, every letter appropriately numbered, the bottom of each page inscribed, 'Copyright Harry Pincus, not for resale.'

In Paris, in the days when we were all broke and collecting rejection slips, we were happy to be listed in Girodias's Traveller's Library. For the then munificent sum of $3,000, we banged out pornographic novels under pseudonyms, making sure to give the most outrageously perverted of our characters the names of remembered high school principals and puritanical aunts and editors who had turned down our short stories. But not Harry. Never Harry. Cornering us one by one, he admonished us for tarnishing our admittedly inferior talents. He invoked the names of the great and the pure and sneered at us for being whores. Then, even as we flinched under his assault, he would ask for a loan of $500, which we were flattered to lay on such a man of principle. Only later, when we compared notes, did we grasp that Harry Pincus, that son of a bitch, had ended up with more than $4,000, having written not a word.

Then, briefly, things seemed to fall in place for Harry. He graciously allowed *New-Story*, a little magazine then edited in Paris, to print a chapter from his novel in progress. An avant-garde New York publisher bit, forking over a $500 advance and actually bringing out Harry's demented novel the following year. The handful of reviews that appeared were devastating. Genuinely sorry for Harry, we took to avoiding the cafés where he was known to hang out, which was a hardship for him, because it meant he now had to pick up his own tabs. In any event, we should have known better, for when Harry finally caught up with us, he read all his reviews aloud with considerable gusto. 'It just goes to prove what I've been telling you for years,' he said. 'The critics don't know a damn thing. To be celebrated by such oafs would be a stigma.'

By this time he was married to the attractive and uncomplaining Gloria, the schoolteacher who would grow old before her time, tending to the needs of Harry and their three children. After a long day at school, Gloria had to do the shopping, the cleaning, the washing. Harry, after all, could not be expected to waste his creative energy on such mundane matters. He has written ten more novels, but has yet to publish another one since the first. However, each typescript has been bound and xeroxed, copies stored in different houses, proof against theft or fire. His short stories do appear in little magazines from time to time, all the other contributors undergraduates. Once, a bunch of us got together and estimated that Harry's literary output earned him an annual $300 max. We invited him out to dinner and urged him, if only for Gloria's sake, to take a teaching job, or even part-time work we could arrange for him as a proof-reader. But that was the year some smart-ass had sent several New York publishers the first chapter of *War and Peace* as well as an outline of the rest of the novel. Only two editors recognized the material. The rest turned it down outright. 'You see,' Harry said. 'You see. You want me, Harry Pincus, to accept the judgment of such idiots. I will not take a job. I have a vocation. But if you're really that concerned about Gloria and call yourself friends . . .'

We hastily put together a pot of $2,500, which we later

discovered had enabled Harry to repair to Barbados for two weeks with a downtown barmaid he fancied.

Harry is still with us, not only writing, but raging. He supports everything, from the Committee Against Acid Rain, through Fair Deal for the Sandinistas, to the Society for the Protection of Baby Seals. He has taken to holding court in a bar where he used to pronounce in the late forties, another generation of students hanging on his words. They consider Harry a saint. And old friends, myself included, still invite him to dinner, taking care first to lock up anything that can't be nailed down. Harry will eat and drink himself into a sorry state, obviously too drunk to stand at 3:00 a.m., but adamantly refusing a lift home. 'I will not drive in a Swedish car. Those bastards were neutral during the war. Remember the Jewish children.' But he will accept the taxi fare, including provision for a large tip, and probably walk home after all.

We continue to put up with Harry, because he is the only fifty-eight-year-old teenager of our acquaintance, and, as Harry says, 'Who can say with any certainty that a hundred years from now I won't finally be recognized for my genius?'

Not me, certainly not me.

June 8

No matter where we've lived (London, Rome, Amagansett, Montreal, etcetera) I've always worked at home and, come five o'clock, repaired to a favoured pub or bar to mull over the day's events with real men, men who actually went to offices and then home to dinner with dazzling tales to charm their wives. Me, descending from my second-floor work-room, I've usually got nothing to say.

'Work hard today, darling?'

'Yeah,' I reply cautiously, because I know when I'm being teased.

'Did it go well?'

'Ah, come on.'

Strangers married to dentists or real estate developers say to my wife, 'Oh, your husband's a writer. You must lead such an interesting life.'

Florence, bless her, is loyal. She doesn't break up laughing, neither does she punch anybody out. Instead she smiles graciously and says, 'Oh yes, yes, of course.'

Actually, being married to a writer must be hell. I count on Florence's judgment. She's not only my wife, but also my editor-in-residence, a most unenviable position. If she doesn't like something I've done, I won't submit it anywhere, but neither will I take her out to dinner or even water the vegetable garden. And if she does approve of what I've done, I'm inclined to doubt her honesty. What if it's just compassion for an aging, often disagreeable novelist?

Out here my bar is The Owl's Nest, a nondescript box slapped together on the 243 roadside. My good companions at the Owl's Nest include Sweet Pea, Dipstick, Buzz, Coz and Buff, most of whom were raised on scratch farms (invariably rocky, the soil shallow) that were lost to the banks years ago. The first thing their struggling fathers sold off, because it was no damn good for anything, was the steeply inclined lake frontage land, now worth a fortune. In winter the regulars at the Owl's Nest plough snow, serve as caretakers to the affluent Montrealers with cottages on the lake, stitch together pick-up carpentry jobs, work at one of the local bobbin mills or hibernate, sitting out the season on welfare. Doreen, who puts in long hours as a cleaning lady, is understandably unimpressed with what I do for a living. 'I could write a book too,' she once told me, 'but I just wouldn't know how to put it into words.'

'That never stopped him,' Sweet Pea said.

I have been drinking at The Owl's Nest for six years now and have got to know and appreciate many of the regulars. Take Vern, for instance. Come March, Vern gets edgy, impatient for the snow to rot so that he can hunt the 105, 243 and 108 for empty beer bottles on the roadside, a whole winter's worth flung from the windows of speeding cars by the rich Montreal kids who have been skiing on Owl's Head. Vern's never bought a round or refused one. Sweet Pea says, 'He's the only guy around here who can come in at noon with a five-dollar bill and leave drunk six hours later with three dollars' change in his pocket.'

Vern's twenty-year-old son is a wild one. Last month he knocked up a waitress at Chez Rob's, the second time he's got a girl in trouble. Vern wasn't pleased. 'You know,' he said, 'when I was your age I never had them kind of headaches.'

'Well, Dad, you don't know what you were missing.'

A couple of summers back, Sweet Pea sidled up to the bar and said to me, 'Write me out a cheque for a hundred dollars.'

'What for?'

'I promised you would contribute it toward the cost of beer for the Austin softball team.'

'Why?'

'Insurance is why.'

I'm the only Montrealer with a cottage on the lake who drinks with the locals at The Owl's Nest, so they take care of me, which can prove compromising on occasion. One afternoon that summer, for instance, I was reading out on our terrace when I looked up and there stood two provincial cops.

'What's the problem?' I asked.

They explained that the neighbour to my right had been robbed the previous week of his 85-horsepower outboard and that the two neighbours to my left were missing their TV sets, a VHS, many bottles of wine and two outboards. 'What have they taken from your place?'

'Nothing,' I had to admit, embarrassed.

Nobody at The Owl's Nest was surprised.

'Hey,' Sweet Pea said, 'we warned 'em, didn't we?'

'Yeah, but now my neighbours give me fishy looks.'

'Tough shit.'

I don't want to give you the impression that we are without the amenities out here. Magog, only twelve miles from my place, boasts a McDonald's, a Colonel Sanders, a liquor store and a topless go-go bar. Gordon's, on the main street, gets the Sunday *New York Times*, maybe only four days late.

When we first moved out here for a summer years ago, I drove in and picked up a copy.

'Hey,' Gordon said, 'you put that right back where you found it. You can't have it.'

'Why not?'

'I only sell reserved copies.'

'Okay, I'd like to reserve for the next ten weeks.'

'Sorry, but you can't do that. I'm not reserving any more copies.'

There's a small grocery shack down the road that has taken to stocking videocassettes. Hard-core porn, mostly. Vern's boy is an enthusiast. 'Now you can watch it and get it at the same time.'

A survival camp has opened down a dirt track off the 243, and now Montreal accountants and salesclerks who want to Rambo it for the weekend pay to sleep out in the open with the blackflies. We are also in touch with the New Age out here. Closer to the border, there is Stanhaven, a holistic centre and spiritual retreat, where Ms. Kristine Nichols, an internationally known teacher, lectures on trance, channelling and healing. If you are so inclined, you can also sit in on a 'Know Thy Self' class, conducted by Nancy Lee Campbell, a professional numerologist. Nancy is big on mandalic symbolism, music reverie, meditation, prosperity and creative visualization, reincarnation and karma and esoteric philosophy.

I expected to find only five or six of the regulars at The Owl's Nest this afternoon, but to my astonishment there were more than twenty men in there, some of them already blasted, others lining up with fists full of quarters for a turn at the Double-Up Poker slots.

'What in the hell's going on here, Pea?'

'Hey, can't you tell? It's Welfare Day. Everybody got their cheques this morning.'

If I may digress briefly, each country has its national day, be it Bastille Day, the Fourth of July, May Day or whatever. In Canada, it comes up once a month and it's called Welfare Day. Once, flying out of Vancouver Island in a small floatplane, hitting the water in Vancouver Harbour, I ducked out of the driving rain into the little air terminal and asked the girl at the counter to call a taxi for me.

'Why, that would be impossible today,' she said.

'What do you mean "impossible"?'

'It's Welfare Day.'

Later it was explained to me that on Welfare Day in Vancouver all the little old ladies order taxis to take them to the bank, wait outside, drive them on to the liquor stores, then back to their apartments. Now I know this is the stuff of a Ronnie Reagan anecdote, ventilated with a sense of outrage on one of his weekly radio chats, but I like it. I'm all for a government that provides for little old ladies to make whoopee once a month.

Our country is different from the other America in more ways than one. That same afternoon, for instance, I unfolded a Toronto *Globe and Mail*, our national newspaper, to check out the page one headline. On a day when Palestinian teenagers were being clubbed, disgruntled Armenians had taken to the streets of Sumgait and there was something like a general strike in Panama, the banner page one headline read: 'DID FAVOURS FOR SPEEDERS, WINNIPEG JUDGE SAYS.'

Forget Hart, Meese, Deaver, Swaggart. Good grief, investigative reporters had discovered that a provincial court judge in Winnipeg had actually fixed a couple of speeding tickets for his buddies.

Judge Allen said: 'I admit that I did it as a favour for them. If I did wrong by doing a 74-year-old man a favour, and a waiter who is of Pakistani descent, then I guess I'm a terrible criminal.'

Today Robert George, the owner of The Owl's Nest, has banged a new notice into the cork board on the wall over the Double-Up Joker Poker machine.

FOR THE 'BENEFIT' OF THE GEORGE CEMITARY ON VALE PERKINS ROAD

"AUX PROFITS' DU CIMETIÈRE SUR LE CHEMIN VALE PERKINS

WRAFFLE: ¼ Beef	TIRAGE: ¼ Boeuf
1 Ticket $1.00	1 Billet
6 Tickets $5.00	6 Billets
10 Tickets including one free meal ticket	10 Billets (1 souper gratis inclus)

I buy six tickets and Robert, appreciative, immediately sends me a double Scotch.

Bad news. A couple of days ago the enterprising Spiderman, a notorious drunk, fell and cracked his head on the pavement outside the Legion Hall in North Troy, and now he can't even recognize his wife. All the same he leaped at her this morning, fists flying, and they had to tie him up and take him away in an ambulance.

Spiderman is rooted in a shack up there somewhere in the hills beyond Lake Nick, three miles past the West Indian lady with a sign nailed into her fence:

HUSBAND WANTED
CHRISTIAN ONY
NO PAPOOSES
APPLY WITHIN

Last winter Spiderman and Jigsaw, another Owl's Nest regular, started a new business. Saturday mornings they drove from one lakeside cottage to another, Spiderman offering to shovel the snow off the roof at minimum wage. 'Guys around here rather sit on their butts and collect welfare, but I'm a war veteran. I got my pride.' And if he knew the owner of the cottage to be Jewish he would lower his eyes and add, 'I want my children to have a better life than I did.'

Once on the roof, Spiderman and Jigsaw would gouge three, maybe four well-spaced holes in the shingles, and then Spiderman would leave his card with the lady of the house. 'Me and my man are also experts at general roof repairs, if you should happen to need us in the spring. Free estimates on request.'

Spiderman, an ugly drunk, never did know any Saturday night satisfaction until he found a fight. His nose has been broken more than once and most of his teeth have been knocked out. His kids are terrified of him. 'Yeah,' Sweet Pea says, 'but if you caught him early enough in the morning, when he was still sober, you could never find a nicer guy.'

Hello, hello. Jigsaw is with us today. Jigsaw reads the Montreal *Gazette*, not only the sports section but even the editorials, and he watches 'The National' on CBC-TV every night. He writes letters to his MP. This afternoon Jigsaw is extremely upset about the free-trade deal soon to be signed by Canada and the United States. Sipping on a Bud, he turns to me, a fellow intellectual, and says, 'If we sign that fucken deal we're gonna lose our fucken national identity. The fucken Yanks will wipe the floor with us. We're gonna become the fifty-first state.'

'About time too,' Sweet Pea says, going on to point out that gas is much cheaper in Vermont, and so is beer and vodka and tires for a grader. All of life's necessities.

Home again, I make another attempt to thin out my books. But I can't let go of my torn Tauchnitz Edition paperback of *Daisy Miller*, which I picked up for sixpence at David's bookstall on the Market Square in Cambridge on a Saturday morning in 1951. A printed note on the first page reads: 'I desire it to be understood that the present is the only edition of "Daisy Miller," 'An International Episode" and "Four Meetings" published on the Continent of Europe with my asent.' It is signed Henry James, Jr., and dated April 1870. A previous owner of the volume has scribbled a note in pencil on the title page: 'a weakness – Giovanelli's dismissal from the plot is contrived by his not having attended Daisy on her illness – most unlikely.'

And what's this? A signed copy of *Edward Gordon Craig, Designs for the Theatre*. Craig presented it to me on the village square in Tourretes-sur-Loup in 1952. In his eighties at the time, he was living in a pension in Vence. Craig said, 'A young man came to see me yesterday and told me that he was my son, but I think he was just trying to make an impression.'

June 10

Happy days ahead. According to today's *Gazette*, Mayor André Auger of St. Lin (pop. 6,000) is pushing through a new by-law to properly reward French-Canadian fertility. Under his innovative scheme, which will do zilch for TV ratings but keep a lot of couples busy elsewhere, a family will now receive $500 for having a third child, $600 for a fourth, $700 for a fifth, and so on. 'I am a Quebec nationalist,' Auger said. 'I believe Quebec should repopulate itself *itself.*'

Quebec's birth-rate, once legendary, is now among the lowest in the Western world, and this has got jolly Jacques Parizeau, the new leader of the separatist Parti Québecois, thinking deep and dirty. He is concerned lest French-Canadians, failing in their conjugal obligations, wake up one morning to find themselves a minority in their own homeland. And so, if elected, Parizeau will stand up for more fruitful fucking, sponsoring a baby-bonus program. Well, okay. Very nice. But like most proposed PQ measures this one does not go nearly far enough. Obviously something will have to be done about randy Jews (I speak as an unapologetic father of five), horny WASPs and what the PQ charmingly calls neo-Quebecers, that is to say Greeks, Italians and Portuguese, all notoriously sex-crazed. In order for the bonus to do its work, I think it should apply to bona fide Québecois, and that the rest of us should be fined rather than rewarded for not being more careful between the sheets.

Look to South Africa or Israel for tragedy. In this room of the North American attic we are living through a farce. Ours is an Alice-Through-the-Looking-Glass province, the only North American territory where so-called anglophones are a threatened minority. Under the terms of Bill 101, the French Language Charter, tradesmen are not allowed to post bilingual signs outside their stores. If, however, they employ four workers or fewer they are allowed bilingual signs inside their stores by the inspectors of the Commission de Protection de la Langue Française, or what we, the oppressed, irreverently refer to as the tongue-troopers.

The issue has now gone to the Supreme Court of Canada, which is expected to rule that Quebec's French-only sign law violates freedom of expression guarantees under the Canadian Charter of Rights. But hold the phone, this won't be the end of it, not in our delightfully loopy country. In Canada, if a province disagrees with a freedom *guaranteed* under the Charter it can simply opt out, invoking something called a 'notwithstanding clause.' And this is precisely what Bobby Bourassa, our slippery Liberal premier, is expected to do. He is being counted on to disallow outside bilingual signs to – as he puts it – keep the social peace, but as a sop to the linguistically deprived it is expected that he will continue to wink at inside bilingual signs. King Solomon would approve. But, speaking as an old hand at Talmudic distinctions, I fear that such a compromise begs further questions. I assume that some of those inside signs will hang in dark corridors and will therefore require lighting from above. A tricky business, one that begs for more legislative guidance. What wattage, for instance, would be considered defiant, a menace to the French face of Quebec, and what would be considered respectful? Would an inspector from the Commission de Protection de la Langue Française take two hundred watts to be subversive, a call to arms? One hundred and fifty watts pushy? Fifty watts sufficiently humble?

Florence is in Montreal today, dealing with our income tax papers which I, being such an artistic fellow, am too pure of heart to cope with. So I'm alone here, which I don't like very much. Alone and guilt-ridden, having laid such a nasty boring job on my wife. I decide to impress Florence by doing another clean-up before she returns tomorrow night, making some room for all the useless stuff that will be coming here from our apartment. Sifting through old letters, pausing to reread just about every one of them, I figure I'm clearing an inch of space an hour, not quite good enough. But at least I do find something I feared was lost. An item sent to me by a bright student in the Maritimes. It is an advertisement he found posted on his university notice board, and I quote it in full.

A
GATHERING OF
JEWISH LESBIAN DAUGHTERS
OF HOLOCAUST SURVIVORS
(and Partners –
Lovers and Lesbian
Friends)
NOVEMBER 13–15 1987

If you are a Jewish Lesbian with one or more parents who have survived the holocaust, or a partner, join us for a weekend in New Hampshire. Workshops, discussion, and support around issues we share. For more information contact:
JLDHS, Box 6194
Boston, MA 02114.

Possibly, there is no longer any need to invent.